The Education of American Leaders

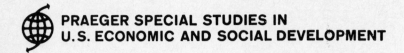

**PRAEGER SPECIAL STUDIES IN
U.S. ECONOMIC AND SOCIAL DEVELOPMENT**

The Education of
American Leaders

COMPARATIVE CONTRIBUTIONS OF
U.S. COLLEGES AND UNIVERSITIES

George W. Pierson

FREDERICK A. PRAEGER, Publishers
New York · Washington · London

The purpose of the Praeger Special Studies is to make specialized research monographs in U.S. and international economics and politics available to the academic, business, and government communities. For further information, write to the Special Projects Division, Frederick A. Praeger, Publishers, 111 Fourth Avenue, New York, N.Y. 10003.

FREDERICK A. PRAEGER, PUBLISHERS
111 Fourth Avenue, New York, N.Y. 10003, U.S.A.
5, Cromwell Place, London S.W. 7, England

Published in the United States of America in 1969
by Frederick A. Praeger, Inc., Publishers

© 1969 by Frederick A. Praeger, Inc.

Library of Congress Catalog Card Number: 69-17173

Printed in the United States of America

CONTENTS

Page

INTRODUCTION   xi

THE FINDINGS--AND THE PROBLEM OF CREDIT   xix

    General Rank Order of Our Colleges and Universities   xx
    Career Emphasis and Success in the College
        Constituencies, 1865-1965   xxiv

Chapter

A. FROM JAMESTOWN TO APPOMATTOX   1

    A-1. The Colleges in the Dictionary of American
          Biography   3
    A-2. 300 "Notable Americans"   6
          400 "Notable Americans"   9
    A-3. The Hall of Fame, 1900-1960   10

B. THE MAKING OF AMERICAN STATESMEN   13

    B-1. The Signers, 1776   16
    B-2. Delegates to the Federal Convention, 1787   18
    B-3. The National Executive, 1789-1962   20
    B-4. "The American Federal Executive," in 1959   22
    B-5. Branches of "The American Federal Executive,"
          in 1959   24
    B-6. Chief Diplomatic Officers, 1946-64   26
    B-7. The Congress of the United States, in 1963   28
    B-8. Justices of the Supreme Court, 1789-1963   30
    B-9. State Governors, 1946-63   32

C. THE PROFESSION OF THE LAW   35

    C-1. Attorneys General, 1789-1964; Solicitors
          General, 1870-1964   38
    C-2. Judges of the United States Circuit Courts
          of Appeal, 1869-1955   40

Chapter   Page

    C-3. Highest State Courts, 1955   42
    C-4. American Bar Association Presidents,
          1878-1955   44
    C-5. The Largest Law Firms in Seventeen Cities,
          in 1955   47

D. THE UNIVERSITIES IN MEDICINE   51

    D-1. The Education of American Physicians--
          Prior to 1900   54
    D-2. Surgeons General   56
    D-3. Heads of Major Professional Medical Societies   58
    D-4. Medical School Deans, Sample Years: 1906-65   60
    D-5. Medical School Alumni: Academic Origins and
          Specializations--Prior to 1950   62
    D-6. Medical Schools: Distribution of Productive
          Efforts--Prior to 1950   64
    D-7. Full-time Faculty in U.S. Medical Schools,
          1960   66
    D-8. Undergraduate Origins of Medical Students,
          1952-60   68

E. PROTESTANT DIVINITY   71

    E-1. Protestant Missionary Organizations, 1810-1910   74
    E-2. Officers of the Major Protestant Denominations,
          1958   76
    E-3. Institutional Sources of Protestant Church
          Leadership, 1958   78
    E-4. Protestant Societies and Interdenominational
          Organizations, 1962-64   80

F. BIG BUSINESS, INDUSTRY, AND BANKING AND FINANCE   83

    F-1. "The Business Elite," 1900-1910   86
    F-2. "The Big Business Executive," 1900-1950   88
    F-3. Presidents of Companies "Excellently
          Managed," 1950   90
    F-4. 505 Big Business Leaders, 1952   92
    F-5. Heads of Billion-Dollar Corporations, 1952   94
    F-6. The 101 Largest Corporations, 1952   96
    F-7. Presidents of the 500 Largest Corporations,
          1956   100
    F-8. "50 Foremost Business Leaders of America," 1957 102
    F-9. Billion Dollar Corporations, 1961   104

F-10. Chief Executive Officers of 750 Major
         Corporations, 1963   106
F-11. The Men in Standard & Poor's, 1964   108
F-12. "The Big Business Executive," 1964   110
F-13. Top Executives of the Largest Nonfinancial
         Corporations, 1955, 1961, 1964   112

           BANKING AND FINANCE   114

F-14. Presidents of the American Bankers
         Association, 1875-1961   114
F-15. New York Stock Exchange, 1817-1963   115
F-16. Officers of the Largest Banks, 1955   116
F-17. The Federal Reserve System (Up to 1956)   118

    SUMMARY: BIG BUSINESS AND THE HIGHER LEARNING   120

Summary Table: Big Business--Colleges   121
Summary Table: Big Business--Universities   122

G. PHILANTHROPY   123

G-1. The Leadership of Major American Foundations,
        1948   126
G-2. Officers of Community Trusts, 1948   128
G-3. Red Feather Charity Drive Chairmen, 1955-57   130
G-4. The Leadership of Major American Foundations,
        1957   132
G-5. The Leadership of Medical Foundations, 1959   134

H. SCIENCE AND ENGINEERING   137

H-1. Starred Scientists, 1903-43   140
H-2. Officers and Council Members of the National
        Academy of Sciences, 1863-1961   142
H-3. Medalists of the National Academy of Sciences,
        1886-1961   144
H-4. Directors of Scientific Museums, 1812-1965   146
H-5. Collegiate Origins of American Scientists,
        1880-1938   148
H-6. Medalists of Certain Professional Engineering
        Societies, 1902-64   150

Chapter   Page

J.   LITERATURE AND THE ARTS   153

     J-1. Former Members of the American Academy and
             the National Institute of Arts and Letters   156
     J-2. 1963 Members of the American Academy and the
             National Institute of Arts and Letters   158
     J-3. The Universities and the Pulitzer Prizes,
             1917-57   160
     J-4. Winners of Two or More Pulitzer Prizes,
             1917-57   161
     J-5. Authors in the White House Library, 1963   162
     J-6. Prizes in History, 1893-1961   164
     J-7. Guggenheim Fellowships for Creative Writing,
             1926-62   166
     J-8. Directors on Broadway, 1952-61   168
     J-9. American Composers, 1620-1965   170
     J-10. Presidents and Gold Medalists of the
             American Institute of Architects   172
     J-11. Fellows of the American Institute of
             Architects, 1913-52   174
     J-12. Fellows of the American Institute of
             Architects, 1953-64   176
     J-13. Prize Fellowships in Architecture   178

K.   EDUCATION AND SCHOLARSHIP   181

     K-1. "Great Educators," from the Earliest
             Settlements   184
     K-2. Headmasters and Principals of 66
             Preparatory Schools, to 1955   186
     K-3. Faculties of 69 Preparatory Schools, 1955   188
     K-4. College and University Presidents, 1961-62   190
     K-5. The Universities and the Learned Societies,
             1948, 1954, 1960   192
     K-6. American Philosophical Society, 1964   194
     K-7. Humanistic Scholarship--A.C.L.S. Prize
             Awards, 1958-62--Education of the 50
             Scholars   196
     K-8. Humanistic Scholarship--A.C.L.S. Prize
             Awards, 1958-62--Faculty Connections of
             the 50 Scholars   197
     K-9. Comparative Ratings of the University
             Graduate Schools, 1925, 1957, 1965   198

Chapter   Page

               THE PROMISE OF LEADERSHIP IN
               EDUCATION AND SCHOLARSHIP   207

     K-10. Rhodes Scholars, 1904-64   208
     K-11. Rhodes Scholars from Harvard, Princeton,
              and Yale by States of Appointment, 1904-64   210
     K-12. Social Science Research Council Fellowships,
              1925-51   212
     K-13. Guggenheim Fellowships: Sample Years   214
     K-14. A.C.L.S. Fellowships and Grants-in-Aid,
              1958-62   216
     K-15. Production of Ph.D.'s, 1861-1956   218
     K-16. Leading Doctorate Producers in the
              Humanities, 1920-61   220
     K-17. College Origins of the Younger American
              Scholar, 1946-51   222

L.   FOR THE TWENTIETH CENTURY: TWO OVER-ALL INDEXES
       OF ACHIEVEMENT   225

     L-1. The Freedom Medal, 1963, 1964   228
     L-2. College Graduates in Who's Who in America,
              1928, 1938, 1950, 1962   230
     L-3. H-Y-P Ratios of Election to Who's Who in
              America, 1928, 1938, 1950, 1962   234

M.   SUMMARY AND CONCLUSIONS   237

     M-1. Summary Table for the Colleges, 1865-1965   242
     M-2. Summary Table for the Graduate and
              Professional Schools, 1865-1965   246
     M-3. Summary Table for the Universities, 1865-1965   248
     M-4. Densities of Contribution, 17 Colleges   253

N.   APPENDIX   255

     N-1. Some Dates of College Founding   256
     N-2. Estimated College Enrollments, 1900-1939   257
     N-3. Estimated University Enrollments, 1900-1959   258
     N-4. Total Living Alumni, 1900-1962   260

ABOUT THE AUTHOR   263

INTRODUCTION

Where have outstanding Americans gone to college? And
to what graduate or professional schools? In what proportion
or relative volume has each of our colleges, and each of our
major universities, contributed to the production of American
leadership? Might it not be of national significance--as well
as a matter of no little personal interest--to ascertain which
institutions of higher learning have had the greatest share in
the education or the technical training of those who later
would achieve high public office, professional eminence,
careers of unusual distinction, or lives of exceptional originality and social usefulness?

This book of tables represents an attempt--a modest attempt yet perhaps the first of its kind--at a broad statistical sampling and comparative numerical evaluation of this
component in the American record.

In a general way we have known that, through the first
250 years of our existence as a people, many of our leaders
were self-made men without the benefit or experience of a
formal education. About twenty years ago Professor B. W.
Kunkel of Lafayette College, by painstaking analysis of the
Dictionary of American Biography (the most inclusive and
authoritative register of distinction from 1607 to the generation born just before the Civil War), effectively demonstrated
that 66 per cent, or almost exactly two thirds of those who
earned recognition by this dictionary, had apparently never
been to college. On the other hand, when he came to look
into the specific institutional connections of the remaining
more highly educated 34 per cent, he found that four colleges
had predominated and that seven others had also made quite exceptional contributions: altogether only eleven out of the
181 institutions involved (see Table A-1). By way of comparison, when Professors B. W. Kunkel and D. B. Prentice investigated sample issues of Who's Who in America for the twentieth
century, they discovered a decreasing percentage of its biographees without at least a bachelor's degree. Yet still
three of the same four colleges were leading the way, while
the contributions of other well-known institutions remained
decidedly subordinate and uneven (see Table L-2).

Admittedly, these were over-all and somewhat miscellaneous measurements. Yet, to turn now from the general to the particular, if we inquire specifically into the education of American statesmen, and tabulate college and university attendance for the Signers of the Declaration of Independence, for the Delegates to the Federal Convention, for all our Presidents and Vice-Presidents, and for all our Cabinet officers from Washington's inauguration to 1962, the returns show strikingly similar disproportions (see Tables B-1, B-2, B-3)--a pattern of distinction repeated and emphasized by the Justices of the Supreme Court through 174 years (Table B-8). One-sided though such distributions may seem, at the top levels of government the historical record is clear, and leaves small room for argument.

What about political leadership in the twentieth century? Have things not changed?

Obviously things have changed--but far less perhaps than many persons have supposed. The more recent samplings of the 88th Congress in 1963 and of the Diplomatic Corps since World War II (Tables B-6, B-7) hint at the wider distribution of talent and educational opportunity which we have come to expect, indeed almost take for granted for the years to come. Yet still the distinction of our great colleges and universities persists.

A broadening of the inquiry into other fields seems even to fortify the disproportions. But the thoughtful layman will wish to judge for himself the results of our sampling studies of twentieth-century leadership: in Law, Medicine, and Divinity; in Business, Industry, Banking and Finance; in the growing field of organized Philanthropy; in Science; in the Arts and Letters; in Scholarship and Education. Finally a brief section on over-all distinction in the twentieth century leads up to a summary of the statistical evidence and gives rise to certain conclusions--conclusions, as it seems to me, of no small moment for society.

Background and Problems of the Study

Before the evidence is examined, or judgments are attempted, I wish to make clear the shortcomings of this study and offer some necessary explanations. As will readily be discovered, the tables here presented leave much to be desired. They fall short of a really satisfactory coverage of occupations and professions. Even in some major categories they provide only samplings of what we might like to know. Indeed certain career lines or occupations of public importance have had to be omitted entirely, or have been covered most inadequately. Again, individual tables have had to be composed sometimes of inadequate materials; they may focus on defective leadership lists, or may measure too limited a segment of a profession for too short a stretch of time. By reason of the circumstances of their manufacture, a few of our statistical constructs will prove inconsistent in criteria and workmanship. It should be added that most of these materials were first put together before the age of computers, by a minimal staff, from time to time, as occasion offered, or as supervision could be provided by a professor with many preoccupations. Even the idea for this inquiry, and the construction of comparative tables, came about accidentally.

It happened in the following fashion. About twenty years ago, just when I had got well launched into research and preliminary writing for a history of modern Yale, a friend and colleague asked me an awkward question. After listening to some of the things I had been finding, he observed: But how do you know Yale's education was effective unless you know what happened to Yale's graduates?

I groaned and changed the subject. The task was patently impossible.

On further and rather painful reflection it seemed, however, that some attempt must be made. And so was undertaken-- by a part-time secretary, a succession of undergraduate bursary students, and myself--a most hopeful, tantalizing, frustrating, and extremely laborious search for the outstanding manpower contributions made by Yale to the many-sided development of American society. That exploration or series of explorations remains unfinished, primarily because before it had made real progress a second challenge complicated the problem. If Yale's graduates should be found to have made genuine contributions, how about the graduates of all the other colleges? Did I not need to learn something also about Yale's _relative_ performance?

A quick rundown of the listed Presidents of the United States, for example, made it almost instantly plain that Yale had contributed (substantially! but only once) in the person of William Howard Taft--whereas William and Mary had sent forward three statesmen of classic stature (Jefferson, Monroe, and Tyler), and Harvard no fewer than five chief executives (now six): two Adamses, two Roosevelts, Rutherford B. Hayes (LL.B), and John F. Kennedy. A quick count of the Justices of the United States Supreme Court, on the other hand, turned up more graduates from Yale, and from Princeton, than from Harvard or any other college--while, among the delegates who drafted our Federal Constitution in 1787, the alumni of Princeton seemed to hold a clear lead.

So began a game--or rather a grim and fascinating man-hunt through the dimly lit corridors of our national hall of fame. This phantom hall proved to have several levels and many chambers. A few on the top floor were in good order, since they had been restricted to holders of a particular high office, and the quite limited number of Presidents or of Supreme Court Justices made our study easy. Certain rooms nearby, however, turned out to be so crowded with Congressmen, or Ambassadors, or State Governors, or some other great army of office holders alive and dead, that a total census seemed beyond our powers and only some sampling counts could be attempted. Still other chambers we found empty and dark, or cluttered with ignoble plaster statues, twice life size. And then below were the great waiting-rooms or public concourses, where almost anyone seemed free to come and go, and where we found lawyers and businessmen, doctors and clergymen, artists and writers, scientists and scholars, most not quite certain of their credentials and all milling around in confusion or jostling each other to get to the elevator doors.

The resemblance of our phantom hall of fame to a modern hotel may not be altogether fanciful, for here, too, advance registration is sometimes repudiated, public entry cannot be restricted, and beds cannot be retained indefinitely or passed along from father to son. Yet our metaphor may be abandoned if it has made clear the basic dilemma. Who are or have been our outstanding Americans? Where are our lists of great men posted, or who is to decide what names to include if the lists have not been made?

Sometimes an office is important enough to justify all its tenants: The Presidency of the United States provides such a list, whatever one may think of Buchanan or Harding. But can one be sure the presidency of the American Bankers Association does the same for banking, or that the presidency of the American Bar Association has not been subverted, now and again, to serve the game of regional politics? With the best will in the world, can anyone hope to establish an honor list for the Christian ministry? And who is to single out for us America's greatest doctors, or architects, or musicians? The office holders, medalists, and honor rolls in some of our scientific or literary societies may offer a slim guidance. Yet, from the start to the finish of this investigation, the most trying problem was always that of identification: of finding valid, defensible lists of those who had

been, or still were the leaders in a given profession.* All
of which will account for the major gaps in our tables, the
entire omission of certain professions, the uneven and seemingly arbitrary character of certain of our samplings.

A second and rather surprising difficulty was that of
discovering a man's college connections. For if an individual
could not be located in Who's Who in America, or in Who Was
Who in America, or in the Dictionary of American Biography,
or perhaps in one of the older and less reliable biographical
dictionaries, we found ourselves at the mercy of the incomplete and inaccurate business or professional directories.
The alumni registers of the colleges themselves proved a
doubtful and most uneven resource. The excellent directories
of graduates and nongraduates published at various times by
Harvard, Yale, and Princeton enabled us to check the attributions to the so-called Big Three, and even to discover additional alumni not properly credited by our original sources--
but after some experiment this particular tool had to be abandoned in the interests of fair play. For, aside from Amherst,
Williams, West Point, Annapolis, Cornell, Swarthmore, Stanford, and a few other institutions of comparable stability
and self-respect, alumni directories for our colleges proved
hard to find. They had been published too rarely or were completely out-of-date. By the same token, the largest state
and land grant universities would have been still more markedly disadvantaged, for, to our astonishment, we learned that
many of them did not have any alumni lists, did not know who
had been their students, in fact did not have the faintest
idea how many students they had taken in or how many graduates they had produced!** It followed that often we could
not be sure we had achieved a complete count of the college-
educated, and in many of our tables had to qualify our

------

*Unfortunately, such has been the provincialism and ig-
norance of our academic constituencies, and so great the mutual
jealousy of our colleges, that no joint honor rolls have been
developed (with the doubtful exception of the Hall of Fame for
Football). Hence, no help from that quarter. Obviously, for
a Yale professor and graduate to attempt to manufacture such
lists for himself would only bring his whole enterprise under
suspicion.

**Recent replies from a number of institutions, both
private and public, suggest a growing recognition of this
lack, and a determination to compile lists of living alumni--
an enterprise likely to be forwarded by the growing reliance
on computers, for alumni relations as for student records.

enumeration of those without college connection by the phrase: "No college or unknown." Happily, the numbers of the unknown were rarely so large as to bring into question the ratios or major institutional attributions in our tables.

A third problem should be noted. Because of its statistical approach, this is in some degree a quantitative rather than a qualitative assessment of the record. A quite different way of measuring the eminence of a college or university would be to ask what geniuses it has produced. To such a challenge Yale could answer: Jonathan Edwards and J. Willard Gibbs. Should Noah Webster and James Fenimore Cooper, Eli Whitney and S. F. B. Morse, William Graham Sumner, Thorstein Veblen (Ph.D.) or Irving Fisher also be mentioned? Discrimination would prove difficult, if not downright impossible. Should the U.S. Military Academy register MacArthur with Grant and Lee, and Whistler with Poe? Could Hamilton College enter Elihu Root in the competition?

Alternatively, we might ask about contributions to the advancement and communication of knowledge--and on that somewhat less exalted level each of our older and more celebrated colleges could marshall a host of great names. To take but one example, Yale's Sillimans and Danas would be matched by Harvard's Asa Gray, with Agassiz, father and son. In Paleontology O. C. Marsh might renew his old feud with Pennsylvania's E. D. Cope. But could the Dwights and Hadleys and Seymours of old New Haven match the James family, the Everett brothers, and all the shining company of Boston's Brahmins? And how would one compare Chancellor Kent with Justice Story, or with Oliver Wendell Holmes? Evidently an intimate knowledge would be required and not just of learning in New England. And eventually one might be reduced to categories and to the impersonal device of counting, even as in this study.

Still another and rather different way would be to compare the reputations of our colleges and universities, nationally and internationally, by their power to draw scholars and students from far and near. Unfortunately, measurements of the regional origins and regional destinations, over any considerable stretch of time, are not only extremely laborious to make, they are often impossible for want of the proper records. Moreover, they would tell us least of all about the quality of the contributions of any alumni group.

So one returns finally to the biographical dictionaries, to over-all comparisons, and to more particular measurements of preselected leadership groups, in business and the professions, in the arts and letters, in science and scholarship.

Acknowledgments

In this extremely onerous but strangely absorbing work I have had the privilege, for short stretches of time, of many helpers, who have carried the chief burdens. And I should like to express my appreciation here to all concerned: to Miss Boatfield and Miss Simison for research help, to Miss Pflueger who kept me on the rails during six years of administrative preoccupations, to my secretaries who have checked and typed and retyped the tables, and to the bursary students who have dug up the facts, and first organized them into intelligible form. In some part the following have all shared in the making of this book:

Helen C. Boatfield, now Associate Editor of the Papers of Benjamin Franklin

Barbara D. Simison, Reference Librarian, Yale University Library

Loueva F. Pflueger, Executive Secretary of Yale's Department of History

Secretaries

Ruth P. Gray
G. Katherine Grimm
Georgialee B. Furniss
Miriam P. Roens
Donet M. Roelofs
Eleanore Doban
Vera M. Ferguson
Judith S. Rowe

Regina M. Stack
Catherine M. Vosburgh
Katharina S. Dresbach
Beth Torrey
Emily W. Boldt
Mary E. Starnes
Jo-Ann Daly
Karen K. Garver
Elise W. Enk

Yale College Bursary Students

	Class of		Class of
Bernard N. Miller	'42	Rushton H. Little	'50
Shepard F. Palitz	'42	James L. Bryan	'50
Joseph W. Neubert	'45	George F. Dole	'52
Edward S. Hermberg	'45	Henry H. Seward	'53
Lee B. Kasson, Jr.	'45	R. H. Babcock	'53
Martin J. Aronstein	'45S	William C. Hollocher	'55
Homer D. Babbidge	'46	Henry S. Sizer	'55
Gerard Mandelbaum	'46M	Douglas W. Smith	'56
Richard J. Selcoe	'47M	Anthony J. Latona	'60
John G. G. Finley	'47	J. V. Hinckley	'61
George L. Thurlow, Jr.	'47M	Fred W. Wakefield	'61
Daniel P. Weinig	'47N	Robert C. Varnum	'64
Daniel A. Austin, Jr.	'48	Shannon B. Ferguson	'64
Robert M. Northrop	'49	Thomas J. Polivka	'65
Paul A. Rinden	'49	David A. Wertheimer	'66
Orville H. Bathe	'49	Geoffrey S. Law	'66
Paul E. Klebe, Jr.	'50F	Harold Chesnin	'68
John J. Schurdak	'50		

For the use of research information and for permission to quote statistical materials published by others (acknowledged in each table with the identification of sources) I am most sincerely grateful. My hope is that, with better records in the years to come, others may be able to carry forward this enterprise of public assessment more fully, more authoritatively, more perceptively, and still without fear or undue favor.

G. W. Pierson

THE FINDINGS--AND THE PROBLEM OF CREDIT

The statistical returns from these prolonged investigations--the photographic reports, so to speak, from repeated probes into the upper stratospheric layers of our most mobile society--will surely surprise many, and may entirely satisfy no one. Yet they are remarkably consistent and clear. What they suggest, and come very close to proving, may be summarized in the following generalizations:

1. Ours has been, and to a striking degree remains, a society of widespread opportunity and achievement.

2. Yet the achievement of leadership has, increasingly since the Civil War, and more and more as the twentieth century has advanced, accrued to those who took advantage of the opportunities of a higher education.

3. In general, a higher education has been the more advantageous if it has been obtained at one or more of the well-established colleges or universities.

4. In particular, these investigations show that it has been, and continues to be, the graduates of certain celebrated colleges (preeminently Harvard, Yale, and Princeton), and the men who pursued further professional or graduate studies at a select group of outstanding universities (led by Harvard, Columbia, and Yale--then Chicago, Michigan, California, Princeton, and Pennsylvania), who up to this moment have made the most numerous contributions to American leadership and in so doing have helped win for their colleges and universities exceptional reputations.

The first two propositions rest largely on certain well-established facts. Prior to the Civil War professional education in this country was undeveloped and hard to come by, and even a college education was valued only by the minority of ambitious young Americans. But after the Civil War, and especially with the coming of the twentieth century, college-going became more popular, while the added opportunity of graduate and professional training after college came slowly to seem more and more advantageous, if still not altogether

GENERAL RANK ORDER OF OUR COLLEGES AND UNIVERSITIES

As producers of leaders and men of exceptional distinction in American life--with emphasis on the twentieth century.

ALUMNI OF THE COLLEGES	ALUMNI: GRADUATE OR PROF'L SCHOOLS	NET TOTALS: ENTIRE UNIVERSITIES
HARVARD	HARVARD	HARVARD
YALE		
	COLUMBIA	YALE
PRINCETON	YALE	
		COLUMBIA
COLUMBIA		
	CHICAGO	PRINCETON
MICHIGAN	MICHIGAN	
		MICHIGAN
	CALIFORNIA	
PENNSYLVANIA		PENNSYLVANIA
CALIFORNIA	PRINCETON	CALIFORNIA
		CHICAGO
	PENNSYLVANIA	
CHICAGO		CORNELL
CORNELL		
	WISCONSIN	WISCONSIN
	CORNELL	
WISCONSIN		
M.I.T.	JOHNS HOPKINS	
DARTMOUTH		M.I.T.
		JOHNS HOPKINS
MINNESOTA	M.I.T.	
	MINNESOTA	ILLINOIS
	STANFORD	
ILLINOIS	ILLINOIS	STANFORD
N.Y.U.		
STANFORD	N.Y.U.	N.Y.U.
		MINNESOTA
WILLIAMS	NORTHWESTERN	DARTMOUTH
		VIRGINIA
	TEXAS	
		NORTHWESTERN
	OHIO STATE	
		WILLIAMS

indispensable to success. In statistical terms this well-
established surge of American youth into higher education may
be represented by some telling figures. In 1870, 1.68 per
cent or 1 in every 60 young men 18-21 years of age was enrolled in some form of higher education; in 1900, 1 in every
25; in 1940, 1 in every 6.5; and in 1962, 1 in every 2.6.
Have the more successful young men (the men who would later
become the leaders in politics, business, the professions,
and the arts) kept in step with this general movement? They
were far ahead. For our tables demonstrate that, even before
the Civil War, one in every three of the men who won through
to enough distinction and leadership to be listed in the Dictionary of American Biography had gone to college. By 1900
these proportions seem to have shifted radically: One guesses
that on the average perhaps only 25-50 per cent of the leaders
at the turn of the century were self-made men, without the
benefit of a higher education. By the 1950's our professional
elite had almost all gone to college and the majority had
taken professional training as well. In the quite different
field of business--where such a preparation had once seemed
to many unnecessary, if not positively deleterious--a good 80
per cent of the top leadership were now college-educated, and
25 per cent had taken further graduate or professional training. Even in the artistic or nonliterary callings, such as
music, a like trend had recognizably begun to take hold. As
both cause and consequence of this general movement, and in
direct response to the particular demands of the more ambitious, the number of our respectable colleges and universities
had increased in a way to astonish the world. So in table
after table of our statistical findings one may discover that
as many as 75, 100, or 125 colleges and professional schools
had contributed to the preparation of top leadership cadres
often numbering only 200-400 all told. From these figures it
is hard to escape the conclusion that the opportunities for
achievement in American life are still wide but are now to be
found through college rather than without. That is, the colleges have offered something that seemed valuable, especially
to those eager for achievement. And the advantages thus
sought have become attainable in many places. There has been
no monopoly. No single college or university, and no exclusive little coterie of such institutions, has preempted the
paths to advancement.

Yet our statistical investigations suggest also that,
among the many hundreds of contributing institutions, a
much smaller group of colleges and graduate or professional
schools have attracted and taught considerably more than
their numerical share of youthful talent--and a few distinguished institutions have obviously produced far beyond
any statistical expectations. The tables for the several

vocations and professions, and particularly the text and summary tables (M-1, M-2, M-3) in our final chapter, "Summary
and Conclusions," will provide the documentary evidence. So
let us simply note here that these distinctions have been
more marked than many a past commentator was disposed to predict or many a contemporary critic will now wish to recognize.
Not only have certain institutions been able to forward more
graduates into successful careers in this or that business or
profession, but they have done so with an impressive consistency and volume, in field after field, and in generation after generation. Rarely are their graduates missing from the
top echelons of any of the vocations which we have examined.
Indeed the regularities of contribution have been so great
that one can calculate and predict for each of these institutions an expected percentage of participation.

Thus, in any carefully selected lists of the most distinguished leaders in the professions, in politics or scholarship or business, one will find that from 2-20 per cent (on
occasion even 25 per cent) of the individuals will have graduated from or studied at Harvard College--the median expectation being just above 8 per cent. For the sons of Yale College* the range appears to have been between 1.3 and 29 per
cent, with a median expectation of around 7 per cent. For
Princeton College the median figure has been about 4.4 per
cent; for the bachelors from Columbia and Michigan, just
above and below 2 per cent; and for California and Cornell
in the neighborhood of 1.5 per cent. Thus in any adequate
sampling of career leaders, up to now, one can expect to find
on the average twice as many Princeton College graduates as
alumni from Columbia or Michigan, and three times as many as

---

*For easy comparison the "College" means the undergradu-
ates. Thus here, as throughout our tables, when Yale College
is listed or referred to, the term is intended to include all
Yale undergraduates, i.e., the students from the College or
"Academical" Department together with undergraduates from the
three-year (Ph.B.) course of the Sheffield Scientific School
(1852-1919), and from the four-year programs (B.S. and B.E.)
of the reorganized Sheffield Scientific School (1920-45) and
the Engineering School (1932-60). In the same way the students from the now defunct Lawrence Scientific School at Harvard, and the engineering programs at Princeton, have been
counted for Harvard and Princeton Colleges, and undergraduates
of a wide range of vocational specialization, if candidates
for the regular bachelor degrees, have been assimilated to
the students in the humanities, social sciences, natural
sciences, and engineering at Michigan, California (Berkeley),
and many another state university.

had studied as undergraduates at either California or Cornell.

In like fashion, if the reader cares to tabulate the _university_ representations (i.e., the net total number of individuals who had studied in the college or in a graduate or professional school or sometimes in all three), he will find that the percentage of leaders who had had some connection with Harvard (whether candidates for the B.A., LL.B. or M.D., for the M.A., M.B.A., or Ph.D.) ranged from 4.5-40 per cent in the various arts and professions, with a median expectation of about 16 per cent. Yale's graduate and professional schools had been markedly less strong, and in general had supplied fewer leaders, giving the alumni of Yale as a university a range of 2.5-26 per cent, and a "normal" leadership participation of around 9 per cent. In turn the Columbia graduate and professional schools, second only to Harvard in many fields, had added enough to the strong phalanx from the college to give Columbia as a university a range up to 20-22 per cent of some leadership groups, and a median expectation of 7.5 per cent. Princeton as a university showed a range up to 14 per cent, and a median expectation of 6.2 per cent; while Michigan's alumni had not figured in certain leadership groups at all, but, where they did, showed a median expectancy of almost 4 per cent. All of which is to say that in a "normal" group of distinguished elder statesmen, 1 man in every 6 was likely to have studied in some school at Harvard; 1 in every 11 might have lived for a time in New Haven; 1 in every 13 had attended Columbia; 1 in every 16 was probably from Princeton; and every 25th man was likely to have had a Michigan connection of some sort; while no other alumni constituency could be counted on to contribute more than 1 leader in 30, on the average, throughout the vocations and professions.

Such averaged calculations can of course be misleading, for nearly all the alumni constituencies have been uneven in their distribution of efforts and more or less irregular in achievement. Many universities--through their graduates-- seem to have done considerably better than one would have anticipated in particular fields, while failing to figure at all in others. Thus M.I.T. has been the outstanding producer of architects as well as of engineers, and a considerable contributor to big business leadership, too, but without influence in a considerable range of significant professions. Thus Pennsylvania has been uncommonly strong in medicine. Thus Princeton was once extraordinarily effective as a nursery of statesmen, but in the twentieth century has seemed relatively more productive in law, diplomacy, big business, banking, and philanthropy. Thus Harvard College has been preeminent in its production (or attraction) of men of letters, scientists, and scholars, while from Yale College have come more

CAREER EMPHASIS AND SUCCESS IN THE COLLEGE CONSTITUENCIES, 1865-1965

Estimates of the comparative intensity of interest, degree of success, and contributions to leadership in the major vocations and professions on the part of the alumni (graduates and nongraduates) of our leading colleges.

Rank	General Leadership Prior to 1865	Government	Law	Medicine	Protestant Divinity
1.	HARVARD	⌈HARVARD ⌊YALE	YALE	HARVARD	YALE
2.	YALE		HARVARD	YALE	COLUMBIA
3.	⌈PRINCETON ⌊U.S. MIL. ACAD.	PRINCETON	PRINCETON	PENNSYLVANIA	PENNSYLVANIA
4.		MICHIGAN	MICHIGAN	PRINCETON	HARVARD
5.	⌈DARTMOUTH ⌊COLUMBIA	⌈COLUMBIA ⌊PENNSYLVANIA	⌈VIRGINIA ⌊PENNSYLVANIA	MICHIGAN	MICHIGAN
6.				COLUMBIA	N.Y.U.
7.	PENNSYLVANIA	⌈STANFORD VIRGINIA ⌊GEO. WASHINGTON	⌈CHICAGO COLUMBIA ⌊WILLIAMS	⌈DARTMOUTH MINNESOTA ⌊N.Y.U.	
8.	⌈BROWN UNION AMHERST				
9.	⌊WILLIAMS				
10.		⌈CALIFORNIA CORNELL MINNESOTA	⌈GEORGETOWN ⌊TEXAS	⌈CALIFORNIA CHICAGO JOHNS HOPKINS	
11.		⌊WISCONSIN		VIRGINIA ⌊WISCONSIN	
12.			⌈CALIFORNIA ⌊DARTMOUTH		
13.					

Source: The statistical materials gathered for this book.

Big Business, Industry, Banking, Finance	Philanthropy	Science	Literature and the Arts	Education & Scholarship	Who's Who in the 20th Cent.
YALE	YALE	HARVARD	HARVARD	HARVARD	HARVARD
HARVARD	HARVARD	YALE	COLUMBIA YALE	YALE	YALE
PRINCETON	PRINCETON	COLUMBIA		PRINCETON	PRINCETON
CORNELL M.I.T.	DARTMOUTH	CALIFORNIA CHICAGO JOHNS HOPKINS MICHIGAN	PRINCETON	COLUMBIA	MICHIGAN
	MICHIGAN		PENNSYLVANIA	CALIFORNIA CHICAGO MICHIGAN	COLUMBIA
MICHIGAN COLUMBIA CALIFORNIA PENNSYLVANIA STANFORD	CALIFORNIA COLUMBIA CORNELL JOHNS HOPKINS PENNSYLVANIA		CHICAGO		CORNELL
			CALIFORNIA MICHIGAN M.I.T. N.Y.U.		CALIFORNIA
		CORNELL M.I.T.		WISCONSIN	WISCONSIN
				CORNELL DARTMOUTH WILLIAMS	PENNSYLVANIA
		PENNSYLVANIA PRINCETON			CHICAGO
WISCONSIN ILLINOIS MINNESOTA	CHICAGO M.I.T. MINNESOTA WISCONSIN		ILLINOIS CORNELL		U.S. MIL. ACAD.
		WISCONSIN		BROWN PENNSYLVANIA	ILLINOIS U.S. NAV. ACAD.
		ILLINOIS	WISCONSIN		

captains of industry and men of affairs, more lawyers, philanthropists, and leaders of the Protestant ministry. For a rough estimate of the degree of interest, effort, and success among our collegiate constituencies, the reader may consult the table: CAREER EMPHASIS AND SUCCESS IN THE COLLEGE CONSTITUENCIES on page xxiv.

How far may one trust such a table? How accurate are the statistics on which it is based, and how much may they be relied on in drawing conclusions? Here we come to a problem or, rather, to a whole series of problems which merit the most careful consideration.

First, as to the accuracy of the statistics. Warning has already been given that our statistical materials were drawn from diverse public sources, and from leadership lists supplied by other hands, and sometimes with educational attributions which could not be completely verified. These uneven materials were then sorted out, supplemented and analyzed by amateur workers, using only partially satisfactory reference tools, over a considerable stretch of time. And in case after case only a very partial or one-sided sampling could finally be achieved. As a result, the vocational survey was often decidedly limited, and the total coverage far short of what could be desired. On the other hand, to avoid bias or institutional loyalty we looked into a considerable range of occupations, and often investigated a group of directors or a list of medalists or a series of prize winners among whom we supposed few representatives of the "Ivy League" colleges or the major universities would be found. Yet again and again we were staggered by the results. And if often we knew the table was imperfect or limited in some way, each table was nevertheless checked and reworked at least two or three times until it was clear that nothing better under the circumstances could be achieved. Unquestionably there will still be some minor inaccuracies, or some additional attributions which could be supplied. But when table after table, limited or defective as it may be, tells much the same story, and that story conforms to what can be learned by other methods or confirmed by the common knowledge of those expert in the field, it becomes hard to withhold belief. Indeed we are confident that later investigators, working from a more complete body of information and with the far wider command made possible by computer technology, will verify and confirm the main findings of this study.

If so, this leaves us still with the problem of interpretation. For statistics are hardly the same thing as scientific truth. And, in any case, they do not tell us how much credit we must give to the colleges and universities to which future statesmen, or captains of industry, or lawyers or writers happened to go. Would not many of these future leaders have become famous regardless of where or even whether they had gone to college?

Obviously the performance of a college constituency, and the record made by that particular college, must have depended not just on what the college had done to the raw material it received, but also on what raw material came its way. And one has the strong impression that this flow of raw material has been quite uneven--with a far larger indraft of ability into some of the very same colleges and universities which had made the outstanding contributions in previous generations.

To put the matter another way: The development of leadership and achievement, in whatever terms we may translate these words, must over a lifetime depend on many things besides the experience of a higher education. And that education itself may turn out to have been more helpful and influential as a social experience than as an intellectual process or a technical training. This is to say that for many individuals what had perhaps counted most were native ability, parental character, inherited money or family connections, and the planned or accidental associations of schooling and growing up. Quite a few successful alumni had perhaps been destined for important positions almost by birth; a number of others had unquestionably been brought up in high-expectation surroundings; while still others, less well endowed or connected, had benefited from competition and friendships with their more fortunate contemporaries while they were together in college or law school. So, if a college could attract young men of means and talent, it could begin to build a reputation for itself which would in turn attract other able young men, both with established backgrounds and without. Achievement would incite emulation, success would breed success, and over the years there would be a "snowball effect." As my colleague James Tobin goes on to comment, "part of the Harvard-Yale-Princeton attraction to the elite, whether it is a social, money, or brains elite, is precisely that the past elite came from H-Y-P, that other members of the future elite are likely to go there, and that a degree from H-Y-P is a good admission ticket to many career ladders." Of course an admission ticket is not enough to get a man to the top. Even in big business, the corporations are now swifter to hire such men than to promote them (cf. commentaries on "The Big Business Executive," Tables F-2 and F-12). Yet "it helps to have a good position to start climbing." It most certainly does.

It also helps if the college itself is wealthier, older,

and larger than its competitors--and for a wealthy and celebrated university it is a still further advantage to be in or
near one of the financial and cultural centers of the nation.
Vice versa there are poor, backward, and intellectually underdeveloped regions in which colleges find it hard to achieve
quality, universities do not flourish, and able young men
have to start their climb from a social subcellar. Or again
many very large and long-established institutions may find
themselves, like the state or city universities, so situated
politically that they depend on legislative favor for their
support, are expected to emphasize the sciences applied to
agriculture, or engineering, or commerce and home economics,
and are compelled to admit all comers regardless of their
talents or motivation. To the degree that such institutions
find themselves dedicated to mass education (or "followership"
training as one land-grant president once defiantly defined
it) they must inevitably restrict the opportunities for the
able and weaken their own determination to make the most of
any talented minority. And this, too, has a multiplying effect. For the company youth keeps (or fails to keep) will
matter. In a college or professional school which is limited
to a selected clientele of the very able, one may miss the
common touch, but much of the best learning comes from the un-
conscious teaching of one's classmates and competitors. The
able learn from each other--and learn too how to deal with
able men.

     Given such inequalities of talent, judgment, and good
fortune, and such imperfect fluidities of region, class, and
race, a statistician would be foolish to claim too much for
his figures and a humanist will be cautious in attributing exclusive influence to the one factor of a particular institutional connection. Yet it would surely be no less foolish to
overlook the common sense of our findings or to insist on
some patent improbabilities.

     In the first place it would be well to recognize that an
institution with little or nothing to offer is hardly likely
to attract outstanding talent indefinitely. If the reputation and popularity of a college can snowball over the years,
snowballs can also melt--as witness the eclipse of William
and Mary, Transylvania, Union College, and many another once
prominent institution. Ability in the first and second generation of students does not necessarily beget ability in the
third and fourth.

     Age alone will not protect a college, nor traditions
guarantee a bright future. Quite a number of our colonial
and early national foundations have never managed to rise
into the ranks of excellence--or, if they have done so, have

known also long stretches of mediocrity.

Money, of course, is likely to be a great help, to a college as to an individual; yet experience shows that income is never adequate to tomorrow's needs, and the most spectacular gifts or endowments soon shrink and shrink again with the expansion of learning and the depreciation of the dollar. If an example or two may be cited, in New Haven in 1858-61 Yale's promising scientific school was given a building, $100,000, and a name by Joseph Sheffield, to which were quickly added the federal land-grant monies for Connecticut--but after Sheffield's death no donor could be found to fill his shoes, and within thirty years the land-grant fund was taken away. In Baltimore in the 1870's Johns Hopkins got off to its brilliant start in part by having more spending money than any other university except Harvard--but, long before the retirement of its first great president, the trustees painfully awoke to find this endowment quite insufficient for the end-of-the-century competition. Again the University of Chicago and Stanford, with the aid each of one millionaire, achieved spectacular debuts in the 1890's--only to encounter financial difficulties afterwards, and also some quite noticeable ups and downs. Money, one may conclude, helps temporarily, not forever. Instead, once an institution is well launched, what seems to the historian to matter more are the enterprise of its presidents and the continuing excellence of its faculty: two commodities by no means easy to secure or to perpetuate.

The ambition of our colleges for reputation, and for the success of their graduates, have had many other hazards to overcome, not least the mobility of American life and the unpredictability of occupational change. For how perpetuate an institution's eminence in the face of the drainage of American energies to the Middle and Far West? How maintain the excellence and variety of academic opportunities against the competition of bigger universities and larger budgets elsewhere? How continue to generate effective candidates for high positions in government, business, and the professions, through a century of accelerating social change? And how pass on such leadership from one generation of alumni to the next?

After all, even the leadership of the moment is confused and qualified and most precarious. Never yet has an alumni constituency achieved majority command; nor has it been internally harmonious. Men also rise to the top in their professions at different age levels, depending on the requirements of their calling and the accidents of good fortune: The poets and physicists may make their great contributions in their thirties, the historians and the jurists, not till two decades later. So the most loyal college class or

constituency can hardly march forward together. Also, whatever the life cycle of each profession, the leaders generally
manage to stay at the top only while at or near the height of
their powers. They rule their roosts, so to speak, for only
the briefest of intervals. Perhaps eight or ten years may
see the passing of a whole ruling generation. And most jobs
are not inheritable.

A rich man may provide advantages for his son, and even
leave him a controlling share in his business--but careful
studies show that big business leadership has long been depending less and less upon such scions. In politics, again,
few families can count on more than a local influence. In
the law and in the judiciary, eminence is not transferable or
inheritable. In the arts and letters distinction has to be
creatively earned. In scholarship, wealth and breeding may
even perhaps rate as a handicap. Indeed, by and large it
seems impossible to imagine a monied conspiracy so successful,
or a social coterie so effective, or an academic nepotism so
deliberate as to be able to capture and pass down more than
the tiniest fraction of the top job opportunities or posts of
honor in this country. Every four to eight years in the Presidency, every five to ten years perhaps in the sciences, every
six to twelve years apparently in big business, every twenty
years at most in the law and the traditional academic disciplines, the old guard is removed and a younger generation
comes into the positions of leadership and of power. With
anywhere from five to twenty-five turnovers in a century--let
us say, with at least ten complete renovations of personnel
since the Civil War--the automatic perpetuation of any academic oligarchy seems almost unimaginable. Rather one is
tempted to believe that most of the successful may well have
earned their advancements. And if more of them kept coming
from this college than from that, then perhaps this college
itself may have made a contribution to the difference.

Is it not reasonable after all to suppose that, if
college-going in general has proven advantageous to American
youth, then attendance at a particularly effective college
may have been even more beneficial? If it does not seem out-
rageous for a young man interested in architecture or engineering to think of M.I.T., or for a gifted young scientist to ap-
ply to Cal. Tech., why should we be troubled or smell a conspiracy or call into action some discredited Marxian suspicion
or paranoid fantasy, when the brightest, most talented, and
most advantaged young generalists resort to some college or
some small group of colleges which have seemed to give their
predecessors in the older generation both the best of liberal
educations and effective social preparation?

One question of bias or handicap still remains to be considered: the question of size. The bystander may surmise, and the champion of one or more excellent small colleges may charge, that the wealthy big colleges have had an unfair advantage in the competition. For they have graduated far greater numbers of alumni, hence been able to garner more than their share of the top honors and appointments. The observation is valuable and the charge has some substance. But its discount value is perhaps less than supposed.

Let us look at the facts. By 1860 Yale, with 521 undergraduates, had become the largest college (Union having declined), and Harvard, with 896 students altogether, the largest university. And their enrollments kept growing, but unevenly. Meanwhile the registrations at the public institutions were growing faster still. By the 1890's Harvard College was again larger than Yale College and some eight state universities were enrolling more students than could be found in all the schools of Yale University. In the next twenty years these eight institutions and at least four others caught and passed Harvard University, too. So it may be observed that since 1920 Harvard and Yale have not ranked in the first ten for size, and only Harvard has been able to rank in the first twenty. If the reader will consult our sample estimates for college and university enrollments (Tables N-2, N-3), he will find that, at the college or undergraduate level, California, Chicago, Cornell, and Wisconsin have been larger than Harvard College since 1900, as have the undergraduate enrollments at Illinois, Michigan, Minnesota, and Pennsylvania since 1910. Our figures for university enrollments in turn show that in 1900 only Chicago was larger than Harvard (a lead it lost after World War I), but by 1910 Illinois and Michigan had passed the Harvard total; by 1920 California, Columbia, Minnesota, and Wisconsin had moved ahead; and by 1940 Texas had jointed the list of giant universities. Such disparities of enrollment built up, much more slowly but none the less decisively, a series of alumni constituencies slightly larger than Harvard's and considerably larger or several times larger than those for Yale or for Princeton. Hence a mathematical advantage to the state and city universities: They had sent more possible competitors into the competition. Pragmatically their advantage may not have been too substantial. The state universities being coeducational, at the undergraduate level as well, many of their alumni were women, and only theoretically candidates for the Presidency or the Supreme Court.*

---

*It should be noted also that the state universities by the accident of their origins and dedication have devoted

As between Harvard, Yale, and Princeton, our figures show that for every 100 undergraduates at Harvard, Yale College in this century enrolled on the average about 90 and Princeton about 62; while for every 100 university registrations at Harvard, Yale over-all averaged about 67 and Princeton just over 30. These differences produced over-all alumni ratios not far from 100:64:29--a substantial difference in the manpower available for the competition. On the same scale by 1962 the alumni constituency of Johns Hopkins stood at about 27, of Dartmouth at 23.6, of Williams and Swarthmore at 8.3, and of Bowdoin and Reed at only 6.6 and 6.7. This is to say that if Reed College managed to produce 7 leaders to Harvard University's 100, it was, man for man, doing quite as well. Vice versa, Princeton would have to generate almost 4 times as many leaders as Bowdoin or Reed, and Yale would have to match Swarthmore's or Williams' contributions 8 times over to be able to say the same. But whenever Harvard could produce 16 leaders to 1 from Reed, and Yale 9 or more for every graduate of Swarthmore, and Princeton 5 for every man from Bowdoin, the so-called Big Three would be doing better in ratio as well as in weight of production. The reader may find it interesting to analyze the statistical tables in this light. As also to consider the following interpretations:

 From the point of view of the individual, it might in the long run be more advantageous to attend a small college with a high ratio than a large university with a ratio as high or even higher;

 But from the point of view of a college it was perhaps more important to generate 100 leaders out of 1,000 matriculants than to make 10 out of 100.

 In any case, what mattered to American society was leaders. So the excellent large colleges and the great productive universities would, by the sheer magnitude of their contributions, come to exercise a great influence on American life.

But it is now time to examine our findings.

---

major energies to agriculture, to the mechanic arts or engineering, and to teacher training: three areas in which we found the making of statistical comparisons either difficult or impossible. Hence an added statistical disadvantage in our tables.

CHAPTER FROM JAMESTOWN
TO APPOMATTOX

For twentieth-century life in the United States there is perhaps no single honor roll or biographical dictionary, not even Who's Who in America, which will be accepted as a really adequate index of personal worth or register of achievement. For the first 250 years of our history, however, the Dictionary of American Biography (D.A.B.) [Charles Scribner's Sons, 20 volumes, 1928-36, with supplementary volumes in 1944 and 1958] comes close to giving complete satisfaction. Not only does it supersede all the preceding biographical dictionaries; it is more scholarly and more discriminating, and it recognizes a wider range of vocation or variety of distinction. A study of the educational backgrounds of the men and women whose lives are recorded in the D.A.B. is therefore the most illuminating way to begin. It should furnish an informative answer to our question: From Jamestown to Appomattox, which colleges contributed the most to American national leadership?

By way of preliminary warning, one caveat may be in order. A number of our more substantial colleges and some of our great twentieth-century universities were founded late: in the early national period or not until after the Civil War. As Table N-1 well serves to remind us, such notable colleges as Williams, Amherst, Bowdoin, or Hamilton and such significant public institutions as the Universities of North Carolina, Virginia, or Michigan enjoyed, so to speak, but a very brief opportunity to qualify their sons for the D.A.B., while Cornell, Johns Hopkins, California, Chicago, and Stanford could hardly hope to figure in an honor list of American leaders until the opening of the present century. Due allowance must therefore be made for the uneven or delayed development of our structure of higher learning. Yet it has been estimated that as many as 500 colleges had been founded before the Civil War, and for these 500 institutions the D.A.B. furnishes an interesting record.

Because of the sheer numbers involved (13,633 persons in the first 20 volumes) the study of the <u>Dictionary of American Biography</u> might have proved extraordinarily difficult. Happily, a most careful chronological and numerical analysis had already been made by Dr. B. W. Kunkel, Professor of Biology at Lafayette College; and the author very generously encouraged us to make use of his data. It should be remarked that Dr. Kunkel's tabulation by dates of birth has the disadvantage of not identifying exactly the dates of graduation. Also, his data do not cover the biographies in the two supplementary volumes; hence the statistics prove fully meaningful only down to the college generation of those born in the last decade before the Civil War. Finally it should be noted that within the period of reliable coverage, that is to say from 1607 to 1860, about two thirds of the men and women destined for leadership never got to college (a balance that began to shift substantially toward the college-educated only from the 1850's forward). Given these limitations and reservations, however, the message of the Kunkel figures is clear and inescapable.

Of those biographees who did attend some college, the ten leading colleges and the U.S. Military Academy at West Point supplied 60.3 per cent. The remaining 39.7 per cent came from 170 other colleges. It appears, therefore, that our educated leadership was drawn very heavily from a limited number of institutions.

The statistics further show that among these eleven institutions Harvard ranked a clear first and Yale an equally clear second, with the U.S. Military Academy at West Point in third place by reason of the extraordinarily heavy contribution of its graduates to national affairs in the periods of the Mexican and Civil Wars. Princeton ranked a strong third for most of the rest of the time, and close fourth over-all. Vertical comparison of the competitive figures shows that West Point ranked in first place for <u>D.A.B.</u> men born in the 1810's and the 1820's (i.e., presumably graduated in the 1830's and 1840's), in second place for the graduates of the 1820's, and in third place for the men reaching maturity in the Civil War. Otherwise, from the college generation of the 1750's to that of the 1880's, Harvard, Yale, and Princeton nearly monopolized the first three places, and together contributed 33.5 per cent of all graduates listed in the <u>D.A.B.</u>

The chronological arrangement of Kunkel's findings illustrates in a striking way how quickly many of our new colleges attracted talent: Again and again they seem to have been able to contribute a substantial number of leaders within a decade of their founding. Holding on to talent, however, or continuing to attract it and educate it, seem to have been somewhat more difficult matters, as witness the irregularities in the Brown record, or the decline of Union College after the college generation of the 1850's.

Not long ago, when eighteen of America's most eminent political and military leaders were singled out from the <u>Dictionary of American Biography</u> for republication as <u>The American Plutarch</u> (edited by Edward T. James, introduction by Howard Mumford Jones, Scribner's, 1964), it turned out that there had been chosen for this special honor five leaders who had never

gone to college at all: Franklin, Washington, Jackson, Clay, and Lincoln.
Of the remaining 13, 3 had attended West Point (Lee, Grant, and Jefferson
Davis), 2 had studied at William and Mary (Jefferson and Marshall), 2 more
at Columbia (Hamilton and Jay), 2 at Princeton (Madison and Wilson), 2 at
Harvard (Theodore Roosevelt and Oliver Wendell Holmes), and 2 at Yale
(Calhoun and Taft).

One background comparison may be of interest. Examination of their
alumni registers indicates that up to 1880 Harvard had graduated approximately 9,692 from its college, Yale 9,199, and Princeton 5,438. If we
eliminate from their respective lists of biographees all those born after
1860, we find that approximately 6.8 per cent of the graduates of Harvard
College achieved recognition in the D.A.B., while for Yale and Princeton
the respective rates of achievement were 5.6 per cent and 4.7 per cent.

The table shows that only forty of Harvard's D.A.B. graduates and
four of Yale's listed alumni are known to have been born before 1700.

Outstanding graduates of American colleges, as listed in the first twenty volumes of the _Dictionary of American Biography_ (before the supplements), and grouped by decade of birth. Each individual has been credited to the liberal arts college or engineering school awarding him the first degree.

Institution	Before 1700	1700-10	1710-20	1720-30	1730-40	1740-50	1750-60	1760-70	1770-80	1780-90	1790-1800	1800-10	1810-20	1820-30	1830-40	1840-50	1850-60	1860-70	1870-80	1880-90	1890-1900	Total
HARVARD	40	14	9	14	19	27	29	26	27	35	49	51	55	50	80	76	55	43	16	3	1	720[b]
YALE	4	3[a]	15	21	14	8	22	28	17	38	51	35	53	52	62	61	34	23	10	--	1	552[c]
U.S. MILITARY ACADEMY										6	14	46[a]	85	98	48	11	10	11	--	--	--	329
PRINCETON				1	19	27[a]	21	15	20	23	22	16	20	23	18	10	22	9	5	2	--	273
DARTMOUTH							5	7[a]	11	20	17	13	21	18	17	12	13	2	--	--	--	156
COLUMBIA					1	8	3[a]	1	13	13	14	14	14	12	12	12	19	6	6	4	--	152
PENNSYLVANIA					5	14[a]	9	6	9	3	13	9	20	12	12	14	5	8	4	--	--	143
BROWN						2	2	3[a]	14	11	15	18	15	14	13	6	7	4	2	--	--	132
UNION									4	5	15[a]	24	28	14	17	7	3	--	--	--	--	117
AMHERST											1	13	19	13[a]	15	17	16	9	4	--	--	107
WILLIAMS									6	10	8[a]	11	13	9	23	15	4	1	--	2	--	102
Total for 11 Colleges	17	17	24	36	58	86	91	86	121	164	219	250	343	321	317	241	188	116	47	11	2	2,783
Remaining 170 Colleges		0	0	1	1	5	8	9	19	33	88	138	193	263	273	258	277	172	63	20	3	1,828[d]
Total College Graduates	17	17	24	37	59	91	99	95	140	197	307	388	536	584	590	499	465	288	110	31	5	4,611
No College Connection or Unknown	63	63	122	142	273	308	264	284	403	399	561	780	1,003	1,041	937	837	473	199	56	10	5	9,022[e] / 13,633

[a]Indicates decade institution was organized.

[b]Includes one whose year of birth is not known and 40 born before 1700.

[c]Includes 4 born before 1700.

[d]Includes 4 whose year of birth is not known.

[e]Includes 299 whose year of birth is not known and 623 born before 1700.

Source: Table adapted by permission from B. W. Kunkel, "Eminent Graduates of American Colleges," _Bulletin of the Association of American Colleges_, December, 1944.

After consultation with specialists, there was drawn up for the biographical section of the <u>Encyclopedia of American History</u> (Harper and
Brothers, 1953) a list that "would constitute well-rounded representation
of the most eminent American men and women in major fields of activity."
Only those who had been citizens of the United States were eligible, and,
to survive the competition, a candidate's contribution "must have been
notable not only for its time and place but still have measurable impact
on our way of life." The Presidents of the United States were all automatically included (and the Wright brothers were counted as one).

Our analysis of this list of 301, after it was published in 1953,
showed Harvard strongly in the lead both as a college and as a university.
Harvard's outstanding contribution of 42 individuals was followed by 23 en-
tries for Yale, 13 each for Columbia and West Point, 10 for Princeton, 8
for Johns Hopkins, and the rest scattering. On closer study, it developed
that a substantial part of Harvard's impressive representation derived
from its 16 Presidents, statesmen, jurists, or lawyers; and another substantial part came from its extraordinary contribution of 16 distinguished
writers, philosophers, social scientists, or architects. By contrast,
Yale fielded 6 names in law and politics, and but 5 in literature or the
arts. In education, despite Yale's reputation as the "mother of colleges
and college presidents," the electors had given the two universities equal
delegations (Eliot and Langdell from Harvard College, with Flexner and
Thorndike from its graduate division, as against Henry Barnard, D. C.
Gilman, and Andrew D. White from Yale College, with William Rainey Harper,
Yale Ph.D.--but no mention of such powerful educational statesmen as
Timothy Dwight or Theodore Dwight Woolsey). Again, the choice of religious
leaders, with Harvard's W. E. Channing, Theodore Parker, and Phillips
Brooks given precedence over all the makers of the New England and American theology between Jonathan Edwards and Reinhold Niebuhr, seemed possibly
open to question, as did also the omission of Benjamin Silliman from the
list of notables in American science. We felt sure that Princetonians
(and others, too) would regret the failure to list Dr. Benjamin Rush, as
in like fashion the sons and friends of many another institution might
find reason to question the omission of other individuals of some note.
However, that was the way the choices had been made, and this table investigated the education of the 300 thus chosen.

Further study showed that the United States Military Academy had
earned its third-place tie primarily, but not entirely, because of the
achievements of its graduates in the Civil War. As for the ranking given
Columbia, this was in part accounted for by the inclusion of De Witt
Clinton and Hamilton Fish among the statesmen, and Nicholas Murray Butler
among the great educators.

It was interesting to observe that, even in times past, at least two
thirds of the scientists had attended more than one institution, and instructive to be reminded of the contribution of European universities to

300 "NOTABLE AMERICANS"

An inquiry into the college affiliations of the "300 Notable Americans"

	HARVARD	YALE	COLUMBIA	U.S.M.A.	PRINCETON	JOHNS HOPKINS	WILLIAM & MARY	BOWDOIN	DARTMOUTH	U.S.N.A.	WILLIAMS	74 Other American Colleges and Universities	European Universities	Attended More Than One Institution	Did Not Attend College	Total Individuals
Individuals	42	23	13	13	10	8	5	4	4	4	4	89	37	56	95	300
Total Graduate and Professional Connections	16	5	8	0	3	6	0	0	0	0	0	26				
Total Undergraduate Connections	31	19	8	13	7	2	5	4	4	4	4	85				
Scientists	1+3=3	2+0=2	2+4=4	1+0=1	0+3=3	1+3=3				1+0=1		20+3=23	9	22	1	32
Inventors		3+2=4										2+1=2	4	1	7	16
Business Leaders					1+0=1							2+0=2	1		14	18
Pioneers and Explorers								1+0=1		1+0=1		2+1=2	1	1	6	10
Journalists, Editors, and Publishers											1+0=1		1		6	8
Social Reformers and Labor Leaders												3+0=3			12	15
Educators	2+2=4	3+1=4	1+1=2			1+0=1						4+0=4	1	3	2	14
Religious Leaders	3+0=3	1+1=2										1+0=1	4		4	14
Musicians and Composers												1+0=1	1		2	4
Theatre and Applied Arts					1+0=1										5	6
Architects	2+0=2	1+0=1										2+0=2	3	2		6
Artists				1+0=1								6+0=6	3	1	4	13
Belles Lettres, Philosophy, and Social Sciences	12+4=14	3+1=4			1+0=1	0+3=3		2+0=2	1+0=1			12+2=11	5	10	11	40
Naval and Military Figures				7+0=7			1+0=1			2+0=2		1+0=1			7	18
Statesmen	4+2=5	2+0=2	3+0=3		1+0=1				2+0=2			11+3=12	3	4	5	33
Jurists and Lawyers	3+3=5	3+0=3	2+2=3		1+0=1		1+0=1		1+0=1		2+0=2	7+2=6	1	6	1	20
Presidents	4+2=6	1+0=1	0+1=1	2+0=2	2+1=2	0+1=1	3+0=3	1+0=1			1+0=1	11+3=13	1	5	8	33

Note: The first number in each column indicates the undergraduate connections; the underscored number represents the graduate or professional connections; and the last figure gives the net total of individuals who were educated at the given institution in that category.

Source: Selected and classified for the biographical section of Encyclopedia of American History, edited by Richard B. Morris, 1953. Cf. article by Morris, "Where Success Begins," The Saturday Review, November 21, 1953.

the education of 37 or 12 per cent of the 300 "Notable Americans." Altogether some 95 individuals or 32 per cent had managed to become "notable" without benefit of higher education--most easily in the fields of business, labor, social reform, journalism, and writing. By contrast, almost the same number, or a net total of 98 individuals, could claim to have achieved a part or all of their preparation for distinction at Harvard, Yale, Columbia, West Point, or Princeton.

In 1961 (or some years after our Table A-2 was originally constructed) the Encyclopedia of American History enlarged its list of "Notable Americans" from 300 to 400, in the process modifying certain of the categories, dropping out some 6 of the original 300 notables, and adding 107 (the Mayo brothers counting as one) to its new roll of honor. Examination of the new names showed that the editors of the Encyclopedia must have shared one or two of the reservations expressed above. For now both Benjamin Silliman and Benjamin Rush were included. The 6 omitted figures turned out to be the "Swamp Fox," Francis Marion; the business leader, Thomas Coleman DuPont; and 4 scientists, Carl D. Anderson of Cal. Tech., Alfred Blalock of Georgia and Johns Hopkins, Ross G. Harrison of Johns Hopkins and Bonn, and Harvey Cushing of Yale and Harvard.

In the expanded list Harvard registered 15 new names, Columbia 10, Yale 6, Princeton 5, Berlin 5, C.C.N.Y. and N.Y.U. each 4, the U.S. Military Academy, Oxford, and California each 3. With allowance made for dropped notables, this gave Harvard a net total of 56 out of the 402 individuals in the new listing. With 6 new names and 1 deletion, Yale's contribution rose to 28. With 10 new names Columbia's figure came close to doubling at 23. The U.S. Military Academy and Princeton followed at 16 and 15, after which came Johns Hopkins at 6, William and Mary at 6, U.S. Naval Academy and Williams College, each at 5.

Close inspection suggested the interest of some of the new choices and underlined the difficulties of the choosing. Thus Princeton added not only Benjamin Rush but John Foster Dulles and three who attended but did not graduate: John Randolph of Roanoke, F. Scott Fitzgerald, and John F. Kennedy (briefly as a freshman). The Yale additions, besides Benjamin Silliman and Samuel J. Tilden (attended) for the nineteenth century, were Robert A. Taft, Archibald McLeish, and John Franklin Enders (all of Yale College), with Joshua Lederberg, Ph.D. (a graduate of Columbia).

Columbia's enlarged list rescued Robert Livingston, B.A. 1765, from neglect, and showed that John Randolph of Roanoke had also tried studying in New York. Its other notables were of more recent instruction: Harlan Fiske Stone, Michael Pupin, Charles A. Beard, Herman J. Muller, Edwin H. Armstrong, Oscar Hammerstein II, and Richard Rodgers (attended). Finally, Harvard's new list began by doing justice to Increase Mather, Thomas Hutchinson, and James Otis; then filled in Wendell Phillips, Samuel Gridley Howe, and Herbert Croly (attended) for the nineteenth century; and for the twentieth century added W. E. B. DuBois, Leonard Bernstein, John F. Kennedy, Felix Frankfurter, and Learned Hand--as well as the Yale graduates Enders (Ph.D.), McLeish, and Taft (both LL.B.).

Another very different and somewhat questionable honor list is provided by the Hall of Fame for Great Americans, which is administered for
the American people by New York University. The great Americans are
selected in some measure by popular ballot. Any citizen may submit a nomination, and every five years these nominations are winnowed by a committee of electors, with all states represented. The rules allow no more
than seven persons to be added to the Hall of Fame in a given election
year, and a majority vote is required. A certain amount of campaigning
seems to precede the election.

The quasi-popular choice, thus achieved, reflects some striking pref-
erences and makes an astonishing contrast with the 402 "Notable Americans."
To begin with, Columbia loses all of its 23 notables, except Alexander
Hamilton. Princeton loses 13 of its 15, retaining only Madison and Woodrow
Wilson. West Point keeps Whistler, Poe, and 3 soldiers, Grant, Lee, and
Sherman. Yale is cut down to 1 theologian, Edwards; 1 lawyer, Kent; 1
author, Cooper; 1 scientist, Gibbs; and 2 inventors, Eli Whitney and S. F. B.
Morse. Harvard gains one inventor not listed among the 402 Notables, the
anaesthetist, Morton, while retaining both Channing and Phillips Brooks as
theologians, as well as its strong cluster of writers. Johns Hopkins drops
out of the list of leading contributors entirely. And once again those who
know their colleges will find reasons to regret omissions from this popular
roll of honor.

By 1960, the Hall of Fame had enrolled 17 statesmen, 17 authors, 9
scientists, 6 educators, 5 inventors, 5 clergymen, and 4 lawyers, with the
rest scattering. Some 33 of these immortals had never been to college,
among them Edwin Booth, Daniel Boone, Elias Howe, Admiral Farragut, John
Paul Jones, Patrick Henry, and no fewer than 6 women: Emma Willard, Mary
Lyon, Maria Mitchell, Harriet Beecher Stowe, Charlotte S. Cushman, and
Susan B. Anthony. The feelings behind such choices are obvious. The Hall
of Fame seems an honor list out of our patriotic past, and out of the
romantic hero-worship of days gone by.

THE HALL OF FAME

1900-60

Educational backgrounds of the individuals
elected to the Hall of Fame

College or University	Undergraduate Connections	Graduate or Professional	Net Total Individuals
HARVARD	14	7	16
U.S. MILITARY ACAD.	6	-	6
YALE	6	1	6
WILLIAM AND MARY	3	-	3
BOWDOIN	2	-	2
DARTMOUTH	2	-	2
PRINCETON	2	1	2
WILLIAMS	2	-	2
25 Other Colleges and Universities	13	13	18
Foreign Universities and Institutions	6	13	9
Totals			
Hall of Fame Members with College or University Connections	46	33	56
Hall of Fame Members with No College or University Connections	-	-	33
Net Total Individuals			89

Source: The Hall of Fame for Great Americans at New York University, edited by Theodore Morello, New York University Press; Dictionary of American Biography.

CHAPTER B THE MAKING OF
AMERICAN STATESMEN

Just as education for greatness had long been the quiet
business of the clustered colleges of Oxford and Cambridge,
so the making of statesmen for this new world became a major
purpose and justification for our scattered colonial colleges.
From its earliest beginnings, Harvard served the settlers of
Massachusetts Bay as a nursery of future governors and great
Puritan divines. In 1701, Connecticut chartered a Collegiate
School wherein youth might be "fitted for Publick employment
both in Church & Civil State"--and before long the graduates
of Yale were guiding that land of steady habits in offices of
public responsibility. In Virginia the College of William
and Mary survived its precarious beginnings to contribute men
of such stature as Thomas Jefferson, Edmund Randolph, and
John Marshall to the making of the new nation. Princeton,
founded as the College of New Jersey as late as 1746, would
generate no fewer than twenty-two members of the Continental
Congress. And King's College, before the Revolution changed
its name to Columbia, had already nurtured Alexander Hamilton
and John Jay.

Notwithstanding such public records, the alumni of our
colonial colleges, and indeed of their nineteenth-century
descendants and rivals--whether colleges or universities,
public or private--proved more eager to celebrate the great
graduates, each of his own alma mater, than to compare such
contributions with the achievements of rival institutions.
In compensation for these understandable loyalties, and in
partial repair of an unfortunate neglect, we offer nine
tables. They will attempt to sample the varieties of
statesmanship, and the differences of alumni contribution
from the Declaration of Independence to today.

Our first table (B-1) analyzes the Signers of the Declaration of Independence with rather interesting results. Half of these bold revolutionaries had apparently never been to college either in the colonies or abroad. To the 28 who had known some higher education Harvard had made the outstanding numerical contribution. Its delegation of 8 members, headed by the 2 Adamses and the elegant penman John Hancock, was twice as large and, oddly enough, rather younger than the next largest delegation of 4 from Yale. William and Mary could boast the incomparable Thomas Jefferson, B.A. 1762, and 3 others who had certainly or probably studied in its halls. Pennsylvania and Princeton each contributed 2 Signers. Benjamin Rush, after graduating at Princeton, had taken his doctor's degree at Edinburgh. James Wilson had attended no American college but 3 universities in Scotland. The University of Edinburgh had seen to the education also of the redoubtable John Witherspoon. Two Signers had studied at Cambridge in old England, but none came from Oxford. Six had taken lawyers' training at Inns of Court. Out of 9 colonial colleges, King's College (Columbia), Queen's College (later Rutgers), Dartmouth, and Brown were not represented.

Between them the 3 most solidly established colleges--Harvard, Yale, and Princeton--had produced 14 of the 17 degree-holding graduates, and 25 per cent of the whole group of Signers.

THE SIGNERS, 1776

Education of the Fifty-six Signers of the Declaration of Independence

In the Colonies

HARVARD
John Adams (A.B. 1755)
Samuel Adams (A.B. 1740)
William Ellery (A.B. 1747)
Elbridge Gerry (A.B. 1762)
John Hancock (A.B. 1754)
William Hooper (A.B. 1760)
Robert Treat Paine (A.B. 1749)
William Williams (A.B. 1751)

WILLIAM AND MARY
Carter Braxton
Thomas Jefferson (B.A. 1762)
Benjamin Harrison (1745)
?George Wythe

YALE
Lyman Hall (B.A. 1747)
Philip Livingston (B.A. 1737)
Lewis Morris (B.A. 1746)
Oliver Wolcott (B.A. 1747)

PENNSYLVANIA
Francis Hopkinson (A.B. 1757)
William Paca (A.B. 1759)

PRINCETON
Benjamin Rush (A.B. 1760)
Richard Stockton (A.B. 1748

In England

CAMBRIDGE UNIVERSITY
Thomas Lynch, Jr. (1767-72)
Thomas Nelson, Jr. (1758-61)

UNIVERSITY OF EDINBURGH
Benjamin Rush (M.D. 1768)
James Wilson (1763-65)
John Witherspoon (1736-43)

UNIVERSITY OF GLASGOW
James Wilson (1759-63)

UNIVERSITY OF ST. ANDREWS
James Wilson (1757-59)

INNS OF COURT
Thomas Heyward, Jr. (1765-   )
Thomas Lynch, Jr. (?1764-67)
Edward Rutledge (1767-   )
Arthur Middleton (1763)
William Paca
Charles Carroll (1757-60?)

Charles Carroll of Carrollton, after being educated by the Jesuits of the Collège de St. Omer, at Rheims, and again at the Collège de Louis le Grand in Paris, studied civil law at Bourges and continued at the Inns of Court, London.

College or University	Graduated	Attended	Total Individuals
HARVARD	8		8
WILLIAM AND MARY	1	?3	?4
YALE	4		4
PENNSYLVANIA	2		2
PRINCETON	2		2
In England or Europe	1	9	10
Net Totals	18	12	28
No College or Unknown			28

The Delegates to the Federal Convention, chosen after a decade of great ventures and trials, could claim an even higher incidence of college attendance than the Signers (in a day when college attendance was still most exceptional). In their company were now also two alumni of King's College (Columbia) in the persons of Gouverneur Morris and Alexander Hamilton. Otherwise the same colleges enter (or are missing from) the table, though with an almost entirely fresh roster of representatives.

Among these constitution-makers the number of the Princeton graduates is exceptional and their role surprising. As the figures show, Princeton contributed more than twice as many delegates as Harvard; and among the alumni of that or any other college none could compare with Princeton's James Madison, the chief architect of the Federal Constitution under which we still live. The odd part is that 5 of Princeton's delegation of 9 would eventually, for one reason or another, not sign--among them Oliver Ellsworth, delegate from Connecticut, who had attended Yale and then graduated at Princeton, A.B. 1766.

Five Signers of the Declaration of Independence--James Wilson, George Clymer, Benjamin Franklin, George Read, and Roger Sherman--had the honor of subscribing the new Constitution as well. The only other Signers on hand were George Wythe, who resigned from the Convention, and Elbridge Gerry, A.B. Harvard 1762, who refused to sign but did submit the document with his protests to the Massachusetts government. Oxford contributed Charles C. Pinckney, who later studied law at the Middle Temple, as did 5 others. Glasgow and Edinburgh had each had a hand in the education of 2 delegates, St. Andrews of 1; but this time no graduate of Cambridge appeared on the scene.

It may be appropriate here to note that Princeton's dedication to the public service and its flair for producing men destined to make a mark in public life would continue with remarkable vitality. Woodrow Wilson's motto of "Princeton in the nation's service" was to be merely a twentieth-century restatement of the University's ingrained habit. Already by 1896 the General Catalogue of the College could claim 1 President, 2 Vice-Presidents, and 13 Cabinet officers; 2 presidents of the United States Senate and 54 Senators; 3 Speakers of the House of Representatives and 135 Representatives; 15 Ministers Plenipotentiary; 31 governors; 5 presidents of provincial congresses; 17 members of state constitutional conventions; 1 Chief Justice of the United States and 5 Justices of the U.S. Supreme Court; 9 Attorneys General and 204 judges; 42 state attorneys general; 14 state chancellors; 7 presidents of state senates; 53 state senators; 23 speakers of state assemblies; 109 state assemblymen; and 28 state chief justices (to say nothing of scientists, physicians, or founders, presidents, and trustees of American colleges).

DELEGATES TO THE FEDERAL CONVENTION, 1787

Education of the 55 Delegates to the Federal Convention of 1787.   Of these Delegates 39 eventually signed the United States Constitution, but 16 did not.   Among the 16, 4 had no institutional connection; 1 had attended Yale and graduated from Princeton; 2 had attended Harvard; 4 had studied at William and Mary; and 5 altogether had attended Princeton.   A tabulation of the college connections of the actual signers would therefore show: Princeton and Yale 4 each; Harvard, Columbia, and Pennsylvania 2 each; and William and Mary 1.

College or University	Undergraduate	Graduate or Professional	Net Total Individuals
PRINCETON	9	1	9
YALE	5	1	5
WILLIAM AND MARY	5	-	5
HARVARD	3	1	4
COLUMBIA	2	-	2
PENNSYLVANIA	2	-	2
Foreign Colleges and Universities	5	8	9
Totals			
Number of Individuals with Some Known College or University Connection	28	10	32
No College or University Connection	-	-	22
Unknown	-	-	1
Net Individuals	-	-	55

Source: Max Farrand, editor, The Records of the Federal Convention, 1911.

The condensed statistics on the National Executive cover the first 173 years of our existence as an independent nation, and reflect the widening opportunities of education and of participation in the executive branch of our federal government. Of our colonial colleges all but Rutgers sent forward at least four alumni to the Presidency or to Cabinet positions. In addition one notes the substantial contributions of the Universities of Michigan, Virginia, North Carolina, Cincinnati, and Texas together with the Colleges of Union, Dickinson, West Point, Transylvania, Amherst, and Brown. Altogether 176 institutions of higher learning had a hand in the shaping of the federal executive. Michigan contributed no Presidents or Vice-Presidents but was strong in Agriculture and Commerce. Columbia did best in State and Treasury. William and Mary made a distinguished record in the Presidency, Vice-Presidency, State Department and Attorney General's office before declining in prestige and output. North Carolina proves to have been prolific of Secretaries of the Navy; Brown, of Secretaries of State. In short, our figures suggest the role played by chance and a considerable irregularity or unevenness of participation.

Notwithstanding, the preeminence of Harvard as a nursery of statesmen is made unmistakable in this table. Princeton College educated Presidents Madison and Wilson and contributed an exceptional number of Secretaries of State, War, Navy, and Attorneys General. Yale College produced 1 President, William Howard Taft; 1 Vice-President, John C. Calhoun; and an average of 5 officers for each of the original major Cabinet positions. Meanwhile, Harvard College generated 5 Presidents (2 Adams, 2 Roosevelts, and J. F. Kennedy) and a great number of Cabinet officers; on top of which the Harvard Law School gave an LL.B. in 1845 to future President Rutherford B. Hayes (a graduate of Kenyon) and in the past eighty years has drawn outstanding future executives from far and near. It is true that four of the individuals thus connected with Harvard had taken their undergraduate degrees at Yale: William M. Evarts, William C. Whitney, Henry L. Stimson, and Dean Acheson. Even so, Harvard as a university had a hand in the education of almost as many statesmen as Yale and Princeton put together.

The third statistical emphasis which emerges from this table is the tremendous cumulative contribution made by these three. Eliminating duplicate names between them, 104 individuals out of a total of 201 for the top 18 colleges and universities owed all or a part of their education to Harvard, Yale, or Princeton. In the major offices of the Cabinet this preponderance is particularly striking. Nine out of 34 Presidents or 26 per cent, 19 out of 53 Secretaries of State or 36 per cent, 10 out of 54 Secretaries of the Treasury or 19 per cent, 19 out of 60 Secretaries of War or 31 per cent, 21 out of 62 Attorneys General or 34 per cent, and 19 out of 47 Secretaries of the Navy or 40 per cent, had been connected with one or the other of these three universities: an over-all average of 31 per cent for the six most important executive functions. When it is realized that a substantial number of individuals appear never to have gone to college at all, the role of Harvard, Yale, and Princeton in producing educated leaders seems all the more remarkable.

In the minor Cabinet offices their contributions were less outstanding. Harvard produced no Secretaries of the Interior, or of Commerce and Labor; Yale none of Agriculture, or of Labor, or of Health, Education, and

THE NATIONAL EXECUTIVE, 1789-1962

College and University connections of the Presidents and Vice Presidents of the United States and the duly-appointed members of the Cabinet

Office / Category	HARVARD	YALE	PRINCETON	MICHIGAN	COLUMBIA	VIRGINIA	WILLIAM & MARY	NORTH CAROLINA	PENNSYLVANIA	DARTMOUTH	UNION	DICKINSON	U. OF CINCINNATI	U.S.M.A.	TRANSYLVANIA	AMHERST	BROWN	TEXAS	Net Totals (top 18)	158 Other Institutions	Net Individuals: All Colleges	No College or Unknown	Individuals: Grand Totals
Net Total Individuals	57	35	28	14	14	12	11	12	10	8	7	7	6	6	6	5	4	5	214	181	347	100	447
Graduate or Professional Connections	30	9	1	7	10	8	0	0	3	0	0	0	5	0	3	0	3	1	83	60	134		134
Undergraduate Connections	37	32	27	7	5	4	11	12	8	8	7	7	1	6	3	5	4	1	179	158	322		322
Total Cabinet & Non-Cabinet Officers																							
Net Individuals	57	35	28	14	14	12	11	12	10	8	7	7	6	6	6	5	4	5	214	181	347	100	447
Total Positions	71	42	33	15	14	12	17	14	12	10	9	9	7	6	6	6	6	6	255	207	411	112	523
Non-Cabinet Officers																							
Net Individuals	4	6	3	1	1	1	0	0	2	2	1	0	0	0	0	0	0	2	16	5	19	2	21
Total Positions	4	6	3	1	1	1	0	0	2	2	1	0	0	0	0	0	0	2	16	5	19	2	21
Sec'y of Army (Est. 1947)	1	2	1	0	0	0	0	0	2	1	0	0	0	0	0	0	0	0	5	1	6	0	6
Sec'y of Navy (Est. 1947)	1	0	0	0	0	0	0	0	1	1	0	0	0	0	0	0	0	2	4	3	6	2	8
Sec'y of Air Force (Est. 1947)	2	4	2	0	1	0	0	0	1	0	0	0	0	0	0	0	0	0	7	1	7	0	7
Cabinet Officers																							
Net Individuals	54	29	25	13	13	12	11	11	9	7	7	7	6	6	6	5	4	4	201	177	331	98	429
Total Positions	67	36	30	14	13	12	17	12	10	9	9	7	6	6	6	6	4	4	239	202	388	110	498
Sec'y of Health, Education, and Welfare (Est. 1953)	1	0	0	0	0	0	0	0	0	0	0	0	0	0	0	0	0	0	1	5	5	0	5
Sec'y of Defense (Est. 1947)	3	1	1	0	0	1	0	0	0	1	0	0	0	0	0	0	0	0	6	3	8	0	8
Sec'y of Commerce (Est. 1913)	1	1	0	2	0	0	0	0	1	0	0	0	0	0	0	1	0	0	7	8	14	2	16
Sec'y of Labor (Est. 1913)	1	0	0	0	1	0	0	0	0	0	0	0	0	0	0	0	0	0	2	8	8	3	11
Sec'y of Commerce and Labor (Est. 1903)	0	1	0	0	1	0	0	0	0	0	0	0	0	0	0	0	0	0	2	2	4	0	4
Sec'y of Agriculture (Est. 1889)	1	0	0	3	0	0	0	0	0	0	0	0	0	0	0	0	0	0	4	13	15	1	16
Sec'y of Interior (Est. 1849)	0	1	0	1	1	0	1	1	0	0	1	0	1	0	0	0	0	0	6	25	28	9	37
Postmaster General (Est. 1789)	6	5	1	2	0	0	1	1	1	1	0	1	0	2	0	1	0	1	22	20	37	17	54
Sec'y of Navy (Est. 1789)	8	5	7	2	1	0	3	0	4	0	1	2	0	0	0	0	0	0	29	9	34	13	47
Attorney General (Est. 1789)	10	7	5	2	1	1	3	4	0	3	1	1	1	0	1	0	1	2	39	26	54	8	62
Sec'y of War (Est. 1789)	10	6	4	1	1	0	2	2	0	1	3	1	1	3	1	0	1	0	32	18	45	15	60
Sec'y of Treasury (Est. 1789)	6	2	2	3	0	1	0	0	2	1	2	1	0	0	0	0	1	0	22	20	39	15	54
Sec'y of State (Est. 1789)	11	5	6	1	3	1	3	0	0	1	1	1	0	0	0	1	0	4	33	18	44	9	53
Vice-President	3	1	3	0	1	1	2	0	0	0	1	0	1	0	2	0	0	0	16	15	27	10	37
President	6	1	2	0	1	1	3	0	0	0	1	1	1	2	0	1	0	0	18	12	26	8	34

Welfare. On the other hand, an analysis of the Office of Secretary of Defense, and of the non-Cabinet offices since that office was created, suggests that the role of the three leaders continues to be one of major proportions. As already indicated, 5 out of their 9 Presidents have held office in the twentieth century. A count showed that 33 out of Harvard's 57, 17 out of Yale's 35, and 6 out of Princeton's 28 federal executives have achieved their positions since 1900.

Note: Ad interim tenants of vacant Cabinet offices have not been counted.

B-4. "THE AMERICAN FEDERAL EXECUTIVE," IN 1959

The interesting study by W. Lloyd Warner and his associates of "The American Federal Executive" as of the year 1959 suggests the still wider distribution of educational opportunities of recent years and the increasing tendency to seek formal academic training as a preparation for (or a road of promotion within) the government service.

This training has been obtained primarily in the public institutions. George Washington, C.C.N.Y., and California (Berkeley) all appear to have produced more bachelors for the federal executive than Harvard; and the next most productive institutions have been the state universities of Minnesota, Illinois, Michigan, Wisconsin, Ohio State, and Washington. Only at the head of the second ten does one find such private institutions as M.I.T., Princeton, Yale, and N.Y.U. At the higher level of the doctorate Harvard, Chicago, Columbia, Johns Hopkins and Cornell do much better, with Wisconsin, California, and Minnesota for the state universities, followed by Yale and N.Y.U.

In interpreting such totals, two cautionary words are in order. First it should be noticed that the survey covered 2,169 members of the foreign service and 1,865 with political appointments, but no fewer than 7,640 from the career civil service (with 69 per cent of the grand total responding to the original questionnaire). In other words, the career civil service counted for almost twice the appointive posts at home and abroad, and quite outweighed them in the balance. Whether civil servants down to GS-14 should be characterized as an "elite" may also be a question.

In the second place the count of four-year degrees (first column) lumped together bachelors of arts and bachelors of science with other four-year bachelor degrees in engineering, business administration, etc. About one third of those responding proved to have engineering degrees, and another 16 per cent reported degrees in administration--subjects either omitted or slighted in most liberal arts colleges. Twenty-five per cent reported degrees in the physical or biological sciences, leaving at most another 25 per cent for the social sciences and the humanities.

The very respectable output of Maryland, George Washington, American University, and Georgetown among the producers of doctoral degrees and the quite extraordinary showing of George Washington on bachelor degrees may reflect the tendency of many government employees in Washington to complete their education by taking courses in engineering or business administration or by adding professional training to their equipment while continuing in the civil service at the nation's capital.

"THE AMERICAN FEDERAL EXECUTIVE," IN 1959

Four-year (bachelor) and doctoral degrees held by "the elite of all departments and all agencies, old and new, from State, Treasury, and Defense to Health, Education, and Welfare, from TVA to the Small Business Administration, in and out of Washington." Questionnaires were sent to "the men and women of the career civil service, the foreign service, and those who have political appointments ranging from Cabinet level to General Schedule (GS) grade level 14 or equivalent: 7,640 from the career civil service, 1,269 from the foreign service, and 1,865 with political appointments (plus 77 unclassifiable)--a total of 10,851 civilian employees." Over 69 per cent of those receiving schedules filled them out and returned them.

Thirty Institutions Which Produced the Largest Number of Four-Year Degrees Reported by Civilian Federal Executives		Thirty Institutions Which Produced the Largest Number of Federal Executives with Doctoral Degrees	
Institution	Number	Institution	Number
GEORGE WASHINGTON	260	HARVARD	85
C.C.N.Y.	180	CHICAGO	70
CALIFORNIA	173	WISCONSIN	64
HARVARD	156	COLUMBIA	51
MINNESOTA	138	JOHNS HOPKINS	49
ILLINOIS	135	CORNELL	44
MICHIGAN	134	CALIFORNIA	42
WISCONSIN	130	MINNESOTA	40
OHIO STATE	128	YALE	36
WASHINGTON	123	N.Y.U.	30
M.I.T.	120	ILLINOIS	29
PRINCETON	115	OHIO STATE	28
YALE	110	MARYLAND	24
N.Y.U.	107	MICHIGAN	23
CORNELL	107	IOWA	23
BENJAMIN FRANKLIN U.	87	M.I.T.	23
PENNSYLVANIA	86	STANFORD	22
MISSOURI	81	IOWA STATE	22
PURDUE	79	PRINCETON	20
GEORGETOWN	77	GEORGE WASHINGTON	18
NEBRASKA	76	PENNSYLVANIA	17
CHICAGO	76	AMERICAN U.	17
STANFORD	76	CAL. TECH.	16
PENN STATE	71	NORTH CAROLINA	12
COLORADO	63	PITTSBURGH	10
IOWA	60	NEBRASKA	10
IOWA STATE	60	GEORGETOWN	9
COLUMBIA	59	NORTHWESTERN	9
KANSAS	59	TECH. U. DARMSTADT	8
SYRACUSE	55	CLARK	8

Source: Statistics reproduced by permission from W. Lloyd Warner, Paul P. Van Riper, Norman H. Martin, and Orvis F. Collins, The American Federal Executive: A Study of the Social and Personal Characteristics of the Civilian and Military Leaders of the United States Federal Government, New Haven: Yale University Press, 1963, pp. 132, 138.

B-5.   BRANCHES OF "THE AMERICAN FEDERAL EXECUTIVE," IN 1959

The statistical breakdown between the three branches of the federal executive--career civil service executives, political executives, foreign service executives--is both informative and revealing of a certain emphasis in the Lloyd Warner study. The weight given to career civil service executives (down to GS-14) is demonstrated by the fact that, of the first 16 producers of such executives (second column), all but the last 3-- Purdue, Missouri, and Nebraska--were found also among the top 16 producers of "all civilian federal executives," and in much the same order. Harvard ranked 21st in career executives; while Yale and Princeton failed to figure in the top 30, and only managed to rise into the top 16 on an overall basis by virtue of their contributions of political executives and foreign service executives.

A second noteworthy feature of this table was the strong showing, not only of George Washington, with its opportunities of instruction at the nation's capital, but of C.C.N.Y. Both George Washington and C.C.N.Y. had produced more political executives than might have been anticipated, while the graduates of California were strong in all categories.

A third feature worth noting is the wide educational spread and opportunity. No longer are the superior offices in government being staffed exclusively by the 9 colonial colleges, or by the more notable college-universities of the nineteenth century, or even by the best known universities of our own day. Among the 30 leaders in the several categories here analyzed, one finds the names of no fewer than 47 institutions. And only for the foreign service had the top 30 generated as much as 50 per cent of the personnel.

The final column on foreign service executives showed Harvard, Princeton, and Yale still in the lead, but by no very great margins, with a combined production of 14 per cent of the personnel. The reader will find it interesting to compare this column (for the sample year 1959) with the more selective but extensive coverage provided by Table B-6, CHIEF DIPLOMATIC OFFICERS, 1946-64.

BRANCHES OF "THE AMERICAN FEDERAL EXECUTIVE," IN 1959

Thirty institutions which produced the largest number of four-year degrees reported by Civilian Federal Executives

Rank	All Civilian Federal Executives		Service Executives		Political Executives		Foreign-Service Executives	
1	G. WASHINGTON	3*	G. WASHINGTON	3*	G. WASHINGTON	4*	HARVARD	5*
2	C.C.N.Y.	6	C.C.N.Y.	6	HARVARD	8	PRINCETON	10
3	CALIFORNIA	8	CALIFORNIA	8	C.C.N.Y.	11	YALE	14
4	HARVARD	10	OHIO STATE	10	YALE	13	CALIFORNIA	17
5	MINNESOTA	12	MINNESOTA	12	CALIFORNIA	16	G. WASHINGTON	20
6	ILLINOIS	14	ILLINOIS	14	PRINCETON	18	STANFORD	22
7	MICHIGAN	15	WASHINGTON	16	MICHIGAN	20	GEORGETOWN	24
8	WISCONSIN	17	WISCONSIN	17	PENNSYLVANIA	22	ILLINOIS	26
9	OHIO STATE	19	M.I.T.	19	M.I.T.	24	CHICAGO	28
10	WASHINGTON	20	MICHIGAN	21	MINNESOTA	25	WISCONSIN	29
11	M.I.T.	22	N.Y.U.	22	WISCONSIN	27	COLUMBIA	31
12	PRINCETON	23	CORNELL	24	WASHINGTON	28	DARTMOUTH	32
13	YALE	25	BENJ. FRANKLIN U.	25	CHICAGO	30	MICHIGAN	34
14	N.Y.U.	26	PURDUE	26	GEORGETOWN	31	MINNESOTA	35
15	CORNELL	28	MISSOURI	27	ILLINOIS	32	CORNELL	37
16	BENJ. FRANKLIN U.	29	NEBRASKA	29	IOWA	34	OKLAHOMA STATE	38
17	PENNSYLVANIA	30	PENN STATE	30	CORNELL	35	NORTHWESTERN	39
18	MISSOURI	31	COLORADO	31	NORTHWESTERN	36	UTAH	40
19	PURDUE	32	PENNSYLVANIA	32	OHIO STATE	37	OBERLIN	41
20	GEORGETOWN	33	IOWA STATE	33	KANSAS	38	SOUTH DAKOTA	42
21	NEBRASKA	34	HARVARD	34	N.Y.U.	40	WASHINGTON	43
22	CHICAGO	35	KANSAS STATE	35	NORTH CAROLINA	40	PENNSYLVANIA	44
23	STANFORD	36	MARYLAND	35	PURDUE	41	NORTH CAROLINA	45
24	PENN STATE	37	TENNESSEE	36	MISSOURI	42	MISSOURI	46
25	COLORADO	38	CINCINNATI	37	STANFORD	43	SYRACUSE	47
26	IOWA	39	SYRACUSE	38	COLUMBIA	44	M.I.T.	48
27	IOWA STATE	39	STANFORD	38	ALABAMA	44	BENJ. FRANKLIN U.	48
28	COLUMBIA	40	ALABAMA POLYTECH.	39	TEXAS	45	BROWN	49
29	KANSAS	41	GEORGETOWN	40	BROWN	46	OHIO STATE	50
30	SYRACUSE	42	OREGON STATE	41	SOUTH DAKOTA	46	U.S. NAVAL ACAD.	51

*Percentage of total accumulated through the rankings.

Source: Reproduced by permission from W. Lloyd Warner, Paul P. Van Riper, Norman H. Martin, and Orvis F. Collins, The American Federal Executive: A Study of the Social and Personal Characteristics of the Civilian and Military Leaders of the United States Federal Government, New Haven: Yale University Press, 1963, pp. 372-73.

Whatever studies of the lower echelons of the diplomatic corps may reveal, in the top-level representation of American interests and American policies abroad the graduates of Harvard, Yale, and Princeton have been preeminent. No fewer than 206 individuals out of a grand total of 513 principal officers of the State Department and chief representatives of the United States abroad in the first 19 years after World War II had obtained some part of their education at one or the other of these three (a net figure of 40.2 per cent: Some 23 had attended both Yale and Harvard or taken graduate work at Yale or Harvard after an undergraduate course at Princeton). The lead of Harvard at the graduate level and of all three institutions in the field of undergraduate education is remarkable. Given the fact that Princeton has been distinctly smaller, with only about 51-72 students to every 85-90 in Yale College and every hundred in Harvard College, it can be deduced that the ratio of undergraduate expectation of high diplomatic office has been even higher at Princeton than at either of the other two (the reader interested in ratios of production is referred to our Tables N-2, N-3, and N-4).

Our count for diplomatic officers included all those institutions contributing at least 9 individuals each, at which point there seemed to occur a kind of break. Only one institution contributed 8: the University of Texas. Following Texas came the American University, Brown University, and the U.S. Naval Academy, each contributing 7. Maryland, Oklahoma, and the University of Cambridge in England each contributed 6; while Minnesota and N.Y.U. placed 5 apiece, and 6 other institutions could each claim 4 representatives.

Unfortunately the sheer magnitude of the task made it impossible to measure the total contributions of our leading institutions throughout our national history since 1789. An earlier study for Yale alone, however, had showed that, out of 1,737 principal appointments in the United States Diplomatic Corps made in the period 1789-1949, some 124, or just over 7 per cent, went to men holding earned degrees from Yale. The fact that 63 out of 513 principal officers or representatives (or more than 12 per cent of the top diplomats for the period 1946-64) had some connection with Yale (59 earned degrees) would seem to suggest that the role of our most productive universities may have grown rather than diminished with the years.

Note on method and sources: A number of persons held more than one principal office, thus reducing 570 principal offices to a net total of 513 individuals. For the years 1953 to 1964 the list of principal officers was taken from the State Department Register; for the years 1946-52 it was determined on the basis of office and rank as given in the Congressional Directory. The ambassadors, envoys, and consuls here represented were listed in the Foreign Service List as being at the highest foreign service rank, if career men. Delegates (with the full rank and status of ambassador) to the United Nations were determined from the Congressional Directory and the State Department Register, and delegates to N.A.T.O. and the European Communities were determined from the Foreign Service List. Biographies were generally taken from the State Department Register with a small number added from Who's Who in America.

Eliminated and not counted in this table were various commercial

CHIEF DIPLOMATIC OFFICERS, 1946-64

Education of American diplomats who held posts of major responsibility, from World War II to 1964. This group of 513 individuals was made up of 164 "principal officers" of the State Department, 394 persons who were the chief representatives of the United States abroad, 6 delegates or first deputy delegates to the United Nations, and 6 representatives having the status of ambassador to N.A.T.O. and the European communities.

College or University	Undergraduate Connections	Graduate Connections	Net Total Individuals
HARVARD	58	72	113
YALE	53	19	63
PRINCETON	49	9	53
GEORGE WASHINGTON	12	20	30
COLUMBIA	11	20	28
GEORGETOWN	11	12	22
STANFORD	9	7	13
CALIFORNIA (Berkeley)	7	5	12
DARTMOUTH	11	1	11
MICHIGAN	6	7	11
PENNSYLVANIA	5	9	11
WISCONSIN	7	7	11
AMHERST	10	–	10
CHICAGO	4	7	10
CORNELL	7	4	10
NORTHWESTERN	4	6	9
VIRGINIA	5	6	9
U.S. MILITARY ACADEMY	9	–	9
156 Other American Institutions	179	78	219
Foreign:			
OXFORD	1	25	26
PARIS	1	12	13
ÉCOLE LIBRE DES SCIENCES POLITIQUES	–	9	9
48 Other Foreign Institutions	15	61	59
No Higher Education			28
Unknown			6
Net Total			513

Sources: State Department Register, Foreign Service List, and Congressional Directory.

institutions and a number of military training schools: the National War
College, the Army War College, the Army Coast Artillery School, the Naval
War College, the Army Information School, the Army Command and General
Staff School, and the U.S. School of Military Aeronautics (of World War I).
Individuals giving the National University as their educational affilia-
tion were credited to George Washington.

B-7. THE CONGRESS OF THE UNITED STATES, IN 1963

Ideally one would like to know the derivations and educational backgrounds of all our Congressmen from the First Congress of Washington's administration to the present. Unfortunately the sheer size of such a research job proved prohibitive. Instead it was decided to test the current
state of affairs by analyzing one of the very recent Congresses; and the
88th Congress, 1st Session (President Kennedy's Congress), was selected as
a representative sample.

This 88th Congress proved to have been drawn from wide backgrounds.
Out of its total membership of 535, some 45 Senators and Representatives
had apparently achieved their honors and responsibilities without benefit
of formal higher education. To the preparation of the remaining 490 Senators and Representatives, no fewer than 333 institutions of higher learning had contributed. Among these institutions certain state universities--
notably Michigan, Alabama, Texas, Minnesota, and Virginia--had each had a
hand in the education of at least 10 Congressmen. The three most productive institutions had been Harvard, Yale, and Columbia, with Yale leading
at the college level and Harvard and Columbia showing the most graduate or
professional connections. Rather surprisingly, Princeton College had produced only 8 Congressmen, which placed it in a tie with Dartmouth and
Missouri for seventh place in this category.

Close analysis of the Senate revealed that, as a group, the 13 land-
grant colleges and public universities (which are shown in our table as
contributing to the education of at least 7 individuals each) had played a
role in the education of no fewer than 25 Senators: an average of 2 Senators per institution. Of these, Minnesota could claim 5, Virginia 4,
Michigan and Washington each 3. Cornell and Pennsylvania, intermediate in
character between public and private institutions, had each educated 1
Senator. By contrast the 10 private universities, here listed, had between them enrolled 36 future members of this most august deliberative
body, with Yale claiming 8 and Harvard altogether 12 (2 Yale B.A.'s
included).

THE CONGRESS OF THE UNITED STATES, IN 1963

Educational background of the 535 Senators and Representatives sitting in the First Session of the 88th Congress, January, 1963.

College or University	Undergraduate Connections	Graduate or Professional Connections	Net Total Individuals
HARVARD	10	37	44
YALE	15	12	25
COLUMBIA	3	21	23
MICHIGAN	11	14	19
ALABAMA	9	10	16
GEORGE WASHINGTON	3	13	16
TEXAS	10	6	14
GEORGETOWN	5	9	12
SOUTHERN CALIFORNIA	2	9	11
MINNESOTA	5	8	10
VIRGINIA	3	8	10
CALIFORNIA (Berkeley)	9	6	9
FLORIDA	5	8	9
PRINCETON	8	1	9
WASHINGTON (Seattle)	4	5	9
CORNELL	6	6	8
DARTMOUTH	8	-	8
MISSOURI	8	1	8
N.Y.U.	4	5	8
OHIO STATE	3	6	8
WISCONSIN	5	7	8
CUMBERLAND	1	6	7
GEORGIA	5	4	7
NORTH CAROLINA	6	4	7
PENNSYLVANIA	2	5	7
STANFORD	5	6	7
U.C.L.A.	6	2	7
301 Other American Institutions	365	180	354
5 Foreign Institutions	-	7	7
No Higher Education			45

Over the span of its first 174 years no fewer than 7 British institutions and 56 American colleges or universities contributed to the education of its 95 Justices. In our table one encounters again the distinguished Universities of Michigan and Virginia, and Union College, while Cincinnati makes its first appearance as a substantial contributor.

The Supreme Court, however, owes most to four universities: Yale, Harvard, Princeton, and Columbia. William and Mary, in the days of its glory, knew 4 future Justices, but no other university or college can claim more than 3, or a third of the number turned out by Princeton. Between them, over the years, Yale, Harvard, and Princeton contributed 34 Justices out of 79 college-educated Justices, or out of 95 Justices in all: a reading in these two categories of 43 per cent and 36 per cent. These percentages were built up in large part during the last hundred years. Only 11 graduates of Yale, Harvard, and Princeton were appointed and served on our highest Bench before the Civil War: 2 from Yale, 3 from Harvard, and 7 from Princeton.

JUSTICES OF THE SUPREME COURT, 1789-1963

College or University	Undergraduate Connections	Graduate or Professional	Net Total Individuals
YALE	11	7	14
HARVARD	7	11	13
PRINCETON	9	-	9
COLUMBIA	3	5	7
WILLIAM AND MARY	3	1	4
CINCINNATI	1	2	3
MICHIGAN	2	3	3
UNION including Albany Law School	1	2	3
VIRGINIA	1	2	3
47 Other Colleges and Universities	41	20	45
7 British Universities and Institutions	1	5	6
Totals			
Justices with College or University Connections	72	53	79
Justices with No College or University Education	-	-	16
Total Justices			95

In the education section of its Sunday edition The New York Times of April 18, 1965, carried a box announcement which read as follows:

EDUCATING LEADERS

The research machinery of the National Association of State Universities and Land-Grant Colleges last week was set in motion to tell the story about the state universities' part in educating the nation's leadership. Computers revealed that 28 of the 50 governors were educated entirely or in part by state universities--26 of them in their home states. Only two did not attend college, indicating that the age of the self-made Governor is passing.

Our own study of 227 state governors from World War II to 1963 confirms in part some of the suggestions made in this announcement. While a number of our older universities have continued to contribute substantially, with Yale the most productive college and Harvard the most productive university, their record seems good rather than outstanding--and Princeton, with Adlai Stevenson and only 2 other B.A.'s, fails to register among the 9 leading institutions. Between them the 4 state universities of Minnesota, Alabama, Michigan, and Virginia produced 25 governors, or 11 per cent of the total, to Harvard's 5 per cent, Yale's 3 per cent, and a combined Harvard-Yale-Princeton production of 20 governors or 8.8 per cent.

The tendency of governors to be regionally educated is also confirmed. Thus the University of Minnesota produced 3 future governors of the state-- Luther W. Youngdahl, Karl Rolvaag, and Orville L. Freeman--as well as Robert B. Crosby for Nebraska, William L. Guy for North Dakota, Edward C. Johnson for Colorado, and Charles M. Dale for New Hampshire.

Yale's 7 governors were Chester Bowles, B.S., and James M. McConaughy, B.A., for Connecticut; Walter J. Kohler, Ph.B., for Wisconsin; Foster Furcolo for Massachusetts, Hugh Gregg for New Hampshire, W. Averill Harriman for New York, and W. W. Scranton for Pennsylvania (all B.A., with Furcolo and Scranton also LL.B.).

Harvard College produced John Davis Lodge for Connecticut and 3 governors for Massachusetts: Robert F. Bradford, Christian A. Herter, and Endicott Peabody. The very striking emphasis of the Harvard list, however, was provided by 9 future governors who attended its law school: H. A. Hildreth of Maine, Hugh Gregg (Yale B.A.) of New Hampshire, Alfred E. Driscoll of New Jersey, A. B. Chandler of Kentucky, Robert B. Crosby of Nebraska, M. S. Simpson of Wyoming, and W. F. Quinn of Hawaii--also Lodge and Bradford, both Harvard College B.A.'s.

By contrast to the 1965 poll reported in The New York Times, a number of states in the years 1946-63 were still electing self-made governors, as witness the 19 who attended no college or university and the 21 who probably had no such connection: an approximate ratio of 1 governor in every 5.5.

Among the substantial contributors to the list of educated governors

32

STATE GOVERNORS, 1946-63

Educational backgrounds of the governors of the forty-eight (fifty) states in the United States, since World War II.

Colleges and Universities	Undergraduate	Graduate or Professional	Net Total Individuals
HARVARD	4	9	11
GEORGE WASHINGTON	2	5	7
MINNESOTA	5	5	7
YALE	7	2	7
ALABAMA	3	3	6
CUMBERLAND	2	4	6
MICHIGAN	3	4	6
VIRGINIA	2	4	6
STANFORD	3	2	5
Totals for 146 Other American Colleges and Universities	147	107	167
Foreign Colleges and Universities	-	4	4
Totals			
Number of Individuals with Some Known College or University Connection	153	128	187
No College or University Connection	-	-	19
Unknown	-	-	21
Net Individuals			227

Sources: List of governors provided by Information Please Almanac and World Almanac. Biographical information from Who's Who in America.

for this period were Boston University, Chicago, Columbia, Georgia, Nebraska, North Carolina, Northwestern, and Wyoming, each 4; Arizona, Arkansas, California, Cornell, Dartmouth, Georgetown, Kansas, Kentucky, Mississippi, Oklahoma, Oregon, Pennsylvania, Princeton, Texas, Utah, Vanderbilt, Washington and Lee, and Wisconsin, each 3.

Altogether no fewer than 159 institutions had contributed to the upbringing of 187 college-educated state governors.

CHAPTER C THE PROFESSION OF THE LAW

Immemorially one of the three learned professions, the Law in this country long labored under great handicaps, circumstantial and psychological. For one thing, it took the English colonists 200 years to transplant the highest learning to this wilderness. For another, lawyers had been for many settlers the agents of dispossession by landlords and enclosures back home; and they continued to be associated with authority, taxation, costly land title claims, and self-serving complications and formalities. Such preparation as there had to be for this necessary learning consisted, for the well-born and more exceptionally ambitious, in residing at the Inns of Court in London; for the remainder, in reading law in the office of some already established but quasi-amateur attorney. Finally this apprentice system was seen to be inadequate. In 1779-80, George Wythe became the first American professor of law, at William and Mary, and gave instruction to John Marshall. In 1784, Tapping Reeve (Princeton, B.A. 1763) established what became the first systematic law school in the United States at Litchfield, Connecticut. In 1815-20, Harvard was able to organize a degree-granting law school; and from 1824 Yale sponsored a regular course of instruction by taking over a private New Haven law school, conducted since 1800 by Yale graduates. It was not, however, until Charles W. Eliot's presidency at Harvard, and the great reform of legal study and instruction under Dean Christopher Columbus Langdell (1870-95), that the era of influence and power for our modern university law schools can be said to have begun; and it was only just before or just after 1900 that the best of these modernized law schools began to demand a college degree for entrance and expanded their curriculum to a thorough three-year course of instruction.

This background underlines the exceptional legal qualifications of certain of the Signers and Delegates to the Federal Convention, who had resided at the Inns of Court (see Tables B-1 and B-2). It reminds us that, while Daniel Webster may have drawn advantages from his college education, most of his contemporaries and many ambitious politicians since his day preferred to get their law without the trouble of a college degree--a practice still known in the South and in the night schools of our northern cities. It will also in some degree account for the extraordinary role played since 1870 by the Harvard Law School in drawing graduates of other colleges to that university for their professional training.

Note: For the legal tables the Yale Historian's office wishes to record its great debt to Carlton B. Schnell (B.A. 1953, LL.B. 1956), by whose almost unaided efforts the researches and analyses were carried through on the Attorneys General and Solicitors General, on the Courts, and on the Largest Law Firms in Seventeen Cities.

C-1. ATTORNEYS GENERAL, 1789-1964
SOLICITORS GENERAL, 1870-1964

Once again a table on governmental office showed the distinguished Universities of Virginia and Michigan, Pennsylvania and William and Mary, contributing substantially to the conduct of high office, with Cincinnati replacing Columbia among the leaders, but with Harvard, Yale, and Princeton contributing most of all. Eliminating duplications, we found that the last-named colleges had provided the undergraduate education of 40 per cent of those Attorneys General and 42 per cent of those Solicitors General who had gone to college; while at the graduate level these institutions had given training to 38 per cent of those Attorneys General and 35 per cent of those Solicitors General who had taken advanced instruction.

Nor was this all ancient history. It may correct some impressions to note that only the graduates of Princeton were prominent in the Attorney General's office before the Civil War. Thus, the second Attorney General of our national history was William Bradford (A.B. Princeton 1772) in 1794-95, who was followed by Charles Lee (A.B. Princeton 1775) for the years 1795-1801, and he in turn by the first Harvard man, Levi Lincoln (A.B. Harvard 1772) for 1801-05. By 1831 there had been appointed two more Princeton graduates, to account for 4 of its 5, but the second Harvard appointment did not come until 1852-57 in the person of the redoubtable Caleb Cushing (A.B. 1817, with a year of Harvard law). There were no Yale-trained Attorneys General before 1868, and no Yale-trained Solicitors General before 1890. By contrast, in 16 of the 96 years since 1868, the Attorney General has been a Yale man; and in 20 out of the 74 years since 1890, the Solicitor General has been a Yale man; and in 1930-33 and 1935-38, Yale graduates carried the responsibility of both offices. In the last 3 years covered by the table, 1961-64, the two offices were for the first time held simultaneously by Harvard graduates (Robert F. Kennedy and Archibald Cox).

ATTORNEYS GENERAL, 1789-1964
SOLICITORS GENERAL, 1870-1964

College or University	Undergraduate			Graduate			Net Total (Individuals)		
	Attorneys General	Solicitors General	Net Total	Attorneys General	Solicitors General	Net Total	Attorneys General	Solicitors General	Net Total
HARVARD	8	3	10	7[a]	5[a,c]	11[b,c]	10[a]	6[a,c]	15[b,c]
YALE	6	7	12	3	2	5	7	7	13
PRINCETON	5	1	6	1	0	1	5	1	6
VIRGINIA	1	1	2	2	1	3	3	2	5
MICHIGAN	0	2	2	2	0	2	2	2	4
CINCINNATI	0	0	0	1	2	3	1	2	3
PENNSYLVANIA	1	0	1	1	1	2	2	1	3
WILLIAM AND MARY	3	0	3	0	0	0	3	0	3
47 Other Colleges and Universities	26	15	40	15	10	22	29	18	45
Net Totals	47	26	71	29	20	47	52	29	78
No College or University or Unknown							11	3	14
							63	32	92

[a]Includes one Yale B.A.
[b]Includes two Yale B.A.'s.
[c]Includes Robert L. Stern, LL.B. 1932, "acting Solicitor General" in 1953.

39

C-2. JUDGES OF THE UNITED STATES CIRCUIT COURTS OF APPEAL, 1869-1955

Our analysis of the United States Supreme Court (see Table B-8) showed Yale with 14, Harvard with 13, and Princeton with 9 Justices: a net contribution of 34 individuals out of the 79 college- or university-educated Justices. Subsequent analysis of JUDGES OF THE UNITED STATES CIRCUIT COURTS OF APPEAL for the shorter stretch of time 1869-1955, showed Harvard far ahead at the graduate or professional level and in clear first place for its university total, while the graduates of Princeton, which has had no law school, could do no better than a tie for fourth. Among the alumni of our colleges the graduates of Yale were outstanding, with almost twice as many judges in their number as Harvard College could muster, and with Michigan and Princeton following Harvard very closely. The Harvard-Yale-Princeton net total of individuals (after allowance for 4 Princeton and 2 Yale undergraduates who went on to the Harvard Law School) showed 56 future Judges of the United States Circuit Courts of Appeal out of 190 Judges with a known college or university connection, or just under 30 per cent.

An interesting feature of this table was the analysis of earned degrees, which showed the considerable number of those who merely attended for a time or failed to graduate.

It should be noted also that a most creditable number of independent liberal arts colleges have earned judiciary laurels in competition with the great public universities: thus Dartmouth, Bowdoin, and Williams--but also Washington and Lee, Hamilton, Westminster, and DePauw. Altogether 107 institutions of higher learning have had a hand in the general education or professional training of 190 judges of the U.S. Circuit Courts of Appeal, in office 1869-1955.

40

JUDGES OF THE UNITED STATES CIRCUIT COURTS OF APPEAL, 1869-1955

College or University	Total Undergraduate	Earned Degree	Total Graduate or Professional	Earned Degree	Net Total Individuals
HARVARD	11	10	30	22	32
YALE	19	19	10	8	21
MICHIGAN	9	7	11	7	14
COLUMBIA	2	2	9	7	9
PRINCETON	9	8	2	2	9
CHICAGO	3	2	7	6	8
WASHINGTON & LEE	5	1	2	1	7
GEORGETOWN	2	1	4	4	6
VIRGINIA	3	1	4	3	6
DARTMOUTH	5	4	1	1	5
BOSTON UNIVERSITY	0	0	4	2	4
CINCINNATI	1	1	3	3	4
CUMBERLAND	1	0	3	2	4
HAMILTON	4	3	2	2	4
INDIANA	2	1	3	2	4
IOWA	3	2	3	3	4
N.Y.U.	1	1	3	2	4
PENNSYLVANIA	2	2	4	4	4
WESTMINSTER	4	2	0	0	4
WISCONSIN	4	3	2	2	4
BOWDOIN	3	3	0	0	3
BROWN	2	2	2	2	3
CORNELL	3	3	1	1	3
DEPAUW	3	2	0	0	3
MISSOURI	3	3	0	0	3
NEBRASKA	2	2	2	2	3
TEXAS	2	0	2	2	3
WILLIAMS	3	2	0	0	3
79 Other Colleges and Universities	68	48	44	38	98
Net Totals	167	127	146	122	190
No Affiliation or Unknown	56		77		33
				Total	223

Note: Upon leaving office in 1801, President John Adams appointed the so-called midnight judges to the Circuit Courts. In 1802, these positions were abolished, and the Supreme Court justices continued to hold court in the circuits by themselves until 1869. Among the judges sitting on the Circuit Courts of Appeal in 1801-02 there was the following distribution:

Harvard	2
Columbia	1
Pennsylvania	1
Princeton	1
Rutgers	1
Yale	1
No College or University	5
Unknown	5
Total	17

When President Jefferson had Congress abolish the other circuit judgeships in 1802, the judges for the District of Columbia, for some reason, were retained. Of the 10 judges who served on the Court of Appeals for the District of Columbia between 1801 and 1863, 1 attended Harvard; 3 are known to have had no college or university training; and no information is available on the other 6. Three judges who were appointed in 1863 served into the period after 1869 and are therefore included in the table of circuit judges above.

The table on the highest state court judges measured only a single year, 1955, but made an interesting comparison with that on the Judges of the United States Circuit Courts of Appeal (Table C-2). The more local nature of the appointments showed clearly in this investigation.

At the college level Harvard had a clear lead over California, Alabama, and Yale; while in the graduate and over-all counts once again its Law School gave Harvard University an extraordinarily commanding position. The strong reputation of the Michigan and Virginia Law Schools is also reflected by the position of these universities on our table, whereas Princeton, with but 3 sons on the highest state courts, falls out of the leadership list entirely.

Thanks largely to the Harvard Law School, the H-Y-P contribution of 45 out of the 279 who had some higher education represented a contribution of 16 per cent to the highest state courts just after the mid-century. Running down the list of producing institutions, one is also struck by the role that the University of Alabama has evidently played in the political life of the South (cf. Tables B-7, B-9). Once again, as for the Circuit Courts (Table C-2), the contributions of Washington and Lee, Georgetown, and Boston University stand comparison with those of Pennsylvania and Chicago. For the preparation of state judges, Kansas and Missouri reappear in the leadership list. And altogether 149 institutions were found to have had a hand in the education of 279 state judges out of a grand total of 303 sitting in the year 1955.

HIGHEST STATE COURTS, 1955

College or university connections of the judges on the highest court in each state.

College or University	Undergraduate	Graduate or Professional	Net Total Individuals
HARVARD	10	30	32
MICHIGAN	2	12	13
VIRGINIA	4	8	10
YALE	5	6	10
PENNSYLVANIA	4	7	9
WASHINGTON AND LEE	4	7	9
CHICAGO	1	8	8
KANSAS	2	8	8
MINNESOTA	4	7	8
MISSISSIPPI	4	8	8
ALABAMA	5	7	7
ARKANSAS	4	3	7
BOSTON UNIVERSITY	3	6	7
CALIFORNIA	6	4	7
COLUMBIA	0	7	7
GEORGETOWN	3	5	7
MISSOURI	4	6	7
OKLAHOMA	3	6	7
131 Other Colleges and Universities	133	134	196
Judges with College or University Connections	200	267	279
Judges with No College or University Training	-	-	14
Judges on Whom No Information Was Available	-	-	10
Total Judges			303

Source: Compiled from the list of judges in the 1955 edition of the Martindale-Hubbell Law Directory.

C-4. AMERICAN BAR ASSOCIATION PRESIDENTS, 1878-1955

The leaders of the American Bar have sometimes, but by no means always, achieved the office of President of the American Bar Association.
This office has been subject to regional and organizational politics;
hence it should not be weighted too heavily as a measurement of distinction. The statistical approach also suffers in this case because the list
of names is so small.

For what the table may be worth, it showed Harvard and Yale in the
lead, and good small colleges like Washington and Lee, Hamilton, and
Williams making honorable contributions. Georgetown reappears, as do
N.Y.U. and Texas (the latter two just beginning to hint at the strength
which they would demonstrate in the latter half of the twentieth century).
Altogether 65 institutions had contributed to the education of 70 American
Bar Association presidents, out of a grand total of 78 men chosen for that
office.

AMERICAN BAR ASSOCIATION PRESIDENTS, 1878-1955

Educational background of the 78 Presidents of the American Bar Association.

College or University	Undergraduate	Graduate or Professional	Net Total Individuals
HARVARD	5	12	13
YALE	5	3	6
COLUMBIA	0	5	5
VIRGINIA	4	1	5
WASHINGTON & LEE	2	2	3
GEORGETOWN	1	2	3
TEXAS	2	2	3
NEW YORK UNIVERSITY	1	2	3
HAMILTON	3	0	3
MICHIGAN	1	2	2
UNIVERSITY OF NASHVILLE	2	0	2
WILLIAMS	2	0	2
ALBANY LAW SCHOOL	0	2	2
GEORGIA	2	2	2
PENNSYLVANIA	2	2	2
Totals for 50 Other Colleges and Universities	32	23	48
Totals			
No Higher Education or Unknown			8
Net Totals	57	53	78

Sources: James Grafton Rogers, American Bar Leaders, 1878-1928 (Chicago, 1932); Reports of the American Bar Association, 1928-55; American Bar Association Journal, vol. 16; Who's Who in America; and Who Was Who in America.

C-5.   THE LARGEST LAW FIRMS IN SEVENTEEN CITIES, IN 1955

This table was constructed by analyzing the membership of 82 law firms, with 1,578 partners, as representative of the legal profession in 17 cities across the country.   The selection was defective in that it gave quite inadequate representation to the South: Only Houston and Miami, with 4 firms in all, were included.   The table was also open to criticism as neglecting all but the largest law firms.   The statistics, however, proved remarkably consistent and persuasive.   They showed in the cities of San Francisco and Los Angeles strong representation from the Universities of California and Stanford, just as one would expect.   Cleveland boasted a large representation of Western Reserve graduates; Philadelphia enjoyed the attentions of an enormous number of Pennsylvania men, and quite a few from Princeton; the University of Michigan dominated in Detroit, etc. Clearly, intending lawyers have found it advantageous, for their future placement and careers, to attend the strongest regional or state law school, and build a future clientele on the foundation of local ac- quaintance.

Reciprocally, it may be noted that many of the important universities of the country seem to have a strong alumni representation in the law only in their own region.   By contrast, Harvard and Yale graduates were found everywhere: Harvard in 16 of the 17 cities surveyed, Yale in 15; moreover, theirs was a balanced representation across the country.   At the under- graduate level Yale had contributed 172 future partners to these major firms, compared to 137 from Harvard College and 121 from Princeton.   At the professional school level Harvard's 471 partners raised its university contribution to overwhelming preeminence, with Yale second, Pennsylvania third, and Columbia and Princeton close together in fourth and fifth places.   For a small college Williams had done very well indeed.   Among the large universities there was considerable variety: 138 out of 149 Pennsylvania alumni were found concentrated in the Philadelphia firms, whereas Michigan's alumni were widely distributed.   One notes also the geographical concentration of the men from Northwestern, Texas, Western Reserve, and Minnesota--the somewhat wider West Coast distribution for Stanford--and the more nearly national representation of Dartmouth, Williams, and Cornell.

The compiler of these and other law statistics commented on the rela- tively large number of men who had attended the Harvard Law School without ever receiving a degree.   He also observed that in the large law firms he found the older partners predominantly Harvard men, while among the younger associates, the graduates of the Yale Law School often equaled or outnumbered the Harvard contingent.   No observation was hazarded on what it takes to become a Philadelphia lawyer.

THE LARGEST LAW FIRMS IN SEVENTEEN CITIES, IN 1955

Survey of the college and graduate or professional school affiliation
of 1,578 partners in 82 law firms in 17 cities

		New York	Chicago	Philadelphia	Cleveland	San Francisco	Los Angeles	Houston	Washington	Minneapolis
Number of Firms Surveyed		19	14	10	5	5	4	3	5	2
Number of Partners in Firms		409	287	200	154	85	75	68	68	45
HARVARD	UG.	61	17	20	14	3	3	0	6	1
	Gr.	157	79	42	51	27	23	6	19	11
	N.T.	178	86	53	53	29	23	6	20	11
YALE	UG.	91	22	8	9	2	4	1	7	5
	Gr.	63	6	2	11	2	7	2	8	3
	N.T.	122	24	10	15	4	8	3	11	6
PENNSYLVANIA	UG.	1	2	54	0	0	0	0	0	0
	Gr.	6	1	128	0	1	0	0	1	0
	N.T.	7	2	138	0	1	0	0	1	0
COLUMBIA	UG.	18	1	0	2	0	1	0	0	0
	Gr.	88	8	2	4	0	3	2	10	0
	N.T.	93	8	2	5	0	4	2	10	0
PRINCETON	UG.	40	15	42	10	0	0	1	4	1
	Gr.	0	0	0	0	0	0	0	0	0
	N.T.	40	15	42	10	0	0	1	4	1
MICHIGAN	UG.	4	23	0	8	5	3	0	2	1
	Gr.	6	31	0	15	5	5	0	2	1
	N.T.	8	39	0	18	5	6	0	3	1
CHICAGO	UG.	5	38	0	2	1	0	0	0	0
	Gr.	5	58	0	3	0	0	1	0	0
	N.T.	6	64	0	4	1	0	1	0	0
NORTHWESTERN	UG.	4	18	0	1	1	1	0	0	0
	Gr.	3	44	1	0	2	1	0	0	0
	N.T.	6	50	1	1	2	2	0	0	0
CALIFORNIA	UG.	1	0	0	0	34	14	0	1	0
	Gr.	0	0	0	0	27	13	0	1	0
	N.T.	1	0	0	0	37	17	0	1	0
TEXAS	UG.	1	0	0	0	0	0	22	1	0
	Gr.	1	0	0	0	0	0	50	0	0
	N.T.	1	0	0	0	0	0	51	1	0
WESTERN RESERVE	UG.	1	0	0	13	0	0	0	1	0
	Gr.	0	0	0	38	0	1	0	0	0
	N.T.	1	0	0	41	0	1	0	1	0
MINNESOTA	UG.	2	1	0	0	0	0	0	1	23
	Gr.	2	3	0	0	0	0	0	0	27
	N.T.	3	3	0	0	0	0	0	1	34
STANFORD	UG.	0	0	0	0	17	10	0	1	0
	Gr.	0	0	0	0	11	7	0	2	0
	N.T.	0	0	0	0	20	11	0	2	0
DARTMOUTH	UG.	13	9	2	6	0	1	0	1	2
	Gr.	0	0	0	0	0	0	0	0	0
	N.T.	13	9	2	6	0	1	0	1	2
WILLIAMS	UG.	15	9	2	3	1	3	0	2	0
	Gr.	0	0	0	0	0	0	0	0	0
	N.T.	15	9	2	3	1	3	0	2	0
CORNELL	UG.	14	3	3	2	1	0	0	3	0
	Gr.	10	2	0	4	1	1	0	0	0
	N.T.	15	4	3	5	1	1	0	3	0

Source: Based on <u>Martindale-Hubbell Law Directory</u>, New York, 1955.

Detroit	Cincinnati	St. Louis	Seattle	Denver	Kansas City	Portland, Oregon	Miami	Totals		
3	3	2	2	2	1	1	1	82		Number of Firms Surveyed
43	28	25	25	23	17	15	11	1,578		Number of Partners in Firms
1	4	4	0	1	2	0	0	137	UG.	HARVARD
8	15	7	4	4	2	4	0	471	Gr.	
9	16	10	4	5	4	4	0	511	N.T.	
3	7	1	0	9	2	0	1	172	UG.	YALE
2	3	0	0	5	4	0	1	119	Gr.	
5	10	1	0	11	4	0	1	235	N.T.	
0	0	0	0	0	0	0	0	57	UG.	PENNSYLVANIA
0	0	0	0	0	0	0	0	137	Gr.	
0	0	0	0	0	0	0	0	149	N.T.	
0	0	0	1	0	0	1	0	24	UG.	COLUMBIA
0	0	0	2	0	0	1	0	120	Gr.	
0	0	0	2	0	0	1	0	127	N.T.	
1	4	1	1	1	0	0	0	121	UG.	PRINCETON
0	0	0	0	0	0	0	0	0	Gr.	
1	4	1	1	1	0	0	0	121	N.T.	
20	0	0	1	1	2	0	0	70	UG.	MICHIGAN
19	1	2	1	0	2	0	1	91	Gr.	
25	1	2	1	1	3	0	1	114	N.T.	
0	0	0	1	0	1	0	0	48	UG.	CHICAGO
0	0	0	1	0	1	0	0	69	Gr.	
0	0	0	1	0	1	0	0	78	N.T.	
0	0	0	0	0	0	0	0	25	UG.	NORTHWESTERN
0	0	0	0	0	0	0	0	51	Gr.	
0	0	0	0	0	0	0	0	62	N.T.	
0	0	0	0	0	0	0	0	50	UG.	CALIFORNIA
0	0	0	0	0	0	0	0	41	Gr.	
0	0	0	0	0	0	0	0	56	N.T.	
0	0	1	0	0	0	0	0	25	UG.	TEXAS
0	1	0	0	0	0	0	0	52	Gr.	
0	1	1	0	0	0	0	0	55	N.T.	
0	1	0	0	0	0	0	0	16	UG.	WESTERN RESERVE
0	0	0	0	0	0	0	0	39	Gr.	
0	1	0	0	0	0	0	0	45	N.T.	
0	0	0	0	0	0	1	0	28	UG.	MINNESOTA
0	0	0	1	0	0	0	0	33	Gr.	
0	0	0	1	0	0	1	0	43	N.T.	
0	0	0	3	0	0	1	0	32	UG.	STANFORD
0	0	0	2	0	0	2	0	24	Gr.	
0	0	0	4	0	0	2	0	39	N.T.	
1	3	0	0	0	0	0	0	38	UG.	DARTMOUTH
0	0	0	0	0	0	0	0	0	Gr.	
1	3	0	0	0	0	0	0	38	N.T.	
2	0	0	0	1	0	0	0	38	UG.	WILLIAMS
0	0	0	0	0	0	0	0	0	Gr.	
2	0	0	0	1	0	0	0	38	N.T.	
2	0	0	0	1	0	0	0	29	UG.	CORNELL
0	0	0	0	0	0	0	0	18	Gr.	
2	0	0	0	1	0	0	0	35	N.T.	

CHAPTER **D** THE UNIVERSITIES
IN MEDICINE

A hall of fame for American physicians and surgeons? Better still would be a limited, selective Who's Who and Who Was Who for all branches of American medicine from the days of Cotton Mather to the Mayo brothers. It would be especially interesting to be able to identify the great medical educators--or to have available an honors list of medical scientists in this century comparable to the winners of the Nobel Prize yet not restricted to a mere handful of men and discoveries. Unfortunately, the scientific and comparative study of the evolution of American medicine has hardly begun to provide materials for such judgments--and the only general honors list we were able to find was a biographical dictionary of American physicians "who have done the noteworthy" and died before 1927 (see Table D-1).

The comparison of medical schools and their products would seem another desirable undertaking. But this instructive line of inquiry requires some understanding of the formal training of American physicians and surgeons from the almost primitive colonial beginnings to the complex and protracted scientific instruction of today. Historically, American medicine was almost invariably second-hand science, a little crude and behind the times. Our settlers began with the traditional apprentice system, enlightened by the occasional import of books, or by the return of some ambitious colonial from Edinburgh, Leyden, or the London hospitals where he had gone to acquire some experience or training in the advancing medical arts. Finally, in 1765 and 1769 the first American medical schools were established at Pennsylvania and King's College, followed by Harvard in 1782 and Yale in 1810-13; after which the nineteenth century saw the proliferation of private or proprietary schools, many without collegiate connections or reliable standards of instruction. The celebrated Flexner Report of 1910 put a virtual end to many shabby and wastefully competitive practices and helped concentrate the major American resources and scientific effort on a comparatively restricted group of university-connected institutions located at strategic points across the country. And some statistical comparison between these medical centers now begins to be possible (see Tables D-4, D-5, D-6).

In studying these comparisons several considerations should be kept in mind. In the beginnings, formal schooling in medicine was not indispensable for a doctor. Then a college education became for physicians a useful foundation, both general and scientific, for their later professional studies in some city institution or abroad--and our colleges were able to make contributions prior to or beyond that of strict professional instruction. By the twentieth century the days of informal study or of proprietary medical institutes were numbered; medicine required so much science, and had so much need of a larger social learning, that a university became the almost indispensable setting for fine medical training. It followed that the quality of the university itself, and of its separate schools, would be matters of no small moment, and would tend to create marked differences of emphasis and attitude on the part of a given medical faculty or group of premedical students. In turn the quality of the medical school would enhance or modify the reputation of its university.

Finally, the presence or absence of adequate hospital facilities, together with a range of pathological materials in the shape of a large and varied human population, either gave encouragement to our medical schools or limited their possibilities. In such circumstances the extraordinarily rich and varied resources of New York, Philadelphia, Chicago, and Boston have found a natural reflection in our tables.

D-1. THE EDUCATION OF AMERICAN PHYSICIANS--PRIOR TO 1900

This table was based on the biographical selection made by Kelly and Burrage, and their choice of those physicians "who have done the noteworthy." In a sense theirs is a medical <u>Dictionary of American Biography</u> but, like that greater work, it is limited in its value to the first three centuries of American history. The absence of Johns Hopkins from the list of 20 leading institutions demonstrates that the emphasis is on the physicians of the eighteenth and nineteenth centuries (Johns Hopkins University was founded in 1876 but did not achieve a medical faculty until 1886 or a formal medical school until 1893. Hence but 9 Hopkins graduates were memorialized in Kelly and Burrage, compared to 26 from Transylvania). Crudely stated, our twentieth-century medicine figures in this table hardly at all.

The same accent on the nineteenth century accounts for the high ranking of Jefferson Medical College and for the considerable contributions of a number of institutions not connected with any college or university. It is nice to see the distinguished professional instruction of the University of Edinburgh (in 6th place) here recognized. Because of this same historical emphasis, Columbia University (in 13th place) is listed separately from the New York College of Physicians and Surgeons (in 3rd place); the two were not nominally connected until 1860, and P. and S. did not come under the full jurisdiction of Columbia until 1890. Rush Medical College did not begin awarding M.D.'s for the University of Chicago until 1897; and Bellevue Medical College was not consolidated with the Medical College of N.Y.U. until 1898.

The exclamation mark of this table is the very great lead of the University of Pennsylvania, which ranked third as an undergraduate source of physicians but which at the professional level trained more than twice as many "noteworthy" doctors as Harvard. Indeed, Pennsylvania contributed more noteworthy physicians than all the medical colleges and hospitals of New York, and almost as many individuals as Harvard, Yale, and Princeton put together. One notes also in this table the distinguished production by Dartmouth College and Medical School, and the balanced contributions of Virginia, as well as of Michigan and of Bowdoin in Maine.

54

THE EDUCATION OF AMERICAN PHYSICIANS--PRIOR TO 1900

American physicians "who have done the noteworthy, dating from the earliest discoverable down to the latest necrology, January 1, 1927."

College or University	Undergraduate	Graduate	Professional	Total Connections	Net Total Individuals
PENNSYLVANIA	62	22	381	465	405
HARVARD	175	23	188	386	255
NEW YORK COLLEGE OF PHYSICIANS AND SURGEONS			171	171	171
JEFFERSON MEDICAL COLLEGE			129	129	129
YALE	101	7	34	142	124
UNIVERSITY OF EDINBURGH	6	1	76	83	82
MARYLAND			68	68	68
DARTMOUTH	31	12	33	76	65
PRINCETON	52	8		60	54
MEDICAL COLLEGE OF OHIO			50	50	50
VIRGINIA	22	1	22	45	42
UNIVERSITY OF THE CITY OF NEW YORK	7	4	31	42	40
COLUMBIA	22	10	15	47	37
NEW YORK UNIVERSITY	4	1	35	40	37
MICHIGAN	16	2	25	43	37
RUSH MEDICAL COLLEGE			31	31	31
BOWDOIN	22	3	12	37	30
BELLEVUE HOSPITAL MEDICAL COLLEGE			30	30	30
BERKSHIRE MEDICAL INSTITUTE			27	27	27
TRANSYLVANIA	9		19	28	26
300 Other Colleges and Universities	504	39	580	1,123	847
No Formal Education					175
Net Total	1,033	133	1,957	3,123	2,048

Source: Howard A. Kelly and Walter L. Burrage, Dictionary of American Medical Biography, New York: D. Appleton and Company, 1928.

In an effort to sample some one branch of medical practice and administration from our earliest national beginnings, we investigated the office of Surgeon General as represented in the military services and more recently in public health. With the aid of the three departments, satisfactory information was finally obtained on 58 of the 61 U.S. Surgeons General (or officers of equivalent rank).

The first "Physician General"--James Craik, 1788-1800--had emigrated to this country after studying medicine at Edinburgh. Thereafter only two future Surgeons General seem to have taken training abroad: E. R. Stitt for the Navy in 1905 and Rupert Blue for the Public Health Service in 1910, both at the London School of Tropical Medicine. Whether this indifference to the universities of the continent in the great age of European medical discoveries derived from ignorance or indifference or feelings of patriotic Americanism our data did not make clear. Perhaps accident or the nature of the office and the Services had something to do with it.

A second remarkable feature of our table is the strong preference shown for the Middle Atlantic region and the colleges and medical schools of the Middle West--with an extraordinary concentration of personnel at the University of Pennsylvania. Harvard ultimately had a hand in the training of 4 Surgeons General and Tufts of 2; but the distinguished university schools and hospitals of New York City seem to have been quite largely neglected by the government services. It may be that a habit became established of looking to Pennsylvania, Maryland, and Virginia for replacements in the Surgeon General's office. In any case, Yale (with 1 alumnus), Princeton (1), Dartmouth (0), Cornell (0), and a number of other leading colleges and universities are conspicuous by their absence from the top 15 in our leadership list.

SURGEONS GENERAL

Surgeons General of the U.S. Army 1778-1966, the U.S. Navy 1842-1966, and the U.S. Public Health Service 1902-66.

College or University	Undergraduate Connections	Graduate or Professional	Net Total Individuals
PENNSYLVANIA	2	16	16
MARYLAND	2	5	7
JEFFERSON MEDICAL COLLEGE	-	6	6
VIRGINIA	2	4	5
HARVARD	1	4	4
MICHIGAN	3	1	4
N.Y.U.-BELLEVUE	1	4	4
COLUMBIA	-	3	3
DENISON	2	-	2
DICKINSON	2	-	2
GEORGETOWN	1	1	2
INDIANA	2	2	2
IOWA	1	2	2
LOUISVILLE	-	2	2
TUFTS	-	2	2
30 Other American Institutions	16	14	21
2 Foreign Institutions	-	3	3
None			1
Unknown			3
Net Total Individuals			61

Sources: Names of surgeons general before 1900 were taken from Historical Register and Dictionary of the United States Army From its Organization September 29, 1789 to March 2, 1903, by Francis B. Heitman (Washington, D.C.: Government Printing Office, 1903), volume 1; and List of Officers of the Navy of the United States and of the Marine Corps from 1775 to 1900, edited by Edward W. Callahan (L. R. Hamersby and Company, 1901). Names of appointees since 1900 were taken from the Official Register of the United States (compiled by the Department of Commerce, Bureau of the Census). Biographical information was obtained from Who's Who in America and from the following offices: Department of the Army, Office of the Surgeon General; Department of the Navy, Bureau of Medicine and Surgery; Department of Health, Education and Welfare, Public Health Service, National Library of Medicine.

D-3. HEADS OF MAJOR PROFESSIONAL MEDICAL SOCIETIES

The leadership of American medical societies since the 1870's reflects a high degree of scientific sophistication and academic involvement--as well as the concentration of American medical science and hospital services in the cities of Philadelphia, New York, Boston, and Chicago. Benefiting from and contributing to this concentration, by the professional training they provided, were certain outstanding institutions: Harvard, Pennsylvania, Columbia, Johns Hopkins, Chicago, Jefferson Medical College, Michigan, N.Y.U. (with Bellevue), and Northwestern. Among the colleges, Harvard, Yale, Pennsylvania, Chicago, and Princeton excelled in the production of future candidates for the leadership of the chief medical societies. Among foreign universities, Vienna evidently attracted the greatest number, followed by the German universities of Berlin and Munich, then Paris.

A study of the professional training of the largest undergraduate delegations shows that out of the 17 Harvard undergraduates 1 took a graduate degree at Harvard and 14 took their professional training at the same university, with only 3 going outside, 2 to Columbia and 1 to Washington University. Out of the 11 Pennsylvania undergraduates, 9 took professional degrees at Pennsylvania and 2 at Jefferson Medical College (which is also to say that the Pennsylvania Medical School attracted 26 from other universities against a figure of 21 for Harvard). Of the 9 Chicago undergraduates, 5 took graduate degrees at Chicago and 8 received their professional degrees from the same university, with only 1 going to Johns Hopkins (Rush Medical College, originally separate, was counted as a part of Chicago University). By contrast, Yale's 14 undergraduates scattered widely, with only 2 taking graduate degrees and 1 his professional degree in New Haven. One Yale alumnus took a graduate degree and 4 took professional degrees at Harvard. Five studied at Columbia and 1 each at N.Y.U., Chicago, Johns Hopkins, and Emory. Out of Michigan's 6 undergraduates, 2 took graduate degrees and 3 their professional degrees at Michigan, with 1 each going to Wayne, N.Y.U., and Chicago. Of Princeton's 8 undergraduates, 1 took a graduate degree at Princeton, while 2 professional degrees were obtained at Columbia, and 1 each at Jefferson, Maryland, Pennsylvania, Harvard, Chicago, and Hahnemann Medical College.

In medicine (as in other disciplines) the home-keeping tendency of Harvard, Pennsylvania, and Chicago students was very marked, while Yale and Princeton, the two earliest of our colleges to achieve a nationwide constituency, perhaps reflected this fact in the dispersion of their students in graduate and professional studies. The local character of Yale's medical school, prior to World War I, and the absence of a medical school at Princeton compelled the intending physicians from these two institutions to go elsewhere for their professional training, but perhaps did not dictate as wide a diversity of selection as was actually practiced. One might, for example, have expected the Princeton undergraduates to concentrate in Philadelphia or New York.

Of the 260 individuals here studied, 137 or 53 per cent had been educated in whole or in part at one or more of the six leading institutions.

58

HEADS OF MAJOR PROFESSIONAL MEDICAL SOCIETIES

The undergraduate, graduate, and professional education of the presidents of the following medical associations: American College of Physicians and Surgeons (1915-63), American Gynecological Society (1876-61), American Society of Clinical Pathologists (1922-65), American Academy of Pediatrics (1948-64), and American Surgical Association (1880-63).

College or University	Undergraduate Connections	Graduate Connections	Professional Connections	Net Total Individuals
HARVARD	17	3	35	38
PENNSYLVANIA	11	3	35	37
COLUMBIA	3	1	23	23
JOHNS HOPKINS	3	1	21	22
CHICAGO	9	5	17	18
YALE	14	2	2	15
JEFFERSON MEDICAL COLLEGE	-	-	14	14
MICHIGAN	6	3	11	14
N.Y.U.	2	-	9	10
NORTHWESTERN	2	3	9	10
PRINCETON	8	1	-	8
CALIFORNIA (Berkeley)	5	3	4	6
MARYLAND	1	5	6	6
LONG ISLAND COLLEGE-HOSPITAL	-	-	5	5
MINNESOTA	3	1	4	5
VIRGINIA	5	-	1	5
WASHINGTON U. (St. Louis)	1	1	4	5
DARTMOUTH	4	-	2	4
MEDICAL COLLEGE OF OHIO	-	-	4	4
OREGON	2	-	2	4
91 Other American Colleges and Universities	72	16	55	103
Foreign:				
VIENNA	-	-	19	19
BERLIN	-	-	12	12
PARIS	-	-	9	9
EDINBURGH	-	-	6	6
McGILL	3	-	5	5
MUNICH	-	-	5	5
21 Other Foreign Institutions	3	1	26	21
No Undergraduate Connection or Unknown	87			
Unknown				1
Total Individuals				260

D-4. MEDICAL SCHOOL DEANS, SAMPLE YEARS: 1906-65

This table is interesting as showing the rather wide distribution of academic origins for the deans of the first-flight medical schools in the past sixty years. Altogether, no fewer than 57 colleges and universities in this country, and 20 abroad, contributed to the educational experience of our group of 107 future leaders in medical administration.

Within this distribution the count shows a modest concentration of production at certain outstanding universities, led on an over-all basis by Harvard and Johns Hopkins. At the successive levels of academic education and professional training, however, the ranking of these major institutions varies considerably. Thus, the colleges most productive of future medical school deans prove to have been Harvard and Yale, followed by Johns Hopkins, Northwestern, and Princeton, then the state universities of Michigan, California, and Wisconsin. A distinctly smaller number of individuals took graduate instruction in the arts and sciences--usually with the M.A. degree--and at this level of instruction the leading institutions were Chicago, Harvard, and Northwestern. Finally, among the professional schools of medicine which trained the leaders in American medical education for the twentieth century, Johns Hopkins and Harvard were clearly outstanding, followed by Pennsylvania, then Chicago, Northwestern, N.Y.U., California, and Michigan.

Abroad, apparently more of our most promising medical students looked to the continent than to England.

MEDICAL SCHOOL DEANS, Sample years: 1906-65

College, graduate, and professional education of the deans of twenty-two major medical schools at selected intervals through the first two thirds of the twentieth century.

College or University	College	Graduate	Professional	Net Total Individuals
HARVARD	7	5	10	17
JOHNS HOPKINS	5	1	12	14
CHICAGO	2	6	6	9
NORTHWESTERN	5	5	6	8
PENNSYLVANIA	2	-	8	8
YALE	7	1	2	8
CALIFORNIA	3	1	5	6
COLUMBIA	2	2	4	6
MICHIGAN	4	2	5	6
N.Y.U.	-	-	6	6
PRINCETON	5	-	-	5
JEFFERSON	-	-	4	4
TULANE	-	-	4	4
VANDERBILT	2	-	3	4
MARYLAND	-	-	3	3
MINNESOTA	2	2	3	3
WISCONSIN	3	2	-	3
40 Other American Institutions	37	6	15	46
Foreign:				
BERLIN	1	-	4	5
HEIDELBERG	1	-	2	3
VIENNA	-	-	3	3
17 Other Foreign Institutions	7	3	13	15
Net Total Individuals				107

Sources: By consulting the American Medical Directory for the years 1906, 1916, 1925, 1934, 1942, and 1956, the deans for the years immediately preceding publication were ascertained. For 1965, resort was had directly to the medical school catalogues. The medical education of the deans was ascertained from the same sources. Further information came from Who's Who in America.

For twentieth-century medicine in this country it has, to our regret, proved difficult to find, borrow, or manufacture any substantial and fully satisfying leadership lists.

Apparently in this ancient art-science (this profession which intermingles experiment with intuition, personal therapy with social engineering, and the highest scholarship with the temptations of commercial exploitation): In modern medicine, apparently, the rewards are so great, the competitions so fierce, the rates of discovery so high, the degrees of specialization so various, and the tools of comparative judgment so imperfect or even arbitrary, that no public agreements have been reached as to who are or have been the great leaders. An honor roll of brilliant surgeons, a list of discoverers or medical pioneers, a society whose membership has been limited to those who have made some outstanding medical contribution--these do not appear to exist. Accordingly, one is driven to detection, to indirect measurements, and even to anticipation. Which schools have educated the most doctors? In what lines? And with what ratios of apparent success? Which of them emphasized medicine as science; which, its practice? In which universities have the researchers and teachers been trained, and which colleges have generated or accommodated the greatest student interest? The answers to such questions will still not identify or locate our most distinguished M.D.'s, but they will give us clues perhaps as to which university medical schools have become promising for the future.

Our first group of university statistics analyzes the alumni of 16 major medical schools for the first half of this century. The figures, borrowed and rearranged from the excellent analysis of Frank G. Dickinson, are already somewhat out-of-date, but they will indicate the quantitative production and the relative distribution of emphasis among some of our leading medical schools, for the first half of the twentieth century.

The medical schools are here listed in order of size, i.e., in each of our two tables the 10 medical schools with the largest living group of alumni are given first, followed by 6 other outstanding but smaller institutions. Thus, in 1950 Johns Hopkins had a living alumni group of 3,118, and ranked 17th in order of size among the alumni groups, while Stanford, Rochester, and Chicago ranked among the smallest of the list of 71 approved U.S. four-year medical schools studied by Dickinson. Specific comparisons are also made possible, e.g., Yale is shown to have produced less than a third the number of M.D.'s graduated from Harvard.

The columns on professional specialization in this first table are interesting as suggesting the relative numbers contributed by the outstanding schools to the several medical specialities, with Jefferson, Illinois, Northwestern, and Minnesota producing the greatest numbers in general practice, but with Harvard, Pennsylvania, and Columbia outweighing them in full-time specialities. Further analysis shows Harvard and Johns Hopkins leading the production of full-time medical school men, Hopkins and Pennsylvania ahead on administrators, Illinois astonishingly productive of doctors for the federal government, and Yale outstanding in no single category except the percentage of its graduates who had become diplomates.

MEDICAL SCHOOL ALUMNI: ACADEMIC ORIGINS AND SPECIALIZATIONS--PRIOR TO 1950

Distribution of living alumni of sixteen major medical schools as of April, 1950.

College or University	Size		Professional Specialization										Diplomates[c]	
	Living Graduates	Rank by Size of Alumni Body	General Practice	Part-time Speciality	Full-time Speciality	Active Private Practice	Administration	Full-time Medical School	Federal Government	Retired and Not in Practice	Interns	Residents	% of Living Graduates	Rank by %
JEFFERSON	5,742	1	1,935	745	1,798	4,478	26	33	286	253	273	393	15.6	24-25
PENNSYLVANIA	5,462	2	1,419	603	2,111	4,133	40	87	224	323	229	426	25.2	5-6
ILLINOIS	5,258	3	1,948	672	1,304	3,924	21	18	350	252	305	388	12.7	39
HARVARD	4,987	4	903	365	2,222	3,490	31	145	242	286	257	536	32.7	2
NORTHWESTERN	4,856	5	1,652	595	1,551	3,798	20	77	277	249	50	385	17.8	16-17
COLUMBIA	4,419	6	990	393	1,902	3,285	26	42	172	320	210	364	27.2	3
N.Y.U.	4,351	7	1,154	521	1,652	3,327	15	21	214	93	257	424	22.0	8
MICHIGAN	4,214	8	1,091	448	1,641	3,180	29	52	137	257	195	364	23.1	7
TULANE	4,053	9	1,298	537	1,200	3,035	18	50	211	171	173	395	14.2	29
MINNESOTA	3,808	10	1,518	377	1,046	2,941	21	103	249	166	18	310	17.8	16-17
JOHNS HOPKINS	3,118	17	418	206	1,524	2,148	45	131	143	220	164	267	37.1	1
CORNELL	2,432	27-28	538	202	988	1,728	17	19	118	116	153	281	25.2	5-6
YALE	1,532	49	327	105	613	1,045	15	35	79	73	97	188	25.7	4
STANFORD[a]	1,400	55	376	128	510	1,014	8	25	77	39	18	219	21.2	9
ROCHESTER[b]	1,002	63	212	65	259	536	8	24	56	35	134	209	15.6	24-25
CHICAGO[b]	839	66	250	28	210	488	6	29	68	26	56	166	15.9	23

[a] Alumni for the years 1910-49 only.

[b] Alumni for the years 1925-49 only.

[c] Diplomates for the American Boards in 1950.

Source: Materials taken by permission from Frank G. Dickinson, Distribution of Medical School Alumni in the United States as of April, 1950, Bulletin 101, American Medical Association, 1956.

This second table, drawn from the same source, provides a fair analysis of specialization by calculating the per cent of effort given to the several specialities within each alumni group, and by then ranking the producing schools in order of relative emphasis. Thus Jefferson Medical College proves to have sent 78 per cent of its living alumni into active private practice (center column), a percentage equaled by two other medical schools and exceeded by 9. By contrast, Rochester, Chicago, Yale, Johns Hopkins, and Harvard sent only from 53.5 per cent to 70 per cent into active practice, but graduated rather more than their ratio of M.D.'s who would later go into full-time medical school work.

A second indicator of differences in emphasis may be found in the percentages of full-time specialists; and still a third measure of the scientific standing of these medical schools has been the percentage of their living graduates who were diplomates of the American Boards (see previous table). Here again Johns Hopkins ranked first, with Harvard 2nd, Columbia 3rd, Yale 4th, Cornell and Pennsylvania tied for 5th, and Michigan 7th. When comparable figures become available for the generation since 1950 it will be interesting to see what shifts, if any, have occurred in the large group of institutions emphasizing the training of physicians for private practice, and in the much smaller group distinguished for their emphasis on medical science.

MEDICAL SCHOOLS: DISTRIBUTION OF PRODUCTIVE EFFORTS--PRIOR TO 1950

Analysis of living alumni of sixteen major medical schools, showing for each school the intensity of production or relative emphasis on the various branches of the profession.

College or University	General Practice		Part-time Speciality		Full-time Speciality		Active Private Practice		Full-time Medical School		Federal Government		Retired and Not in Practice	
	Rank	%	Rank	%	Rank	%	Rank	%	Rank	%	Rank	%	Rank	%
JEFFERSON	39	33.7	16	13.0	19	31.3	10-12	78.0	34-37	0.6	51-52	5.0	21-24	4.4
PENNSYLVANIA	62	26.0	41-42	11.0	7	38.7	28-29	75.7	9-10	1.6	62-64	4.1	8	5.9
ILLINOIS	28	37.0	18	12.8	48	24.8	36	74.6	57-63	0.3	15-17	6.7	15-18	4.8
HARVARD	70	18.1	58	7.3	2	44.6	55-56	70.0	4	2.9	53-54	4.9	10	5.7
NORTHWESTERN	38	34.0	24-25	12.3	16	31.9	8-9	78.2	9-10	1.6	34-35	5.7	12-13	5.1
COLUMBIA	66	22.4	52	8.9	3	43.0	38-39	74.3	20-24	1.0	65	3.9	3	7.2
N.Y.U.	60	26.5	29	12.0	8	38.0	20-22	76.5	38-43	0.5	53-54	4.9	53	2.1
MICHIGAN	63	25.9	44-45	10.6	6	39.0	30	75.5	14-18	1.2	67	3.3	7	6.1
TULANE	46-47	32.0	12-14	13.3	26-27	29.6	35	74.9	14-18	1.2	46-48	5.2	25-26	4.2
MINNESOTA	15	39.8	48	9.9	31	27.5	15-17	77.2	5	2.7	20-23	6.5	21-24	4.4
JOHNS HOPKINS	71	13.4	61	6.6	1	48.9	57	68.9	1	4.2	59	4.6	4	7.0
CORNELL	67	22.1	54	8.3	4	40.6	51-52	71.0	26-32	0.8	55	4.8	15-18	4.8
YALE	68	21.3	59	6.9	5	40.0	59	68.2	7	2.3	49-50	5.1	15-18	4.8
STANFORD[a]	57	26.9	50	9.1	9	36.4	47	72.4	8	1.8	40-42	5.5	45-47	2.8
ROCHESTER[b]	69	21.2	62-63	6.5	42-43	25.8	68	53.5	6	2.4	36-39	5.6	33	3.5
CHICAGO[b]	54	29.8	68	3.3	46-47	25.0	67	58.1	2	3.5	7	8.1	39-40	3.1

[a] Alumni for the years 1910-49 only.

[b] Alumni for the years 1925-49 only.

Source: Materials taken by permission from Frank G. Dickinson, Distribution of Medical School Alumni in the United States as of April, 1950, Bulletin 101, American Medical Association, 1956.

D-7. FULL-TIME FACULTY IN U.S. MEDICAL SCHOOLS, 1960

In 1961 the Division of Basic Research of the Association of American Medical Colleges published two tables analyzing the medical education of the full-time faculty members of U.S. medical schools: the first, for the entire faculties; the second, for the younger generation or for those members of the faculties who had graduated from medical school in the preceding twenty-five years, 1934-58. Both tables (reproduced exactly from the original Datagrams) showed Harvard clearly in first place with Johns Hopkins next. A study of the two, however, reveals that Harvard's lead over Johns Hopkins had derived primarily from weight of numbers rather than intensity of research and teaching interest on the part of the graduating medical students. In the table for the full-time faculties of all ages, the University of Pennsylvania ranked third in quantity of production, followed by Columbia, Chicago, Michigan, and Rochester, with Cornell and Yale occupying tenth and eleventh places respectively (somewhat below the ranking of these two universities as producers of prospective medical students).

In the table for the younger generation, however, the University of Rochester ranked in third place, with Yale fourth, considerably ahead of Columbia, University of California at Los Angeles, Vanderbilt, and Cornell. The implication would seem to be that certain schools of intermediate size have inculcated a greater interest in teaching and research and produced a greater number of future full-time faculty, per hundred graduates, than have such large medical institutions as Pennsylvania, Michigan, Minnesota, or N.Y.U. Comparisons of this junior faculty table with the table for Undergraduate Origins of Medical Students, and with the earlier table on the Education of Physicians, suggest a number of interesting differences of quality as well as quantity. In general, however, it is disappointing to find how few indexes of excellence our medical scientists have been able to provide.

FULL-TIME FACULTY IN U.S. MEDICAL SCHOOLS, 1960

Medical education of the full-time faculties of U.S. medical schools: the first table for all classes; the second table for the more recent classes (1934-58).

FULL-TIME FACULTY MEMBERS* BY SCHOOL OF GRADUATION
(Top 15 Schools)

School	No. of Graduates who Reported Holding Full-time Faculty Positions in All U.S. Medical Schools as of July, 1960	Full-time Faculty by School of Graduation as a Per Cent of Total Full-time Faculty in All U.S. Medical Schools in July, 1960
Harvard Medical School	568	9.87%
Johns Hopkins University	331	5.46
University of Pennsylvania	252	4.16
Columbia University	240	3.96
University of Chicago	188	3.10
University of Michigan	185	3.05
University of Rochester	165	2.72
University of Minnesota	158	2.61
New York University	156	2.58
Cornell University	154	2.54
Yale University	152	2.51
Washington University, St. Louis	137	2.26
Northwestern University	117	1.93
Vanderbilt University	114	1.88
Duke University	111	1.83
Total from top 15 schools	3,028	49.96%
Total from all other schools	3,031	50.03%

*100% = 6,059 (1,269 full-time faculty members did not specify school of graduation or were graduated from foreign medical schools).

Note: Per cents do not add to 100 due to rounding.

PER CENT OF GRADUATES OF EACH MEDICAL COLLEGE WHO REPORTED THEMSELVES AS FULL-TIME FACULTY MEMBERS IN CONTINENTAL UNITED STATES MEDICAL SCHOOLS AS OF JULY, 1960: CLASSES OF 1934 THROUGH 1958
(Top 25 Schools)

School	Total Number of 1934-58 Graduates	No. of Full-time M.D. Faculty Teaching in 1960 Who Graduated from Their Medical School Between 1934 and 1958	Percentage of 1934-58 Graduates Teaching Full-time in 1960
Harvard Medical School	3,603	477	13.24%
Johns Hopkins University	1,901	240	12.62
University of Rochester	1,490	161	10.81
Yale University	1,429	136	9.52
Columbia University	2,733	212	7.76
University of California, L.A.	145	11	7.59
Vanderbilt University	1,315	99	7.53
Cornell University	1,954	139	7.11
Duke University	1,708	110	6.44
University of Pennsylvania	3,361	212	6.31
University of Chicago	2,784	172	6.18
University of Washington	557	27	4.85
Western Reserve University	1,886	90	4.77
University of Michigan	3,148	148	4.70
University of California, S.F.	1,823	84	4.61
University of Wisconsin	1,621	73	4.50
Washington University, St. Louis	2,479	110	4.44
University of Minnesota	3,152	139	4.41
University of Utah	642	28	4.36
Stanford University	1,540	67	4.35
University of Virginia	1,629	70	4.30
New York University	3,243	135	4.16
University of Cincinnati	2,092	76	3.63
Bowman Gray School of Medicine	743	26	3.50
State University of Iowa	2,083	71	3.41

Source: DATAGRAM published by Association of American Medical Colleges, Division of Basic Research AAMC #2586 (reproduced by permission).

Rosters of premedical students, or tabulations of the undergraduate
origins of entering medical students, hardly constitute a reliable index
of distinction or future leadership in the profession. Nevertheless, they
may provide clues to the reputation of an institution, to its ability to
attract intending physicians, or to the intensity of interest in medicine
within a given academic community. As such, they hint at the possibilities of leadership in the years to come.

The Datagram's tabulation of returns on entering medical students, by
two-year intervals from 1952 to 1960, suggests some striking distinctions.
In the first place, these figures show that medicine, in the past decade,
has continued to exercise the very strong attraction for Harvard students
which distinguished that college in the nineteenth century and earlier (as
witness its contribution to the education of American physicians in the
eighteenth and nineteenth centuries, Table D-1). The second major producer of medical students through the 1950's was the undergraduate body of
the University of Michigan; the third proved to be Illinois; Columbia College generally ranked fourth; and Princeton has recently risen to fifth
place, followed by Cornell and Yale, with Indiana, Pennsylvania, Wisconsin,
and others close behind.

If the total sizes of the respective undergraduate bodies are taken
into account, it becomes clear that medical interest has recently been in-
tense at Princeton, moderately high at Yale and obviously, because of the
greater numbers potentially involved, much less compelling at the large
state universities.

Another fact demonstrated by this table is the wide spread of premedical education. The top 25 schools supplied only 28-30 per cent of
such candidates (and it required a steady 45 per cent of all the schools
thus engaged--i.e., 327-349 institutions--to account for 90 per cent of
the first-year classes).

UNDERGRADUATE ORIGINS OF MEDICAL STUDENTS, 1952-60

Analysis of the source of first-year men and women studying medicine in United States medical schools. This table "shows the 25 undergraduate institutions that supplied the largest numbers of entering first-year medical students in 1952, 1954, 1956, 1958, and 1960, and the number of students who came from each of these schools each year. Although some students obtained their premedical education at two or more institutions, for purposes of this report each student has been assigned to only one school. If the student held a baccalaureate degree (or degrees), he was credited to the school from which he received the degree (or the first such degree). If the student had no degree he was assigned to the college at which most of his premedical course work was taken."

1952		1954		1956		1958		1960	
School	No. of Ent. Med. Stud.	School	No. of Ent. Med. Stud.	School	No. of Ent. Med. Stud.	School	No. of Ent. Med. Stud.	School	No. of Ent. Med. Stud.
*Harvard	169	Harvard	174	Harvard	162	Harvard	182	Harvard	164
*Michigan	155	Michigan	136	Illinois	151	Michigan	164	Michigan	145
*Columbia	121	Illinois	105	Michigan	145	Illinois	121	Illinois	135
*Emory	98	Columbia	96	Columbia	145	Columbia	120	Columbia	131
*Indiana	96	Cornell	93	Wisconsin	122	Princeton	106	Princeton	120
*N.Y.U.	96	Yale	92	Cornell	107	Yale	101	Cornell	96
*Minnesota	96	Indiana	90	Yale	94	Penn.	98	Yale	96
*Illinois	95	Ohio State	90	Texas	91	Notre Dame	94	Wisconsin	93
*Yale	87	Cal. S.F.	90	Princeton	87	Cornell	94	Indiana	91
*Stanford	86	Minnesota	90	Cal. S.F.	87	Cal. S.F.	92	Dartmouth	91
*Princeton	85	Penn.	90	Minnesota	87	Wisconsin	87	Texas	89
*Penn.	83	Texas	84	Indiana	80	Dartmouth	84	Penn.	86
Pittsburgh	83	Wisconsin	79	Emory	78	Texas	83	Cal. S.F.	84
*Cal. S.F.	83	Emory	78	N.Y.U.	76	Cal. L.A.	82	Minnesota	84
*Wisconsin	82	Pittsburgh	78	Dartmouth	76	Stanford	81	Duke	83
*Texas	82	Princeton	76	Penn.	75	Emory	81	Stanford	81
Alabama	73	N.Y.U.	72	Stanford	74	Indiana	79	Ohio State	78
*Cornell	73	Stanford	70	Iowa	73	Minnesota	77	Cal. L.A.	73
Cal. L.A.	73	Alabama	70	Ohio State	72	Ohio State	76	Tulane	69
Kansas	71	Tulane	66	Cal. L.A.	71	Wayne	74	Wayne	69
Iowa	64	Dartmouth	65	Tennessee	68	N. Carolina	66	Emory	68
La. State	63	Duke	63	N. Carolina	64	Tulane	64	Iowa	63
Vanderbilt	62	Kansas	62	Notre Dame	62	Pittsburgh	62	Kansas	62
*Ohio State	61	N. Carolina	61	La. State	61	N.Y.U.	61	N.Y.U.	61
Duke	60	Holy Cross	59	Alabama	59	Duke	61	Notre Dame	56
Top 25 Schools Total	2,198		2,129		2,287		2,290		2,288
All Schools Total	7,381		7,424		7,835		7,925		8,075
Per Cent from Top 25 Schools	30%		29%		29%		29%		28%

*Among top 25 schools in all 5 years.

Source: Association of American Medical Colleges, DATAGRAMS, Vol. 3, no. 4, October, 1961 (reproduced by permission).

69

CHAPTER **E** PROTESTANT
DIVINITY

The statistical study of the educational backgrounds of religious leadership in this country presented an almost insoluble problem. For the first 200 years (with the exception of small groups of Catholics, as in Maryland, and an occasional seaport synagogue) the religious loyalties, practices, and organizations of the colonists and founding fathers were exclusively Protestant. Then in the nineteenth century things changed. Starting in 1830, the massive immigration of Irish and Germans poured life and vitality into the Roman Catholic Church in this country; and after 1880 the influx of Jewish peoples from Central and Eastern Europe did the same for the Hebrew faith. By World War I the three major Jewish denominations had become important in many ways, while the Roman Catholic Church was emerging as the largest single religious body in the U.S.A. Theoretically it would seem to follow that we should measure the early Protestant leadership in this country, and then attempt for the twentieth century an assessment of the education of the Catholic and Jewish leadership as well.

Unfortunately, a moment's reflection suggested that the more newly arrived religious bodies had been even more jealous of their orthodoxy, more fearful of contamination, and more exclusive in the education of their priesthood than had been the early Dissenters from the Church of England, or most of the sects which had splintered off from the Congregational and Presbyterian Churches, or emphasized a Methodist or Baptist persuasion, or come in with special immigrant groups from Scandinavia, Central Europe, or elsewhere. In consequence, one could hardly expect to discover any future Roman Catholic bishops taking their B.A.'s at the best private (Protestant) church-related colleges, or even at such non-denominational universities as Harvard (with its liberal-Unitarian tradition) or Yale (once the mother of Congregational churches and colleges) or Princeton (so long a fountainhead of American Presbyterianism). Given our deliberate separation of church and state, and the "godless" character of American public education, one could expect the secular state universities to exercise a hardly greater appeal. Jews and Catholics did begin to come to many of these institutions, and in increasing numbers to Columbia, Chicago, Harvard, and other urban universities--but hardly as a preparation for the priesthood or rabbinate. For the Roman Catholic Church, therefore, an educational historian would be reduced to a separate statistical analysis of their own seminaries in this country or in Europe; and for the rabbinical learning, likewise. These studies we have not attempted.

What can be said, in defense of the brief and quite inadequate tables here offered on the Protestant denominational leadership, is that the Protestants were the moving force, and together still constitute the majority of believers in this country. Protestant attitudes and the Protestant code not only shaped the moral structure of our early republican culture, but have continued to exercise the strongest moral and rational influence on our ways of believing and our attitudes toward man. So it remains of some interest to ask: Which colleges have helped generate the fervor? And what role have our universities been playing, yesterday and today?

E-1. PROTESTANT MISSIONARY ORGANIZATIONS, 1810-1910

Who were the chiefs of staff or major generals of the great Protestant missionary movement? Our investigation of the executive officers of six American Protestant missionary organizations proved an interesting but frustrating exercise.

To begin with, many of the leaders and organizers of foreign missions could not be identified in the standard biographical dictionaries. Altogether 128 eluded classification out of the 425 officers involved. By way of a test run these "unknowns" were read against the catalogue of Yale graduates and ultimately another 4 Yale men were identified. Resort was then had to the alumni registers of Brown, Columbia, Wesleyan, Princeton, Harvard, and Amherst, with the results given in our table. A complete knowledge of the biographical backgrounds (were such studies possible) would unquestionably add to the attributions of a number of the other institutions here listed. On the other hand, it would apparently still leave quite a group of individuals more noted for their piety and enterprise than for their higher learning.

The second bias or peculiarity of emphasis in this table was dictated by the rather uneven numbers from the several denominations, with the Methodists (116), Episcopalians (109), and Baptists (88) outnumbering the Presbyterians (27), the Congregationalists (41), and the interdenominational American Bible Society (38).

Those whose education can be identified give evidence of an interesting distribution. Evidently three distinct groups of institutions made substantial contributions to the conduct of the American mission movement: (1) the great colonial colleges: Harvard, Yale, Princeton, Pennsylvania, Columbia, Dartmouth, and Brown--with Brown, surprisingly, in the lead; (2) the theological seminaries; and (3) a select group of liberal arts colleges led by Wesleyan, Union, Amherst, Dickinson, Trinity, and Williams.

The specific denominational contributions of the leading colleges were: Brown--18 Baptist, 6 Episcopal, 1 Congregational, and 1 Methodist; Yale--12 Congregational, 6 Episcopal, 4 American Bible Society (1 of whom was also Congregational), 2 Presbyterian, and 1 Baptist; Columbia--14 Episcopal, 7 American Bible Society (including 1 Presbyterian), and 1 Methodist; Wesleyan--18 Methodist, 2 American Bible Society (1 of whom was also Methodist), and 1 Episcopal.

PROTESTANT MISSIONARY ORGANIZATIONS, 1810-1910

The educational backgrounds of the executive officers of six
American Protestant missionary organizations during the great mission-
ary century, 1810-1910. The organizations: the American Baptist
Foreign Mission Society, the American Bible Society, the American
Board of Commissioners for Foreign Missions, the Methodist Episcopal
Church Board of Foreign Missions, the Presbyterian Church in the U.S.A.
Board of Foreign Missions, and the Protestant Episcopal Church in the
U.S.A. Board of Missions.

College or University	Undergraduate Connections	Graduate or Professional	Net Total Individuals
BROWN	26	4	26
YALE	23	1	24
COLUMBIA	20	5	22
WESLEYAN	20	1	20
GENERAL THEOL. SEM.	-	17	17
PRINCETON	16	2	16
HARVARD	10	5	15
UNION	14	-	14
PRINCETON THEOL. SEM.	-	13	13
AMHERST	12	-	12
ANDOVER THEOL. SEM.	-	10	10
THEOL. SEM. OF VA.	-	10	10
NEWTON THEOL. SEM.	-	9	9
UNION THEOL. SEM.	-	9	9
PENNSYLVANIA	7	1	8
DICKINSON	7	-	7
DARTMOUTH	5	1	6
N.Y.U.	4	2	6
TRINITY	6	-	6
WILLIAMS	6	-	6
ROCHESTER THEOL. SEM.	-	5	5
SOUTH CAROLINA COLL.	5	-	5
75 Other American Institutions	81	28	91
5 Foreign Institutions	1	6	4
No Higher Education			67
Unknown			92
Net Total Individuals			425

Sources: Educational information from various biographical dictionaries and from the alumni catalogues of Amherst, Brown,
Columbia, Harvard, Princeton, Wesleyan, and Yale.

E-2. OFFICERS OF THE MAJOR PROTESTANT DENOMINATIONS, 1958

After fruitless efforts to find some honor list for the Christian ministry or some accepted categories of distinction, our office undertook an analysis of the current leadership in 1958 of the largest churches comprising the eleven major Protestant Christian religious bodies in this country. Only churches with an individual membership of over 600,000 were considered, and by no means all of these were investigated and tallied. To avoid needless distortions or the inflation of the figures under "None or Unknown" the Negro Baptist and Methodist churches were not included. Investigation then showed that apparently none of the officers of the Jehovah's Witnesses had attended college or university, so that large and vigorous church was dropped from our final total. The Evangelical and Reformed Churches had united with the Congregational Christian Church in 1957 but still in 1958 retained separate governing bodies--hence the retention of a distinction in this table. The Lutheran churches themselves seemed to go rather separate ways, e.g., all the graduates of Capital University and Seminary belonged to the American Lutheran Church; almost all the students at Concordia Seminary and Concordia College were United Lutheran, as were all six of those who attended the Philadelphia Theological Seminary; while in turn Luther Theological Seminary had devoted its efforts to the Evangelical branches.

For once in our returns Harvard did not seem to stand out in any way. It participated in the leadership of the Christian Scientists but it missed a great opportunity with the Latter Day Saints. By contrast the Yale Divinity School had apparently produced two or more leaders for at least three different Protestant religious bodies as had also the Union Theological Seminary. Columbia contributed two or more leaders to two denominations but individual leaders to five others. For an over-all count of institutional contributions to the leadership of the Protestant churches the reader is referred to the next table.

OFFICERS OF THE MAJOR PROTESTANT DENOMINATIONS, 1958

Educational backgrounds of the officers of the largest churches composing the eleven major Protestant Christian religious bodies. Only churches with an individual membership of over 600,000 in the United States were considered.

Institution	Undergrad. Connects.	Grad. or Prof'l.	Net Total Individuals
BAPTIST CHURCHES (27):			
Southern Baptist and American Baptist Conventions			
Southern Baptist Theological Sem.	-	8	8
Oklahoma Baptist U.	5	-	5
Baylor	3	2	5
Mississippi College	3	-	3
Southwestern Baptist Sem.	-	3	3
36 Other Insts.	21	21	22
None or Unknown			3
INTERNATIONAL CONVENTION OF CHRISTIAN CHURCHES (5):			
Yale	-	2	2
7 Other Insts.	5	3	4
None or Unknown			1
CHURCH OF CHRIST SCIENTIST (12):			
Harvard	-	3	3
Columbia	-	2	2
Oxford	-	2	2
Other Insts.	10	-	10
None or Unknown			2
CONGREGATIONAL CHRISTIAN CHURCHES (28):			
Columbia	1	8	8
Yale	2	4	6
Union Theolog. Sem.	-	5	5
Chicago Theolog. Sem.	-	5	5
Oberlin	4	1	4
U. of Chicago	1	2	3
Hartford Sem. Found.	-	3	3
32 Others	19	14	22
EPISCOPAL CHURCH (11):			
General Theolog. Sem.	-	3	3
Yale	1	2	3
Eastern Theolog. Sem.	-	2	2
13 Other Insts.	8	5	7
None or Unknown			2
EVANGELICAL AND REFORMED (5):			
Evangelical and Reformed Sem.	-	2	2
Union Theolog. Sem.	-	2	2
8 Other Insts.	6	3	5
EVANGELICAL UNITED BRETHREN (8):			
Bonebrake Seminary	-	3	3
Evangelical Seminary	-	2	2
Otterbein	2	-	2
8 Other Insts.	3	5	5
None or Unknown			2
LATTER DAY SAINTS (34):			
University of Utah	15	6	19
Brigham Young	6	2	7
Utah State (Logan)	4	-	4
Latter-Day Saints U.	3	-	3
23 Other Insts.	12	15	16
None or Unknown			5
LUTHERAN CHURCHES (56):			
American Lutheran Church, United Lutheran Church of America, Lutheran Missouri Synod, Evangelical Lutheran Church, Evangelical Lutheran Synodical Conference of North America			
Concordia Sem. (Mo.)	1	11	11
Capital U. and Sem.	7	5	7
Philadelphia Theolog. Sem.	-	6	6
Concordia Coll. (Wis.)	5	-	5
Luther Theolog. Sem.	-	5	5
45 Other Insts.	39	33	41
None or Unknown			10
THE METHODIST CHURCH (4):			
11 Institutions	4	7	4
PRESBYTERIAN CHURCHES (8):			
United Presbyterian Church in the U.S.A. and Presbyterian Church in the U.S.A.			
Pittsburgh-Xenia Sem.	-	3	3
Union Theolog. Sem.	-	2	2
8 Other Insts.	7	2	7
None or Unknown			1

Sources: Names from Yearbook of American Churches, 1958. Information from Who's Who in America and from correspondence with church officers.

E-3. INSTITUTIONAL SOURCES OF PROTESTANT CHURCH LEADERSHIP, 1958

This table was based on the same data supplied by the inquiry into
the officers of the major Protestant denominations in 1958. However, only
those institutions which had contributed to the leadership of at least
three different denominations were considered, for the reason that the
accident of a single church with many officers might quite distort a profile of educational backgrounds (e.g., the University of Utah, with a net
total of nineteen individuals helping to govern the Church of the Latter
Day Saints, would have to be placed at the head of the list of institutions supplying Protestant leadership, even though no other denomination
drew an officer from that university).

Given the requirement of interdenominational importance, our analysis
for the year 1958 underlined the significance of Columbia, Yale, Chicago,
and Union Theological Seminary. The large number of graduate connections
at Columbia gave that university the distinction of first place (instead
of Union Theological Seminary as one might have expected). The strong
showing of Yale and Chicago seemed to confirm the reputations of their
faculties. As in many other tables, the Universities of Pennsylvania and
Michigan made a decidedly respectable showing, but California here replaced Virginia as an additional contributor.

It may be suggestive of the lesser importance of certain denominations, and the declining role of the Protestant Churches in general, that
many of their officers proved hard to locate in any biographical dictionaries. Ultimately the education of one quarter of the Protestant leadership could not be determined.

INSTITUTIONAL SOURCES OF PROTESTANT CHURCH LEADERSHIP, 1958

Contributions of the leading universities and theological schools to the education of the officers of the major Protestant Christian religious bodies in the United States. Only those institutions which had contributed to the leadership of at least three different denominations were considered in this table.

Institution	Undergraduate Connections	Graduate or Professional	Number of Denominations	Net Total Individuals
COLUMBIA	2	16	7	17
YALE	4	10	6	14
CHICAGO	4	9 (14)	5	10 (14)
UNION THEOL. SEM.	0	10	4	10
HARVARD	0	8	5	8
PENNSYLVANIA	4	2	3	6
CALIFORNIA	3	1	4	4
MICHIGAN	1	3	3	4
For All Other American Institutions	178	148 (143)	10	169 (165)
Foreign Institutions	6	13	6	10
Men with Some Known College Connection	-	-	-	176
None or Unknown	-	-	-	43
Total	203	225	10	219

Note: Figures in parentheses are corrected totals to be used if Chicago Theological Seminary (affiliate of University of Chicago) is to be considered part of the University of Chicago.

Sources: Yearbook of American Churches, 1958, and Who's Who in America.

E-4. PROTESTANT SOCIETIES AND INTERDENOMINATIONAL ORGANIZATIONS, 1962-64

This table analyzes the educational backgrounds of the officers of the following societies and organizations: World Council of Churches (United States officers only) and National Council of Churches; also American Association of Theological Schools, American Bible Society, The American Tract Society, Inc., The Associated Church Press, Association of Council Secretaries, Evangelical Press Association, General Commission on Chaplains and Armed Forces Personnel, International Society of Christian Endeavor, National Association of Christian Schools, The National Association of Evangelicals, National Council of the Y.M.C.A., National Holiness Association, National Lutheran Council, National Service Board of Religious Objectors, Pentecostal Fellowship of North America, Religion in American Life, Religious Newswriters Association, Religious Public Relations Council, Inc. (formerly National Religious Publicity Council), Young Women's Christian Association of the U.S.A.

Perhaps the two most striking facts turned up by our analysis are the high degree of education of this Protestant leadership and its wide institutional distribution. Thus, out of 234 individual officers, only 10 are known not to have gone to college, with 7 others uncertain. By our count, from relatively complete information, the remaining 217 officers had had 235 educational connections at the undergraduate level and 325 at the graduate or professional level: altogether they had studied at no fewer than 242 institutions here and abroad. It seems clear that the officers of our Protestant societies and interdenominational organizations have been drawn from a wide variety of backgrounds and educational experiences. The statistical returns do confirm the preeminence of Columbia, Yale, Union Theological Seminary, and Chicago, but no single university can claim credit for more than 10 per cent of this leadership group.

PROTESTANT SOCIETIES AND INTERDENOMINATIONAL ORGANIZATIONS, 1962-64

Educational backgrounds of the officers of twenty American
Protestant societies and interdenominational organizations.

College or University	Undergraduate Connections	Graduate or Professional	Net Total Individuals
COLUMBIA	3	20	23
YALE	8	18	22
UNION THEOL. SEM.	-	18	18
CHICAGO	-	15	15
HARVARD	4	11	14
COLGATE-ROCHESTER THEOL. SEM.	1	11	12
N.Y.U.	1	10	11
BOSTON U.	3	8	10
PENNSYLVANIA	3	5	8
CHICAGO DIVINITY	-	7	7
NORTHWESTERN	2	5	7
SYRACUSE	4	3	7
GETTYSBURG THEOL. SEM.	-	6	6
LUTHERAN THEOL. SEM. (Phila.)	-	6	6
MINNESOTA	4	2	6
AUGUSTANA	5	-	5
DREW THEOL. SEM.	2	4	5
GENERAL THEOL. SEM.	-	5	5
GETTYSBURG	5	1	5
MICHIGAN	2	3	5
WHEATON (Ill.)	5	-	5
198 Other American Institutions	167	141	165
Foreign: EDINBURGH	-	9	9
22 Other Foreign Institutions	16	17	25
No Higher Education			10
Unknown			7
Net Total Individuals			234

Sources: Information on officers taken from Yearbook of American Churches
and Bulletin of the American Association of Theological Schools.
Education determined from Who's Who in America and correspondence with offices of the organizations.

CHAPTER **F** BIG BUSINESS, INDUSTRY,
AND BANKING AND FINANCE

Since time out of mind our outstanding businessmen, our
great traders and captains of industry, have excited in their
fellow Americans astonishment, exhilaration, envy and fear,
admiration or grudging respect, above all an almost feverish
curiosity. Who were they? Out of what backgrounds had they
sprung? How had they managed to make so much money? What
great deeds or hidden crimes had they committed? What were
the secrets of their success? For here were the millionaires
and the men of power. By any pragmatic reckoning here were
"the champs" in America's biggest league: the winners of the
game anyone could and many did try to play.

Originally, one may recall, America had been the destina-
tion, the promised land, for three quite different migrations
or orders of human aspiration. There were those who had come
to be free, to practice representative self-government, and
to achieve that protection and power under law to which a
free man might of right aspire. Again there were those who
had been moved by an idealism that was religious and moral
rather than political, who came to save their church, to set
a city on a hill, to plant in the howling wilderness the good
society, to make this a land of character and faith. But
finally there were also the others, the many others, who came
to this continent, or learned to value it, for its economic
opportunities, for its fabulous riches in furs and tobacco
and fish, for its virgin timber and its inexhaustible free
land, for its gold strikes and its silver lodes, for the king-
doms to be built and the fortunes to be made in cotton or
cattle, in coal, iron, or oil.

Of course, the men who succeeded in these pursuits, the
big businessmen of the first century of our nationhood, were
not all of a stripe, but ranged from daring adventurers or in-
genious tinkerers to shrewd traders and able managers or individuals of a monumental patience and persistence. There were
inventors and entrepreneurs like Eli Whitney and Cyrus
McCormick, S. F. B. Morse and Thomas A. Edison. There were
great traders and railroad builders named John Jacob Astor
and Commodore Vanderbilt, Gould, Hill, or Villard. There
were the big bankers and financiers like J. P. Morgan; the
steel and oil men like Andrew Carnegie and John D. Rockefeller;
the automobile inventors, makers, and sellers who matched
resources and wits with Henry Ford. Their kind were empire
builders. They made money but also more important things--
and in the process became the real lords of American creation.
They captured the imagination not only by the magnificent daring of their work but often as well by the generosity of their
gifts afterwards. Their power and influence were not to be
trifled with. A president of a transcontinental railroad
could seem, and with some justice, almost as great as the
President of the United States. A captain of industry like

Andrew Carnegie could preach his gospel with an authority unknown to many of the clergy.

In the intervals of business depression, or in areas of overexpansion and falling prices, the giants of American industry and finance could come under suspicion, vilification, and political attack. But, aside from such spasmodic revulsions, here were the men many Americans admired and wanted to imitate: the models for the ambitious younger generation. But what were their secrets? How had they achieved such success? Who taught them what to do?

The answers have never seemed adequate. Horatio Alger himself represented no more than the pale and ghostlike literary image of a drama with live actors far more impressive. Biographers and novelists alike struggled to capture the heroic spirit of these builders or mined the great mother lode of economic enterprise for ever more sensational exposés-- and fell short of reality.

Perhaps it should not surprise us, then, that in our more sober and systematic twentieth century the personnel of American business leadership has apparently intrigued many analysts and attracted attention from an unusual number of economic historians. Every few years there has burst into print a fresh rash of articles and statistical comparisons on the make-up of American business leadership. From certain of these materials, recast into appropriate form, some thirteen tables have been composed or selected for reproduction here--to which will be added some particular commentaries and statistics on banking and finance.

The disadvantages of such measurements are clear. They were made by many hands. We could have no control over the methods of analysis or the accuracy of each count. The prejudice of individual compilers might skew particular samplings or results. When a group of such inquiries, however, is spread over sixty years and, no matter how composed, consistently exhibits similar patterns or discovers and rediscovers the same contours of performance in the education of our business leadership, then the individually imperfect tables collectively come close to carrying a massive kind of persuasion.

Our series begins with a table on the aristocracy of American business in the first decade of this century, derived from manuscript studies by the economist and economic historian William Miller. According to Mr. Miller's biographical lists, Harvard dominated "the business elite" in the first decade of this century both as a college and as a university, with Columbia following well ahead of Princeton and Yale, and with M.I.T., Pittsburgh, and Rensselaer tied for fifth, followed by a mixture of religious, poly-technical, and state-supported institutions. Altogether forty-six colleges and universities had had a hand in the general education or the engineering training of seventy-seven members of this so-called aristocracy of top executives. Evidently there was no monopoly. Representatives of all three major streams of colonial settlement were participating. And institutions both religious and secular, alike liberal and technical in their instruction, had contributed to the making of our management class. Yet a substantial majority of these business leaders (or almost 60 per cent) turned out to have had no college education at all. It will be interesting to follow these social strands through the next half-century.

"THE BUSINESS ELITE," 1900-1910

College connections of 189 prominent business leaders as identified
by William Miller, historian of business.

College or University	Undergraduate Connections	Graduate or Professional	Total Connections	Net Total Individuals
HARVARD	17	7	24	18
COLUMBIA	6	8	14	11
PRINCETON	6	4	10	6
YALE	5	1	6	5
M.I.T.	3		3	3
PITTSBURGH	3		3	3
RENSSELAER	1	2	3	3
BROOKLYN POLYTECHNIC	2		2	2
CORNELL	2		2	2
GEORGETOWN	1	2	3	2
LOYOLA	2		2	2
MICHIGAN		2	2	2
RACINE	2		2	2
RUTGERS	2	1	3	2
VIRGINIA	1	1	2	2
KNOX	1	1	2	1
30 Other Colleges or Universities with One Connection	27	3	30	27
Totals	81	32	113	77
No College Training				110
Unreported				2
				189

Sources: The names were taken from the unpublished business biographies compiled by William Miller for his chapter, "The Business Elite in
Business Bureaucracies: Careers of Top Executives in the Early
Twentieth Century," pp. 287-305 in Men in Business: Essay in
Entrepreneurship, ed. William Miller, Harvard University Press,
1952. The author kindly permitted us full use of his manuscript
and schedules.

F-2. "THE BIG BUSINESS EXECUTIVE," 1900-1950

In 1955 Mabel Newcomer, in her book The Big Business Executive--The Factors That Made Him, 1900-1950, attempted to throw fresh light on the educational origins and changing character of American business leadership in the first half of the twentieth century. Her tables attracted considerable attention as did her suggestion that the days of inherited wealth and influence, of family and educational elites, were passed or passing.

For 1900 the Newcomer figures showed Harvard well ahead (just as had the schedules of William Miller). Yale, however, ranked second, with Columbia, M.I.T., and Michigan following. The figures for 1925 quite surprisingly showed Columbia and M.I.T. in the lead, with Harvard, Yale, and Princeton following, and Lehigh, Michigan, and Amherst also contributing substantially.

By 1950 Columbia and M.I.T. had dropped back again behind Princeton, Cornell, and Michigan and were contributing less than half as many top executives to big business as Harvard and Yale. Meanwhile, at every census, the number of substantial producers among the competing universities had evidently been growing. This Newcomer's statistics make abundantly clear. Her comments on H-Y-P social prestige and the importance of technical schools, however, invite further reflection.

The suggestion that social prestige had tended to produce business leadership, and vice versa, has obvious appeal. In the days of the Lawrences and the Lowells, as in the later days of the Whitneys, Harknesses, and Vanderbilts, everyone knew that a self-made businessman, having piled up a fortune, was apt to send his sons to a prestigious institution, not so much because he could afford it (the tuition and expenses were ridiculously low) as because he wished for his sons' acceptance into the social world. Having achieved this entrance almost painlessly, the sons would then inherit their father's money, and might go on to build a small business into something much larger, often with the aid of able college mates who had become their society brothers and perhaps married their sisters. The sons and grandsons of such partnerships would in their turn resort to the old college--and in such fashion collegiate loyalties, moneyed enterprises, and a kind of self-recruiting, always enlarging "business elite" might develop. Certainly inherited wealth and connections helped enormously. And the students at Harvard, Yale, and Princeton must have benefited no little (however spare and simple their own backgrounds) from the presence in each class of at least a few scions of the business aristocracy.

Having recognized this factor, however, let us not exaggerate it or allow suspicion and envy to cloud our judgment. Success was not automatic. The capacity to dissipate often ran not far behind the capacity to accumulate. And the growth of industry, the expansion of business enterprise, the opportunities for a liberal or an engineering education have always exceeded--and in the past sixty years have further and further outrun--the power of any college or of any "Ivy League" of colleges to absorb or to dominate, let alone monopolize. On the ever-widening diffusion of opportunity, Newcomer was unquestionably right.

This brings us to her further remarks about the Harvard and Yale

"THE BIG BUSINESS EXECUTIVE," 1900-1950

His educational institutions and professional training.

"The universities most frequently attended by the executives are listed below, together with the number of top executives educated in each. The total number of institutions represented are 51 in 1900, 92 in 1925, and 170 in 1950. The 'Ivy League' holds no monopoly. One third of the degrees of the 1950 group come from state and municipal institutions, as compared with one sixth from these institutions among the 1900 group. There is no question as to the social prestige of such institutions as Harvard, Yale, and Princeton. But Harvard's law school and school of business administration and Yale's engineering school* are largely responsible for their top-ranking positions."

PRINCIPAL UNIVERSITIES AND NUMBER OF EXECUTIVES ATTENDING EACH[a]

1900		1925		1950	
Institution	Number of Executives	Institution	Number of Executives	Institution	Number of Executives
HARVARD	22	COLUMBIA	18	HARVARD	74
YALE	12	M.I.T.	14	YALE	62
COLUMBIA	10	HARVARD	13	PRINCETON	34
M.I.T.	5	YALE	12	CORNELL	33
MICHIGAN	4	PRINCETON	10	MICHIGAN	31
		LEHIGH	8	COLUMBIA	29
		MICHIGAN	6	M.I.T.	23
		AMHERST	5	WISCONSIN	17
				PENNSYLVANIA	15
				CALIFORNIA	14

[a] If one executive attended two institutions, both were counted.

*Miss Newcomer's breakdown to support the above statements concerning Harvard and Yale (letter of April 13, 1956):

	1900	1925	1950
HARVARD			
Law	9	5	21
Business	-	-	12
Other	13	8	41
YALE			
Engineering	-	3	20
Other	12	9	42

Source: Data estimated in Mabel Newcomer, The Big Business Executive--The Factors That Made Him, 1900-1950, New York: Columbia University Press, 1955, pp. 72-74. (Quoted by permission.)

technical or engineering schools. In reply to our inquiry, Newcomer supplied the breakdown given at the bottom of our table. Her figures showed that at each census Harvard owed approximately 40 per cent of its top executives to its law school (or in 1950 to the law and business schools combined)--a tribute surely to their priority and effectiveness of instruction rather than to inherited wealth or social prestige. On the other hand, Yale's engineering school (the Sheffield Scientific School) only in 1950 supplied as much as a third of Yale's group of top executives (a ratio below its numerical expectations and one destined to deteriorate). In 1950 Yale, even without its engineers, and Harvard even without its lawyers and business administrators, could muster more executives than any other institution. This silent commentary on the values of a general academic education may be worth noting.

F-3. PRESIDENTS OF COMPANIES "EXCELLENTLY MANAGED," 1950

In its article on "Facts About Presidents," The Corporate Director for June, 1950, commented that, of the 6 leading colleges, 5 were in the East with a total of 59 company presidents; while Eastern colleges in general supplied over 42 per cent of the chief executives--all this in spite of the fact that 80 executives had been born in the Middle Western states, 69 in the Middle Atlantic states, 15 in the Southern states, and only 13 in New England (4.19 per cent each for Connecticut and Massachusetts). It added:

> In more than one case, there can be no doubt, family intentions rather than educational qualifications have destined a man for high corporate office. The families of many such men have traditions extending over generations as to where their sons should go for schooling. This tends, in families of industrial influence, to cause no little concentration upon specified seats of learning and, therefore, is to some extent responsible for the preponderance of Yale and Harvard men.
> Company officers confirm the fact that industrial leaders pay close attention to the quality of the graduating material of leading universities. However, this loyalty seldom extends beyond original hiring. Thereafter, in most instances, merit and capacity determine promotion.
> In younger companies, it appears, executive promotion is less influenced by abstract reasoning as to what sort of human material is worthy of grooming for the post of chief executive. Non-graduates, the moral emerges, should get into the new and growing companies. In long established firms, the college degree emphatically counts.

A comparison of this A.I.M. table with the Newcomer table for the same years is instructive on another point. Both tables suggest that for the business world of 1950 the Yale undergraduate constituency (Yale College and Scientific School) had been considerably more productive of top executives than had Harvard College (though the ratio of living alumni favored Harvard 100 to 80.3: cf. Table N-4). Why Michigan failed to place in the A.I.M. table is not clear; but it is interesting to note the participation now of some of the newer engineering schools such as Penn State and Purdue.

PRESIDENTS OF COMPANIES "EXCELLENTLY MANAGED," 1950

Analysis of 204 top executives whose organizations have been designated "excellently managed" by the American Institute of Management.

College Attended	Number of Presidents	Per Cent
No College Reported	51	25.00
YALE	25	12.25
HARVARD	18	8.82
CORNELL	6	2.94
COLUMBIA	5	2.45
PRINCETON	5	2.45
CALIFORNIA	5	2.45
M.I.T.	4	1.96
WISCONSIN	4	1.96
N.Y.U.	3	1.47
PENNSYLVANIA STATE	3	1.47
MINNESOTA	3	1.47
PURDUE	3	1.47
All Others	69	33.82
Total	204	99.98

Note: Forty-two per cent of college-educated company presidents had attended the first six universities listed.

Source: Taken by permission from The Corporate Director, published by American Institute of Management, June, 1950.

91

In this fractional sampling of substantial businessmen (505 individuals out of 8,300 usable questionnaire returns) once again Yale, Harvard, Princeton, and Cornell rank at the top among the colleges--with the Harvard graduate or professional schools outdistancing all others, followed by Columbia and by Yale. The rest of the list shows Pennsylvania and Michigan once again among the leaders; Illinois is ranked for the first time; and Williams College achieves the same production as the University of California at Berkeley.

In their study, which paid considerable attention to paternal backgrounds, to occupations, and to geographical distribution, the authors noted (p. 55) that 505 sample executives had received 596 degrees divided as follows: B.A. 211, B.S. 232, B.Bus. 9, M.A. and Ph.D. 72, LL.B. 59, nonclassifiable 13: a reading of only 12 per cent for the law but a clear indication that, outside of the "Ivy League" colleges, engineering and business training were playing an important role in the education of business executives.

"Of the 505 business leaders in our sample, 216 went to only fourteen different colleges; and these same fourteen colleges were mentioned 87 times as the ones attended secondarily, either for graduate work or as a transfer college."

Institution	First or Only Attended	Graduate or Second Undergraduate College Attended
YALE	36	9
HARVARD	27	28
PRINCETON	20	1
CORNELL	18	2
PENNSYLVANIA	16	4
ILLINOIS	13	3
M.I.T.	13	6
MICHIGAN	13	6
N.Y.U.	12	4
MINNESOTA	11	4
WILLIAMS	10	0
CALIFORNIA (Berkeley)	10	0
CHICAGO	9	7
COLUMBIA	8	13
Total	216	87

Methodology note: In 1952, a four-page form was sent to 17,546 big business leaders, defined as presidents, vice-presidents, chairmen of the board, treasurers, and owners of businesses large enough to be of more than local significance. Approximately 8,300 usable replies were received. The 505 men for the college study were selected at random from the study group. (Summarized from W. Lloyd Warner and James C. Abegglen, Occupational Mobility in American Business and Industry, Minneapolis: University of Minnesota Press, 1955, p. 222.)

Source: Estimated in W. Lloyd Warner and James C. Abegglen, Big Business Leaders in America, New York: Harpers, 1955, pp. 50-51.

This analysis of the Billion-Dollar Corporations for 1952 produced a profile of leadership with a number of resemblances to the tables already given, but also with some striking differences. To begin with, only the sixty-six largest corporations were studied and only their two chief officers (i.e., presidents and chairmen) were analyzed, as distinguished from the wider and more random coverages, or the otherwise selective samplings, of Newcomer, A.I.M., and Warner and Abegglen. In close agreement with the A.I.M. study, Pollard found that just over one quarter (29.2 per cent) of his top management group had achieved their offices of power and responsibility without having enjoyed the advantages (or disadvantages) of a college education--a far cry from the self-made elite of Miller's study for 1900-1910. Among the colleges, once again Yale led, followed by Harvard, Cornell, and Princeton (for a combined production, this time, of 28.3 per cent). But after Princeton came Dartmouth and Stanford, with Wooster College instead of Williams now matching giant California. One notes also the contributions to the Billion-Dollar Corporations of such liberal arts colleges as DePauw, Union, and Whitman. Altogether, according to Pollard's estimates, 58.5 per cent of these top executives were graduates of private colleges or universities, only 12.3 per cent had come from tax supported institutions (cf. Newcomer's figure of "one third").

Note: It would appear that this study was made entirely on the basis of college affiliation without regard to graduate or professional school record. For a more detailed analysis of a similar group nine years later, see Table F-9, BILLION-DOLLAR CORPORATIONS, 1961.

HEADS OF BILLION-DOLLAR CORPORATIONS, 1952

Institutions represented in the top management group of 106 men in the 66 Billion-Dollar Corporations identified for 1952 by the United Press, April 22, 1953.

AMHERST	1	M.I.T.	2
BALTIMORE POLYTECH. INST.	1	MICHIGAN	1
BAYLOR	1	MINNESOTA	1
BROWN	1	MISSOURI	1
CALIFORNIA	2	NEBRASKA	1
CHICAGO	2	NORTHWESTERN	1
COLGATE	1	OHIO NORTHERN	1
COLUMBIA	1	PENNSYLVANIA	1
COOPER UNION	1	PRINCETON	5
CORNELL	6	SIMMONS UNIVERSITY	1
DARTMOUTH	3	STANFORD	3
DePAUW	1	SYRACUSE	1
DRAKE	1	TEMPLE	1
GEORGETOWN	1	UNION COLLEGE	1
HARVARD	9	U.S. MILITARY ACADEMY	1
ILLINOIS	1	UNIVERSITY OF WASHINGTON	1
IOWA	1	WESTERN RESERVE	1
JOHN MARSHALL LAW SCHOOL,		WHITMAN	1
Chicago	1	WISCONSIN	1
KANSAS	1	WOOSTER	2
LEHIGH	1	YALE	10

RECAPITULATION

Institution	Per Cent
YALE	9.4
HARVARD	8.5
CORNELL	5.7
PRINCETON	4.7
Other Private Colleges	30.2
Tax-Supported Colleges	12.3
Noncollege Men	29.2

Sources: Calculation by Council for Financial Aid to Education, Inc. Table originally verified by John A. Pollard, Director of Research, and reproduced with his permission.

This table was the only business table made almost entirely in the office of the Historian of Yale, but the work was very carefully done, covered an impressive number of individuals, and analyzed their connections both educational and corporate very thoroughly. The results will repay considerable study.

The table demonstrated, first of all, the value of college training in the production of top personnel for the great industries and corporations of the country in the 1950's. The statistics showed that nearly one half (49 per cent) of the officers and directors had reached their posts without the aid of college or university training; however, these men had been much less successful in reaching the positions at the very top. Thus, the college-trained men held three chairmanships and three presidencies to every one for the noncollege men (once again, just 25 per cent of real management power). Only in the lower offices did the noncollege men predominate.

In the second place, this table exhibited the extraordinary position of Harvard, Yale, and Princeton in Big Business: At the top levels the alumni of these universities seemed without immediate rivals. The men of Cornell had dropped back to a tie with the alumni of M.I.T. and Columbia. Michigan, California, Illinois, and Wisconsin had produced less than forty executives and directors each, while Stanford, Chicago, Pennsylvania, and Dartmouth were close together in the mid twenties. When we asked about undergraduate education, we found that 27 per cent of the college-educated executives, officers, and directors of the 101 largest corporations had attended Yale, Harvard, or Princeton. Again, 35 per cent of those with any university connection whatever had had some connection with one or more of these three.

Comparisons Between Harvard, Yale, and Princeton

At the graduate and professional level, Harvard had walked away with the show: It could claim some connection with 34 per cent of all the individuals who had had graduate or professional training. Its extraordinary record was a tribute by executives to just two professional schools: the Harvard Schools of Law and of Business Administration. The School of Law had enrolled 19 graduates of Harvard College, 11 graduates of Yale College, 3 from Princeton, and 37 from other colleges. In turn the Harvard School of Business Administration had awarded 2 M.B.A.'s to Harvard graduates, 2 to men from Yale, 2 to men from Princeton, and 39 to the graduates of other institutions. By contrast Princeton, without a school either of law or of business, had attracted only 2 future executives to graduate study. Yale had also offered no school of business administration, and its law school, which only began to achieve a more than local reputation after World War I, had been somewhat jealously restricted in numbers. Looked at in another way, the figures showed that the Harvard graduate and professional schools had 14 men who had earned their undergraduate degrees at Yale and 5 more from Princeton, while 1 Princeton undergraduate had come on to the Yale Law School, but no prospective executives from Harvard College had gone either to Princeton or to Yale for postgraduate work.

96

THE 101 LARGEST CORPORATIONS, 1952

The education of the officers and directors of the 100 largest corporations--as identified in July, 1953, by the National City Bank of New York--with the Ford Motor Company added.

College	Undergraduates	Graduate and Professional	Net Total Individuals	Chairmen of Board	Presidents	Directors	Other Officers
HARVARD	93	127	193	3	12	140	91
YALE	148	13	154	6	9	124	51
PRINCETON	73	2	75	4	5	57	28
CORNELL	34	14	45	4	2	33	21
M.I.T.	29	18	45	6	3	35	27
COLUMBIA	18	32	44	0	2	28	21
MICHIGAN	31	11	38	2	1	29	24
CALIFORNIA	27	9	34	0	1	22	16
ILLINOIS	29	8	34	0	0	17	25
WISCONSIN	31	5	33	2	3	21	17
STANFORD	24	3	26	0	2	20	13
CHICAGO	13	15	25	1	3	16	15
PENNSYLVANIA	19	9	25	1	3	18	11
DARTMOUTH	23	2	23	1	2	12	13
Other U.S.	580	120	628	25	36	414	353
Foreign	14	13	24	0	1	17	11
Net Totals	1,140	377	1,205	53	76	827	620
No College or Unknown			1,146	18	25	451	887

Sources: Information from Poor's Register of Directors and Executives (1953), Who's Who in America for 1952-53, and the alumni directories for Harvard (1948), Yale (1948), and Princeton (1939, 1952). Our extensive files and the resulting table were largely the work of my bursary aide Douglas W. Smith (Yale B.A. 1956).

97

At the undergraduate level Yale had clearly been preeminent. In fact
her primacy had been greater than appeared on the surface, for, as of 1948,
Yale College had graduated approximately 80 living alumni to every 100 for
Harvard College and 58 for Princeton. Another way of understanding this
is to note that for every 10 chances a Harvard undergraduate had had of be-
coming an officer or director of one of these 101 companies, the Princeton
undergraduate had enjoyed 13 chances and the Yale undergraduate 20.

When we inquired into the postgraduate training of the Harvard and
Yale business leaders, we found that 31 of Yale's 148 undergraduates in
this table had continued on into graduate work: 7 at Yale, 14 at Harvard,
4 at Columbia, 3 at New York Law School, 2 at M.I.T., 1 at Albany Law
School. For Harvard 30 out of 93 had continued, of whom 27 kept on at
Harvard, and 1 each went to M.I.T., San Francisco Law School, and Trinity
College, Cambridge. The home-staying propensities of the Harvard men had
once again been underlined.

Looking into the corporate connections of the leading universities,
we found that Harvard had the widest representation, there being 1 or more
Harvard College or Harvard University men in a top post in 80 of the 101
companies. Yale University alumni were found among the officers and
directors of 69 of these companies, and Princeton alumni in 51 companies.
Altogether only 8 companies out of the 101 were without some representative of Y-H-P in the year 1952.

Analyzing by individual corporation, it appeared that Princeton had 4
or more representatives in Firestone Tire and Rubber Company, Jones and
Laughlin Steel Corporation, and Pennsylvania Railroad. Yale had 4 or more
representatives in 12 corporations, and in 9 of them was particularly
strong: in the American Can Company, American Metal Company, General
Electric, General Foods, Gulf Oil, International Paper, National Distillers,
New York Central Railroad, and United Aircraft. Harvard had 4 or more representatives in no fewer than 24 corporations, and was strongest in American Can, DuPont de Nemours, General Electric, Pittsburgh Plate Glass,
R.C.A., Allied Stores, Pennsylvania Railroad, and American Telephone and
Telegraph. In 16 companies either the president or the chairman of the
board was an alumnus of Harvard, Princeton, or Yale, and in 10 more companies both the president and the chairman of the board were alumni of one
or the other of these three.

Going down one step further to the individual names, it was found
that the university affiliations of the Harvard men were less firm than in
the cases for Princeton and Yale: that is, not only were many of the
Harvard men law school or business school alumni, with prior attachments
to other colleges, but quite a number merely took a period of technical
training at Harvard without obtaining their degrees.

One returns to the over-all impression that Yale, Harvard, and Princeton were in 1952 beyond challenge the "Big Three" in Big Business.

F-7. PRESIDENTS OF THE 500 LARGEST CORPORATIONS, 1956

Four years after our detailed study of the 101 largest corporations, Business Week published an analysis of the presidential leadership of 458 of the 500 largest publicly owned mining and manufacturing companies ranked according to annual sales. By comparison with our own table (F-6) this represented five times as many companies but only one fifth as many executives and these only from mining and manufacturing. The returns showed that 369 of the presidents (or 74 per cent) had attended a college or university and, on the basis of the highest degree earned, or institution last attended, Harvard had given instruction to 40 presidents, Yale to 30, Cornell and M.I.T. to 16 each, followed by Princeton with 15 and Illinois with 14. This represented a climb by M.I.T. and Cornell into the top 4 and a remarkable showing also for Illinois. Once again Columbia, Pennsylvania, Michigan, Stanford, and California ranked as significant producers, but this time no small liberal arts college or polytechnic institute made the top group.

Had the bar graph represented all earned degrees or all institutions attended (instead of just the highest degree and the last institution), it would have made possible a more complete picture for mining and manufacturing. Even so this Business Week study makes possible some interesting comparisons.

PRESIDENTS OF THE 500 LARGEST U.S. CORPORATIONS, 1956

Education of the presidents of the 500 largest U.S. mining and manufacturing corporations (ranked according to annual sales). Adequate returns had been gathered on 458 of the 500 presidents; 369 of the presidents proved to have attended college, and 280 of them held earned degrees. For those attending more than one institution, only the institution of the highest earned degree was counted. A colored bar graph showed the 11 colleges with the largest representation of college-educated presidents. The figures here given for earned degrees and attendance (first two columns) represent estimates based on a reading of the published bar graph.

College or University	Highest Earned Degree[a]	Number Attending	Per Cent of Total Presidents	Per Cent of 369 College-educated Presidents
HARVARD	33	40	8.0	10.8
YALE	26	30	6.0	8.1
M.I.T.	14	16	3.2	4.3
CORNELL	12	16	3.2	4.3
PRINCETON	14	15	3.0	4.1
ILLINOIS	11	14	2.8	3.8
COLUMBIA	9	12	2.4	3.3
PENNSYLVANIA	10	11	2.2	3.0
MICHIGAN	8	9	1.8	2.4
STANFORD	7	8	1.6	2.2
CALIFORNIA	5	8	1.6	2.2
	149	179[b]	35.8	48.5

[a] This column indicates the number of degrees earned. Thirty-three of the forty who attended Harvard earned their highest degree at Harvard. The remaining seven attended Harvard but earned no degree.

[b] The remaining 190 (51.5 per cent) of the college-educated presidents had been generated by 109 institutions in this country and ten abroad.

Source: Survey made by Business Week and published under the title "The Corporate Presidency. How Top 500 Presidents Set Off on Their Long Climb," June 9, 1956.

F-8. "50 FOREMOST BUSINESS LEADERS OF AMERICA," 1957

On November 6, on the occasion of its fortieth anniversary, <u>Forbes Magazine</u> gave a dinner in tribute to Fifty Foremost Business Leaders in America, chosen by the members of leading business and trade associations and the readers of <u>Forbes Magazine</u> in an "independent and impartial poll . . . representative of the American Way of Life." The list of "50 Foremost Business Leaders of America" was published, with photographs, in <u>The New York Times</u>, November 8, 1957.

Upon educational analysis, it proved that Harvard, though contributing only one former undergraduate, had had the greatest number of connections by virtue of 3 LL.B.'s and 1 M.B.A. Yet the most arresting contribution was perhaps made by the University of Texas, with its delegation of 4. In general, the college attendance had been widely scattered, no fewer than 36 institutions having contributed to the education of 46 business leaders. Of the total group of 50 men, only 4 (8 per cent) acknowledged no college training.

College or University	Undergraduate Connections	Graduate or Professional	Net Total Individuals
HARVARD	1	4	5
TEXAS	3	1	4
YALE	3	1	4
COLUMBIA	1	2	3
M.I.T.	2	1	3
MICHIGAN	2	1	3
STANFORD	2	1	3
CORNELL	2	-	2
MINNESOTA	2	-	2
PRINCETON	1	1	2
26 Other Colleges or Universities with Only One Person on List	22	5	26
Totals	40	17	46
No College Training			4
Grand Totals			50

"50 FOREMOST BUSINESS LEADERS OF AMERICA," 1957

It may be of interest to recall the names of the 50 captains of industry who had been singled out for this banquet honor--with their academic connections.

William M. Allen, Boeing Airplane Company (B.A. Montana State, LL.B. Harvard)
Stanley C. Allyn, The National Cash Register Co. (B.A. Wisconsin)
Stephen D. Bechtel, Bechtel Corporation (studied at California)
S. Clark Beise, Bank of America N.T. & S.A. (B.S. Minnesota)
John D. Biggers, Libbey-Owens-Ford Glass Co. (studied at Washington, B.A. Michigan)
Roger M. Blough, United States Steel Corporation (B.A. Susquehanna, LL.B. Yale)
Harold Boeschenstein, Owens-Corning Fiberglas Corporation (B.A. Illinois)
General Lucius D. Clay, Continental Can Company, Inc. (B.A. U.S. Military Acad.)
L. L. Colbert, Chrysler Corporation (B.A. Texas, LL.B. Harvard)
John S. Coleman, Burroughs Corporation (LL.B. Georgetown)
John L. Collyer, The B. F. Goodrich Company (M.E. Cornell)
Ralph J. Cordiner, General Electric Company (B.S. Whitman)
Charles R. Cox, Kennecott Copper Corporation (grad. N.Y.U.)
Harlow H. Curtice, General Motors Corporation (studied at Ferris Institute)
Harry A. deButts, Southern Railway System (B.S. V.M.I.)
Morse G. Dial, Union Carbide Corporation (M.E. Cornell)
Leland I. Doan, The Dow Chemical Company (studied at Michigan)
Donald W. Douglas, Douglas Aircraft Company, Inc. (studied at U.S. Naval Acad., B.S. M.I.T.)
Cyrus S. Eaton, Banking, Iron Ore, Steel, Coal, Transportation (B.A. McMaster)
Frederick W. Ecker, Metropolitan Life Insurance Company (B.A. Harvard)
Henry Ford II, Ford Motor Company (studied at Yale)
Crawford H. Greenewalt, E. I. duPont deNemours & Co. (B.S. M.I.T.)
Eugene Holman, Standard Oil Company (N.J.) (B.A. Simmons, M.A. Texas)
Theodore V. Houser, Sears, Roebuck & Company (B.E.E. Iowa State)
George M. Humphrey, National Steel Corporation (LL.B. Michigan)
W. Alton Jones, Cities Service Company (studied at Vanderbilt)
F. R. Kappel, American Telephone and Telegraph Company (B.S.E. Minnesota)
James M. Kennedy, Revere Copper and Brass Inc. (LL.B. Kent College of Law)
Henry R. Luce, Time Incorporated (B.A. Yale)
David L. Luke, West Virginia Pulp and Paper Company (B.S. Yale)
Leonard F. McCollum, Continental Oil Company (B.A. Texas)
John E. McKeen, Chas. Pfizer & Co., Inc. (Chem. E. Polytech of Brooklyn, studied at Columbia)
Richard K. Mellon, Mellon National Bank and Trust Company (studied at Princeton)
Frank Pace, Jr., General Dynamics Corporation (B.A. Princeton, LL.B. Harvard)
Donald C. Power, General Telephone Corporation (studied at Denison; B.S., LL.B., M.A., Ohio State)
Donald J. Russell, Southern Pacific Company (studied at Stanford)
General David Sarnoff, Radio Corporation of America
Carrol M. Shanks, The Prudential Insurance Company of America (B.B.A. Washington, LL.B. Columbia)
C. R. Smith, American Airlines, Inc. (studied at Texas)
Winthrop H. Smith, Merrill Lynch, Pierce, Fenner & Beane (B.A. Amherst)
Philip Sporn, American Gas and Electric Company (E.E. Columbia)
Norman H. Strouse, J. Walter Thompson Company
Gardiner Symonds, Tennessee Gas Transmission Company (B.A. Stanford, M.B.A. Harvard)
Edwin J. Thomas, The Goodyear Tire and Rubber Company (LL.D. Akron)
Thomas J. Watson, Jr., International Business Machines Corporation
Sidney J. Weinberg, Goldman, Sachs & Company
Charles M. White, Republic Steel Corporation (B.A. Maryland)
William K. Whiteford, Gulf Oil Corporation (studied at Stanford)
I. W. Wilson, Aluminum Company of America (B.S. M.I.T.)
Robert R. Young, New York Central System (studied at Virginia)

Eight years after his 1953 study of Billion-Dollar Corporations, John
A. Pollard repeated and deepened his analysis of America's largest business enterprises. The new investigation revealed a wider distribution of
origins, but no great surprises. Altogether 60 (instead of 41) American
institutions had contributed, but 32 of the 95 executives who went to college had attended one or more of the Ivy League universities, with a
preference for an undergraduate degree at Harvard, Princeton, or Yale.
At the professional level Harvard had awarded 4 M.B.A.'s, 2 LL.B.'s, and
an M.S. to the graduates of other colleges; and Michigan and M.I.T. had
also attracted a significant number of executives into graduate study.

Beneath the surface of these basically harmonious returns one should
sense an ever changing personnel. For example, a comparison of these 106
executives for 1961 with the "50 Foremost Business Leaders" of 1957 showed
only 13 repeaters. Again, in contrast to his 1953 figure of 12.3 per cent
for tax-supported colleges, Pollard's new tabulation indicated that of the
1961 group 43 had attended publicly controlled institutions and 73 had
been connected with private colleges or universities: an indication of
the growing participation by graduates of tax-supported institutions in
American big business. The appearance of Ohio State among the 9 leading
institutions is illustrative.

BILLION-DOLLAR CORPORATIONS, 1961

Educational background of the two top executives of the fifty-three companies with a billion dollars or more of sales, 1961.

College or University	Undergraduate Connections	Graduate or Professional	Net Total Individuals
HARVARD	6	7	13
PRINCETON	6	-	6
YALE	5	1	6
MICHIGAN	3	4	5
M.I.T.	2	3	4
OHIO STATE	3	-	3
CORNELL	2	1	3
STANFORD	3	-	3
WISCONSIN	3	1	3
Totals for All Other American Colleges and Universities	61	10	61
Foreign Colleges and Universities	-	1	1
Totals Individuals with Some Known College or University Connection			95
No College			11
Net Individuals			106

Institutions with 2 Individuals	Institutions with 1 Individual	
Akron	Austin	Montana State
Alabama	Berkeley	N.Y.U.
Brown	California	Northeastern
Carnegie Institute of Technology	Colgate	Oklahoma
Chicago	C.C.N.Y.	Pittsburgh
Iowa State	Columbia	Pratt Institute
Kansas	DePauw	Rochester
Nebraska	George Washington	South Carolina
North Carolina	Hardin Simmons	Southern California
Pace	Idaho	Susquehanna
Pennsylvania	Illinois	Texas
Stevens Institute	Indiana	Union
Texas A & M	John Marshall Law	U.S. Military Academy
U.S. Naval Academy	Lawrence	Utrecht
Washington (Seattle)	Lehigh	Washington (St. Louis)
Williams	Massachusetts	Wesleyan
	Minnesota	Wichita
	Missouri	

Sources: The list of these companies was published in Business Week for June 16, 1962, page 94. The educational backgrounds were compiled by John A. Pollard, and are reproduced with his permission.

The original Stewart Howe Services Inc. release stated: "Only about 80% of the top executives attended college. Among those who had had college preparation, 60% attended the Big Ten Conference universities, the eight Ivy League schools, Massachusetts Institute of Technology, Stanford University and the University of California."

A quick retabulation shows 264 for the eight so-called Ivy League colleges, 169 for the so-called Big Ten, and 77 for M.I.T., Stanford, and Berkeley: a strong showing for the state universities, with Michigan once again surpassing Cornell, and Illinois, M.I.T., Pennsylvania, Stanford, California, Dartmouth, and Wisconsin all making substantial contributions.

Analysis of the proportion of leaders to student enrollment would of course tell much more heavily in favor of the private colleges (cf. Table N-2). Witness a larger delegation from Princeton than from Michigan despite the enormous enrollments at Ann Arbor; also, as large a representation from Williams as from Columbia, Ohio State, or N.Y.U. Many of the other "good small colleges" also appear, though toward the bottom of the table. Rather surprisingly, the Naval Academy at Annapolis ranks twenty-first among the contributing institutions while the U.S. Military Academy at West Point does not appear among the top eighty. Heading the whole list are Yale, Harvard, and Princeton, in their expected order. This table, of course, lists only the undergraduate connections, but goes beyond mining and manufacturing to sample finance, transportation, and public utilities as well.

The college connections of the presidents and chairmen of boards of the nation's 500 largest industrial firms and fifty each of the largest banking, insurance, merchandising, transportation, and utility companies as listed by _Fortune_ magazine in 1963.

YALE	85	GEORGIA TECH	7	ARKANSAS	3
HARVARD	53	INDIANA	7	AUBURN	3
PRINCETON	44	PITTSBURGH	7	COLORADO	3
MICHIGAN	37	WASHINGTON	7	DENISON	3
CORNELL	34	AMHERST	6	DENVER	3
ILLINOIS	29	C.C.N.Y.	6	DePAUL	3
M.I.T.	27	STEVENS TECH.	6	EMORY	3
PENNSYLVANIA	26	WASHINGTON, St. L.	6	FORDHAM	3
STANFORD	26	BOSTON U.	5	GEORGETOWN	3
CALIFORNIA (Berkeley)	24	BROWN	5	HAMILTON	3
DARTMOUTH	24	DAVIDSON	5	IDAHO	3
WISCONSIN	23	IOWA STATE	5	IOWA	3
MINNESOTA	16	LAFAYETTE	5	KNOX	3
CHICAGO	14	LEHIGH	5	LAKE FOREST	3
NORTHWESTERN	14	NEBRASKA	5	MIAMI, OHIO	3
COLUMBIA	13	SOUTHERN CALIFORNIA	5	NOTRE DAME	3
N.Y.U.	13	TEXAS A & M	5	OHIO WESLEYAN	3
OHIO STATE	13	TULANE	5	OREGON STATE	3
WILLIAMS	13	UNION	5	R.P.I.	3
TEXAS	12	ALABAMA	4	U.C.L.A.	3
U.S. NAVAL ACAD.	11	ARIZONA	4	V.M.I.	3
PURDUE	11	CARNEGIE TECH.	4	V.P.I.	3
MISSOURI	10	GEORGE WASHINGTON	4	WESLEYAN	3
KANSAS	9	ILLINOIS TECH.	4		
VANDERBILT	9	MARYLAND	4	40 colleges, each 2	
VIRGINIA	9	OREGON	4	93 colleges, each 1	
NORTH CAROLINA	8	SYRACUSE	4		
PENN STATE	8	SWARTHMORE	4		
		TENNESSEE	4	Total	1,004

Source: The figures are here taken by permission from the tabulation made by Mr. Carroll L. Lurding for Stewart Howe Services Inc., which issued a public release on their results together with comments on the fraternity backgrounds of many of the executives. The news release indicated that only about 80 per cent of the top executives had attended some college and by no means all of these had graduated. Altogether, 213 out of the approximately 1,300 degree-conferring four-year colleges had contributed to the education of the nation's top executives.

"If you want to succeed in business, either don't go to college at all or attend one of the top 25 schools." So began the news release from Standard & Poor's Corporation analyzing the college, university, or professional school connections of its listed 72,153 executives and directors for 1964. The Corporation seemed to regard the distribution of 23,389 to the top universities, 24,804 to all other colleges or universities, 23,690 to no college or university, as somewhat remarkable. In point of fact these statistics merely brought out what other samplings have shown, with the additional indication that, by 1964, a smaller percentage than ever before of the <u>top</u> executives and directors of the smaller companies were without college education.

With this study of the education of more than 70,000 businessmen, Standard & Poor's achieved the broadest and most inclusive analysis of the species of which we have knowledge. Unfortunately, no breakdown was achieved between college, graduate school, or professional school connections, but one may reasonably assume that most of the Columbia contingent and a large number of the Harvard men had had professional rather than undergraduate connections at the universities named. If the proportions were at all comparable to those in our table for the 101 Largest Corporations in 1952 (Table F-6), then we may estimate that Harvard's grand total of 3,465 represented roughly in the neighborhood of 1,700 undergraduates, while Yale University's 2,446 meant better than 2,200 undergraduates, and almost all of Princeton's 1,506 undoubtedly had their Princeton experience at the same level. Worth notice, incidentally, are the unusually large representations from Pennsylvania and N.Y.U., and the appearance of Northwestern, C.C.N.Y., Toronto, and Washington in the top 25.

Finally, this study should have unusual value in helping to lay a ghost: the specter of an elite conspiracy or Ivy League monopoly. How monopolize the opportunities of 72,000 jobs? It is true that Harvard seems to have contributed ten times as many executives as Washington, the twenty-fifth ranking university. On the other hand, H-Y-P together seem to have been able to contribute only 10 per cent of the management of the corporations listed in Standard & Poor's. And one smiles a little to think of 3,400 Harvard men working harmoniously together or of management bargains between Yale and Ohio State or Princeton and C.C.N.Y. To put the matter another way, American business has been too vast and various to yield to the social and economic dictation of any limited number of men.

THE MEN IN STANDARD & POOR'S, 1964

Analysis of the college, graduate school, or professional school connections of the 72,153 executives and directors listed in Standard & Poor's.

Name of Institution	Number of Individuals Attending
HARVARD	3,465
YALE	2,446
PRINCETON	1,506
PENNSYLVANIA	1,393
MICHIGAN	1,292
N.Y.U.	1,183
CORNELL	1,077
COLUMBIA	969
DARTMOUTH	902
ILLINOIS	902
M.I.T.	885
WISCONSIN	843
CALIFORNIA	821
NORTHWESTERN	811
MINNESOTA	590
OHIO STATE	578
STANFORD	557
CHICAGO	526
WILLIAMS	438
C.C.N.Y.	380
PITTSBURGH	380
PURDUE	375
TORONTO	368
PENN. STATE	359
WASHINGTON, ST. LOUIS	344

Totals

Top 25 Institutions	23,389
Other Than Top 25	24,804
No College or University	23,690

Source: Register of Corporations, Directors and Executives as given to the press, February 20, 1964 (cf. Time, February 28, 1964, p. 96).

This study represents a very interesting attempt to measure the backgrounds--educational, financial, occupational--of the new generation of industrial executives. The returns showed that less than 10 per cent of the 1,001 principal officers had never been to college. Instead, some 38 per cent of America's big businessmen now reported technical backgrounds, i.e., degrees in engineering or natural science or equivalent job experience; and the published returns illustrated in striking bar-graph fashion the rapidity of the shift toward technical background as a qualification for higher corporate responsibility. The decreasing role of inherited wealth or position, and the increasing opportunities for those with limited family backgrounds, were also emphasized.

Another feature, not remarked in this inquiry, was the continued leadership of the same universities as had figured in many earlier tables. On an over-all basis the number of contributing universities seems to have grown remarkably since 1900. A comparison with Newcomer's earlier tables, or with our analysis of The 101 Largest Corporations in 1952 (Table F-6) will indicate immediately, however, that this has not been entirely at the expense of the leading institutions. In 1964, with 88 alumni out of 1,001 executives, Harvard University was still able to demonstrate a connection with more than 8 per cent of the top personnel, while at the undergraduate level Yale was still supplying better than 6 per cent and Princeton almost 4 per cent. Together they had managed to generate not quite 20 per cent of the top officers of the 600 largest U.S. nonfinancial corporations (by contrast with their 10 per cent for all the corporations in Standard & Poor's). So they were still contributing more heavily to the major corporations than to business in general. Paradoxically, in the new era of increasing technical specialization, Yale had seen the decline of its own scientific and engineering schools, yet had managed to maintain its performance notwithstanding. The substantial contributions of Illinois, Stanford, Dartmouth, Missouri, and Lehigh seem also worthy of remark.

"THE BIG BUSINESS EXECUTIVE," 1964

In 1965, Scientific American, Inc. published <u>The Big Business Executive/1964:</u> <u>A Study of His Social and Educational Background</u>. This study, conducted by Market Statistics, Inc. in collaboration with Dr. Mabel Newcomer, was undertaken to bring up to date Dr. Newcomer's well-known <u>The Big Business Executive--The Factors That</u> <u>Made Him: 1900-1950</u> (cf. Table F-2). The analysis concerned itself with the backgrounds of the top officers (president and chairman or principal vice-president) of the 600 largest U.S. nonfinancial corporations. The figures here given represent effective returns on 1,001 officers of 593 companies.

College or University	Undergraduate Connections	Graduate or Professional	Net Total Individuals
HARVARD	46	52	88
YALE	66	12	74
M.I.T.	30	16	43
PRINCETON	39	1	39
CORNELL	24	12	33
ILLINOIS	27	5	29
COLUMBIA	11	15	25
STANFORD	23	6	24
PENNSYLVANIA	19	1	20
MICHIGAN	13	13	19
WISCONSIN	18	2	19
DARTMOUTH	18	-	18
CALIFORNIA	14	4	17
MISSOURI	11	3	14
U.S. NAVAL ACADEMY	14	-	14
LEHIGH	11	1	12
MINNESOTA	10	3	12
N.Y.U.	10	2	12
NORTHWESTERN	10	2	12
CHICAGO	8	5	11
TEXAS	8	3	10
OHIO STATE	6	6	9

Source: Figures quoted by permission of Scientific American, Inc., are taken from <u>The Big Business Executive/1964: A Study of His Social and Educational Background</u> (1965), Table 10, page 41, entitled "Principal Universities and Number of Executives Attending Each," as revised to eliminate duplications. The new tally was supplied to me by the kindness of Allan Wittman, Research Director, whose aid is gratefully acknowledged.

F-13. TOP EXECUTIVES OF THE LARGEST NONFINANCIAL CORPORATIONS, 1955, 1961, 1964

The research materials supplied by John A. Pollard showed that the 100 largest nonfinancial corporations were dominated by manufacturing but included also public utilities, trade, and transportation. Over the nine-year period there had taken place also some replacement of giant corporations by corporations which had grown still larger; thus, three lists of 100 corporations produced 151 corporations in all, and these 151 corporations had as chairman and president, or president and executive vice-president, some 438 individuals. If a man appeared in more than one year or served as one of the chief officers in more than one company, his name and affiliation were counted only once. The figures in our table may, therefore, be taken as a fair sampling of the top management of big business in America over the nine-year period.

This sampling reaffirms the leadership of Yale College and the very strong contributions made by Harvard, Princeton, Cornell, and M.I.T. At the professional level Harvard once again towers over the field, with M.I.T., Michigan, Columbia, and Yale following far behind.

It may be noted that M.I.T. and Cornell make a stronger showing in this table than they did in our table for the 101 largest corporations in 1952. Deductions from an apparent shift should be made, however, with some caution, inasmuch as a breakdown for the three sample years (1955, 1961, and 1964) showed Cornell and M.I.T. strongest in 1955, and Y-H-P regaining their leadership in 1961 and 1964.

The same figures make unmistakable the rapid turnover in top personnel within a period of less than ten years. For example, the preliminary tabulations for 1955, 1961, and 1964 turned up the names of 24 executives who had been undergraduates at Yale, and these 24 individuals appeared as presidents or chairmen just 29 times: a figure for repeaters of only 5 (i.e., it took 24 individuals to hold 29 offices). For the four other top colleges (Harvard, Princeton, M.I.T., and Cornell) the continuity in office seems to have been somewhat though not very markedly higher. Thus, in the three tabulations some 64 individuals were encountered altogether 94 times. For the whole group of 151 corporations, some 438 officers had been required. Had there been perfect immobility in office, 302 officers would have sufficed. Had there been complete replacement of officers between the first and second inquiry and between the second and third, then presumably some 600 chief executives would have been required. The intermediate figure of 438 individuals suggests a fair but not excessive turnover of top personnel, a finding confirmed by our previous studies whenever there was an opportunity to make comparisons.

Mr. Pollard's calculations indicate that the number of men without college experience had by 1964 dropped to 10 per cent of the top executives. Of the 177 attending college, 70 had graduated B.A., 55 B.S., 22 with an engineering degree, 2 B.B.A., and 1 Ph.B. His biographical researches also reveal that the numbers of those taking graduate or professional degrees or at least enrolling for postgraduate study have likewise been growing and have now passed the 25 per cent figure. Calculations for each of the sample years suggested that the public institutions as a group had slowly been catching up to the total contributions of all the private institutions, yet in the leadership lists of 1961 and 1964 their contribution was still in the ratio of 3 to 5.

112

TOP EXECUTIVES OF THE LARGEST NONFINANCIAL CORPORATIONS, 1955, 1961, 1964

Education of the two top executives of the 100 largest nonfinancial corporations (measured by total assets reported) for three sample years: 1955, 1961, and
1964.

College or University	Undergraduate Connections	Professional and Graduate Connections	Net Total Individuals
HARVARD	17	32	43
YALE	24	4	26
M.I.T.	15	8	23
PRINCETON	17	2	18
CORNELL	15	3	17
MICHIGAN	7	8	13
CALIFORNIA (Berkeley)	11	2	12
STANFORD	12	2	12
MINNESOTA	8	2	9
COLUMBIA	2	7	8
ILLINOIS	7	1	8
PENNSYLVANIA	7	1	8
TEXAS	7	1	8
LEHIGH	6	1	7
N.Y.U.	7	-	7
U.S. NAVAL ACADEMY	7	-	7
PURDUE	7	-	7
WISCONSIN	6	1	7
DARTMOUTH	6	1	6
NORTHWESTERN	4	3	6
CHICAGO	4	1	5
IOWA STATE	5	-	5
KANSAS	5	1	5
MISSOURI	4	1	5
NORTH CAROLINA	5	-	5
OHIO STATE	4	3	5
103 Other American Institutions	144	28	149
10 Foreign Institutions	7	4	10
None or Unknown			74
Net Individuals			438

Sources: The original lists were published by the First National City Bank of New
York in its monthly economic letter (September, 1955, July, 1961, and
August, 1964) and represented estimates of the standing of the largest
corporations at the end of the preceding years. The names of the two
top executives of each of these corporations were then determined and
their education ascertained by Mr. John A. Pollard, vice-president of
the Council of Financial Aid to Education Inc. Mr. Pollard has let
us have the benefit of his researches, which are hereby gratefully
acknowledged.

Our study has reproduced an unusually large number of tables on American business and industry, in part because they were available, in part because they provided unusual opportunities for comparison across a time span of sixty years or between kinds of industry or size of corporation. Trends in the numbers of contributing institutions, their location and shifting focus of interest, emerged rather clearly. When we turned from mining, manufacturing, industry, and business in general, however, to attempt a comparable study or two in the fields of banking and finance, we found ourselves in some trouble. To establish satisfactory categories in finance, or to find adequate leadership lists in the formally recognized occupation of banking, were not easy. When finally a given list of leaders was analyzed, we found it impossible in many cases to identify an individual or ascertain his educational experience. The presidency of the American Bankers Association became a case in point--as also did the management of the New York Stock Exchange.

F-14. PRESIDENTS OF THE AMERICAN BANKERS ASSOCIATION, 1875-1961

Of 76 American Bankers Association Presidents, 39 seemed to have had no college education and one was unreported. The majority of the remainder had attended college, but had received no degrees. Four had had some experience at Harvard; 2 at the University of Georgia; and 38 other institutions had seen one future Bankers Association President each: among them the Universities of California, Chicago, Columbia, Cornell, Princeton, Stanford, Texas, Virginia, and Yale. These figures seemed hardly to warrant a statistical table.

A second inquiry was into the management of the New York
Stock Exchange. The presidents and secretaries of the Exchange
were easy to identify, but their educational backgrounds proved
extremely elusive. After searching a number of biographical
dictionaries, we found that Yale and Harvard had contributed 7
individuals out of 62 officers in the 146-year history of the
Exchange; but for 40 individuals no educational information was
obtainable and 11 others had definitely not gone to college.
The first president of the Exchange with an identifiable college education proved to be William Alexander Smith, Princeton
A.B. 1838, who held the office in the first year after the
Civil War, 1866-67. He was followed in 1872-73 by Edward King,
Harvard A.B. 1853, and in 1878-80 by Brayton Ives, Yale B.A.
1861. The first two college-educated secretaries of the Ex-
change who could be identified as such were Ashbel Green, Yale
B.A. 1891, who held the office in the years 1928-36, and Robert
L. Fisher, Yale B.A. 1920, who succeeded him for two years. In
addition the Albany Law School, Cornell, Oxford, Trinity, the
U.S. Military Academy, the University of the City of New York,
and Williams College each contributed one president or one secretary to the Exchange.

In order to sample the top management of our largest banks, a list was taken of the 50 largest banks as of December 31, 1953, and their chairmen, presidents, and executive vice-presidents were subjected to scrutiny. Promptly one of the 50 banks ate up another bank in the list, so a fifty-first bank was added; but before letters of inquiry could elicit the information we desired from the 51 banks, several others had been cannibalized. Ultimately, we therefore had to content ourselves with a sampling of the major officers of 39 of these 51 banks, both for 1955 and for previous years--and the results are given in this table.

Altogether 242 out of 545 officers either had no college training or their educational connections could not be ascertained (by correspondence or through the biographical dictionaries).

The 303 identifiable college or university men distributed themselves into what had begun to seem to our office a representative order. Once again it turned out that Yale led as a college and Harvard led as a university, with Princeton a very respectable third, and California, Columbia, Dartmouth, Chicago, Michigan, Cornell, and Wisconsin among the lesser leaders. The strength shown by Pennsylvania, however, was worthy of remark; while the absence of M.I.T., Stanford, and Illinois from the list of major producers of bank presidents seemed in puzzling contrast to their production of industrial leadership in recent decades.

On close analysis, the survey of officers for the year 1955 yielded substantial returns. Cumulatively, it turned out that 10 out of 23 chairmen, 14 out of 38 presidents, and 31 out of 88 executive vice-presidents (or 30 per cent of all the chief officers) had been educated wholly or in part at H-Y-P. On the other hand, the sampling for officers and years prior to 1955 was gravely handicapped by faulty bank records, often an astounding absence of information on the part of the bank itself, and not infrequently a total indifference. Despite such impediments, a substantial number of names was finally analyzed; and the results indicated a distribution similar to that for 1955, but with a far larger number of noncollege men, and less than 18 per cent from H-Y-P.

OFFICERS OF THE LARGEST BANKS, 1955

College and university connections of the officers of 39 of the 51 largest banks (as of December 31, 1953) with a sampling of officers from earlier years and predecessor banks.

College or University	Officers as of 1955			Officers Prior to 1955			Total	Academic Connections		Net Total Indivi-duals
	Chmn. of Board	Pres.	Exec. V-Pres.	Chmn. of Board	Pres.	Exec. V-Pres.	Offices	Under-grad.	Grad. or Prof.	
HARVARD	4	5	10	10	25	4	58	34	22	48
YALE	2	7	17	10	19	7	62	45	2	46
PRINCETON	4	3	4	6	14	3	34	23	1	24
PENNSYLVANIA	1	2	1	6	15	1	26	15	4	18
CALIFORNIA	1	3	1	2	7	1	15	11	3	14
COLUMBIA		1	1	5	6	1	13	4	7	11
DARTMOUTH		2	5		2	1	10	9	1	9
CHICAGO		1	3		2	2	8	4	4	8
MICHIGAN		1	2	1	4	1	9	2	5	7
N.Y.U.	1		1	2	6		10	4	3	7
CORNELL		2		2	3	1	8	6		6
VANDERBILT	1	2	1	2	3	2	11	4	1	5
VIRGINIA			3		2		5	3	3	5
AMHERST	1		1	2	2		6	4		4
MINNESOTA		1		1	1	1	4	4	1	4
NORTHWESTERN		1	3			1	5	3	2	4
UNIVERSITY OF ST. LOUIS			2		2		4	2	2	4
WASHINGTON (Seattle)	1		1		2		4	3	1	4
WISCONSIN			3		1		4	3	2	4
84 Other Institutions	6	7	20	19	44	12	108	82	11	82
Foreign Study		1	3	2	3	4	13	6	5	11
Others*	2	2	5	5	16	5	33	18	8	25
Gross Totals	22	40	88	75	179	47	451	287	89	
Net Total Individuals										303
No College Training or Unknown	7	6	18	47	193	33	304			
Gross Totals	29	46	106	122	372	80	755	618		242
Net Total Individuals	23	38	88	115	357	73	694			545

*Including the Babson Institute, Rutgers Graduate School of Banking, and institutions of undetermined status.

In this highly important field a survey was made of the college and university connections of the chief officers of the Federal Reserve System and the Twelve Federal Reserve Banks so as to include, if possible, all officers from the inception of the system.   Ultimately 355 names were analyzed, of which 211 proved to have college or university connections.

In general, in part because of the number of individuals with no college or university connections, but perhaps also in part because of the regional requirements of the Federal Reserve System, the educational backgrounds of the Federal Reserve men seemed to show a wide scattering of affiliations.   The ranking of Pennsylvania and Missouri in 5th and 6th places and the appearance also among the top 21 institutions of Chicago, Georgia, Western Reserve, George Washington, Atlanta Law School, and Temple will be noted in this table--as well as the absence of Cornell and Dartmouth, M.I.T. and Stanford from the leadership list.   Altogether the top 21 had a hand in the education of more than half of the college-educated group (i.e., 131 as against 121 credited to the 130 other colleges or universities participating).

A more detailed analysis showed Harvard in the lead as a university; Yale as a college; and California, Columbia, and Pennsylvania ahead of Princeton.   For unexplained reasons not a single Yale undergraduate had gone on to professional study in New Haven.   Instead a detailed study of the universities with substantial graduate or professional connections showed that, of the 18 students who had graduate connections with Harvard, 7 had been undergraduates at Harvard, 2 at Yale, and 1 at Princeton.   Of the 5 at California, 3 had been undergraduates at California, and none at either Harvard, Yale, or Princeton.   Of the 9 at Columbia, 2 had been undergraduates at Columbia, 3 at Yale, and none at either Harvard or Princeton.   Between them, Harvard, Yale, and Princeton had contributed to the college or graduate education of more than 20 per cent of the college-educated officers in the Federal Reserve System up to the year 1956.

THE FEDERAL RESERVE SYSTEM (UP TO 1956)

College and university connections of the Federal Reserve Board and officers of twelve Federal Reserve Banks.

College or University	Board of Governors		Presidents or Governors		Federal Reserve Agents		Vice-Pres. or Dep. Governors		Other Officers		Total Persons		Net Total Individuals
	Under-grad.	Grad. or Prof.	Under-grad.	Grad. or Prof.	Under-grad.	Grad. or Prof.	Under-grad.	Grad. or Prof.	Under-grad.	Grad. or Prof.	Under-grad.	Grad. or Prof.	
HARVARD	3	4	2	4	2	1	3	8	1	1	11	18	22
YALE	3		3		6		3		1		16	0	16
CALIFORNIA	2	1	3			1	4	3			9	5	11
COLUMBIA		1	1	1		1	1	6	1		3	9	10
PENNSYLVANIA	1	1	2	2		1	4		1		8	3	9
MISSOURI			1	1	2	2	5	3			8	6	8
PRINCETON			1		2		6				8	0	8
CHICAGO			1	1			1	1	1	1	3	5	7
ILLINOIS			2	1	1			2	2	3	5	5	7
N.Y.U.	1		1				1	2	2	2	4	4	7
TEXAS	2						1	2	4	2	5	4	7
GEORGIA			1	1	1		3	1	1		5	2	6
WESTERN RESERVE			1		1		2	1	1	1	5	2	6
WISCONSIN							2	4	2	1	2	5	6
GEORGE WASHINGTON	1	1	1				1	1	1	2	2	5	5
IOWA							3	3			3	3	5
MINNESOTA	1		2				2	2	1		3	2	5
ATLANTA LAW SCHOOL							3	3		4	0	4	4
MICHIGAN	1	1			1	1	1		1		3	1	4
NORTHWESTERN	1		1				1	1	1	3	2	3	4
TEMPLE					1		2	1			3	1	4
Top 21 Colleges or Universities	16	8	19	14	16	7	43	44	17	15	103	73	131
130 Other Colleges or Universities	21	12	18	4	15	4	50	16	23	11	109	33	121
Foreign Study	1	2	1				4	1			6	3	9
Total Affiliations	38	22	38	18	31	11	97	61	40	26	196	103	211
American Institute of Banking			1				18		16				36
Rutgers Grad. School of Banking							16		3				19
Commercial Business College	1		3				15		10				29
No College Training	3		17		11		37		18				86
No Educational Records	2		3		2		3		8				18
Persons in Survey	39		56		40		149		79		196	103	355

SUMMARY: BIG BUSINESS AND THE HIGHER LEARNING

Since this study devotes fifteen tables (with nineteen distinct measurements altogether) to Business, Industry, Banking and Finance, there will be those who will object to so much attention to the economic occupations, and some who will wonder what leadership in money-making has to do with the true spirit of the university. These two questions have philosophic implications worth sober exploration, but too complex for settlement here.

The justification for what has been attempted, and for the two summary tables which follow, may be stated as follows: (1) Ours has been to a remarkable degree an economic culture, a society geared to production. In 1950 about 20 per cent of the biographees in Who's Who in America had come from the world of business, as against 6 per cent for the law and 25 per cent for education. (2) For understandable reasons, the subject of business leadership continues to enlist public interest and concern. (3) This interest has generated data of unusual volume and time-span, so that it becomes possible to compare the findings across sixty-five years--to discover some of the differences between the men of business, of industry, and of finance--and to study the variations of educational preparation between chairmen-presidents and lesser officers, or between leadership lists as small as fifty men and as large as 70,000. (4) Contrary to our expectations, these successive top management lists seemed to contain little name duplication--the tables confirming and at times overlapping but seldom replicating each other. (5) Comparisons between big businesses in general and the very biggest of all these American corporations show that it is in the top management of the latter that the graduates of Harvard, Yale, and Princeton have achieved the greatest influence and the largest share (at times 20 per cent to 30 per cent) whereas in all the businesses listed in Standard and Poor's Register of Corporations the H-Y-P top management delegations together do not equal 10 per cent. (7) Given these minority quotas, and given the further fact that the men of Harvard (or Yale or Princeton) do not necessarily work together, let alone forward the careers of their former arch rivals, then it becomes clear once again that the charges of monopoly or the suspicions of conspiracy are misconceived. (8) Finally these tables, when taken together as in our summaries, indicate explicitly and unmistakably the rank order of our college and university constituencies.

120

SUMMARY TABLE: BIG BUSINESS--COLLEGES

Condensed table showing the relative participation, or number of listings at each rank, for the alumni bf the seventeen major producing universities at the college level. This table represents a cumulative recording of the undergraduate production for fifteen of the preceding tables on big business and industry, banking and finance.

College or University	Number of Listings at Each Rank										Total in First 10	Total Mention
	1	2	3	4	5	6	7	8	9	10		
YALE	10-T*	1	1	2							15	15
HARVARD	2-T	9-T			1			T			15	15
PRINCETON	T	TT	7	1-TT				T			14	14
CORNELL			2-T	3-T	1	1	1-T	T			12	12
M.I.T.		1	T	2-T	T	T	2-TTT	T			13	13
MICHIGAN			T	1-T	2-T	T	1		T		9	12
COLUMBIA	1	T	1	T		1		TT			7	14
CALIFORNIA		1		T	1		1-T		1	1-T	8	10
PENNSYLVANIA				1-T	1			1-T	1-T		7	9
STANFORD			T	T	T	1	1	T		1	7	7
WISCONSIN				T	T		T	1	T		5	10
ILLINOIS					1	1-T	TT	T			6	8
MINNESOTA			T					1-T	T	1	5	10
DARTMOUTH					T	1		T		T	4	6
N.Y.U.								T	1-TT		4	8
CHICAGO							T	TT			3	9
TEXAS	T						T	T			3	6

*The numeral indicates an undisputed rank, the "T" a tie at that rank. Thus 10-T means ten undisputed first places and one tie for first.

Condensed table showing the relative participation, or number of listings at each rank, for the alumni constituencies (net total of individuals who had attended the college, graduate or professional schools) of each of the thirteen major producing universities. This table represents a cumulative recording for fifteen of the preceding tables on big business and industry, banking and finance.

College or University	Number of Listings in Each Rank										Total in First 10	Total Mention
	1	2	3	4	5	6	7	8	9	10		
HARVARD	13	3	1								17	17
YALE	3	10-TT*		2							17	17
PRINCETON		T	6-T	3-T	2	T		T			16	16
COLUMBIA	1	1	1-T	1-TT		3	2	1		T	14	17
M.I.T.		1	2-T	1-TT	1-T		2-TTT				14	15
CORNELL			2-T	1-T	3-T	T	1	TT			13	14
MICHIGAN			2-T		3	1	2-T	T	1-T	T	14	16
PENNSYLVANIA			2	1-T				1-T	2	TT	10	12
CALIFORNIA			1	T	1		TT	T		1-TT	9	13
ILLINOIS						3		TT	TT	T	8	10
STANFORD			T		T	T	T	1-T		T	7	9
WISCONSIN						T	T	1		1-T	5	11
N.Y.U.					1			T	TTT		5	9
CHICAGO							T	1-T	T	T	5	10
MINNESOTA								T	1-T		3	11
TEXAS		T						T		T	3	6
DARTMOUTH					T		1		T	T	4	7

*The numeral indicates an undisputed rank, the "T" a tie at that rank. Thus in this instance 10-TT means ten undisputed second places and two ties for second.

122

CHAPTER G PHILANTHROPY

When Alexis de Tocqueville visited this country in
1831-32, he was surprised to find how many good works--ordi-
narily left to the central administration in France, or even
not attempted at all--we Americans carried in our own hands.
Not only did private citizens man juries, found and support
the churches, supervise the schools, and see to the building
of turnpikes or repair of the roads; individually or in volun-
tary association they seemed to be engaged in an almost in-
credible variety of activities for the physical, moral, economic, and social betterment of humankind. In addition to
the antislavery movement, Tocqueville encountered several organized swarms of penitentiary enthusiasts or prison reformers,
some newly established houses of refuge for juvenile delin-
quents, the temperance crusaders, a variety of frontier preach-
ers and missionaries, a Shaker community near Albany, and some
individuals in Hartford who had started to care for the deaf,
dumb, and blind. Then he was told of the group of prominent
citizens who were organizing a convention in Philadelphia to
do away with the evils of the protective tariff, and of another group in New York who were going through the same mo-
tions to promote American industry. Voluntarism was in our
blood. Private and cooperative efforts for the improvement
of man's lot seemed knit into the structure of our society.
Coming from Catholic and authoritarian France, Tocqueville
quickly recognized that here was something quite different:
something essentially Protestant and republican: something
that aided and abetted our federalism and decentralization:
something perhaps in the long run indispensable to personal
and group freedoms in a democracy.

     Today things have changed. So great have grown the prob-
lems and the needed resources that we organize, direct, and
subsidize improvement far more than ever before from Washington. The problems of poverty, old age, medical care, and
human rights can no longer be left to volunteer groups or
private philanthropists unaided. The nation has too serious
a stake in quick relief, reasonably and uniformly applied.
Yet still, if he were to return, Tocqueville would find us
far from the mood or the political stance of the socialists
of Europe. Almost instinctively our "great society" believes
in private effort as well as in public action. Our efforts
to help the developing nations are a mixture--at their best a

happy blend--of official loans and subsidies and food and material with the private efforts of individuals, church groups, and philanthropic foundations. Like the abolitionists and prison reformers of yesteryear, the Peace Corps and the Civil Liberties Union are a traditionally Protestant and characteristically American phenomenon. Indeed, if in the centuries ahead our society is to be remembered for something other than its innocent mistakes and its power, it may well be because we still believed in, still knew how to organize, and still took a personal part in an extraordinarily diversified and very generous philanthropy.

Reflecting on such distinctions, it seemed worth asking: Who have exercised for us these responsibilities? Who, for example, have governed our major foundations? From what backgrounds have come some of our twentieth-century captains of charity? And who have voluntarily shouldered the burdens of looking after the welfare of our new city communities?

G-1. THE LEADERSHIP OF MAJOR AMERICAN FOUNDATIONS, 1948

Our first inquiry was into the educational backgrounds of the officers of twenty-six of our most distinguished and influential foundations as of the year 1948. Would the graduates of our smaller, rural, church-related colleges perhaps step into the forefront of our national efforts where matters of charity and public welfare were concerned? It required only a brief study of the educational affiliations of some 341 individuals to uncover instead and once again the celebrated and established names of the great colleges and universities of this country. On balance the topography of philanthropy betrayed a striking resemblance to the maps already charted for federal office, the professions, big business, and finance.

As can be seen at a glance, at the undergraduate level Yale College had produced the greatest number of officers for the foundations, followed closely by Harvard, with Princeton a strong third, Dartmouth a very respectable fourth, and Columbia, Chicago, Virginia, Johns Hopkins, Michigan, and Wisconsin following. Together, the thirteen leading colleges had contributed more than all the 167 other institutions involved, here and abroad.

At the graduate or professional level Harvard and Columbia were far in the lead, followed by Yale, Chicago, Johns Hopkins, Pennsylvania, and Wisconsin. Altogether, in one capacity or another, 23 per cent of all the officers and directors of the 26 major foundations in the United States had some connection with Harvard University, 15 per cent some connection with Yale. And at the undergraduate level 117 out of 326 with some known college education (or just under 36 per cent) had studied at Yale, Harvard, or Princeton. It is interesting to note finally that the role of foreign colleges and universities had for future philanthropists been much more substantial than in the upbringing of our businessmen or our lawyers.

THE LEADERSHIP OF MAJOR AMERICAN FOUNDATIONS, 1948

An analysis of the educational backgrounds of the officers and directors of twenty-six leading foundations in the United States. These foundations were selected on the basis of national reputation and relatively high endowments.

College University	Undergraduate Connections	Graduate or Professional	Net Total Individuals
HARVARD	46	66	95
YALE	52	18	62
COLUMBIA	9	41	45
PRINCETON	21	6	25
CHICAGO	8	15	21
JOHNS HOPKINS	6	13	15
DARTMOUTH	11	2	11
PENNSYLVANIA	5	9	11
WISCONSIN	6	9	11
MICHIGAN	6	7	9
VIRGINIA	7	2	9
CALIFORNIA	2	7	8
CORNELL	4	5	7
Totals for 125 Other American Colleges and Universities	145	78	166
Foreign Colleges and Universities			
OXFORD	11	5	11
CAMBRIDGE	3	4	5
Totals for 20 Others	7	20	21
Totals			
Number of Individuals with Some Known College or University Connection	326	231	341
No Institutional Connection, or Unknown	--	--	68
Net Individuals			409

Source: Listings in _American Foundations and Their Fields_, vol. 6, 1948.

Who has been concerned for the general welfare of the local community? In an effort to ascertain what kind of men have been carrying on the quiet and unrewarded work of planning for the needs and of safeguarding the social health of some of our more enterprising urban communities, an analysis was made of the trustees and governors of 43 community trusts as listed in the year 1948.

The results, as shown in our table, were hardly adequate or satisfying. The dearth of alumni directories for many colleges and universities made it impossible to determine the educational connections of more than half of the individuals involved: For 154 such trustees and governors we could obtain no information. For 87 we found student associations with Harvard, Yale, Princeton, Wisconsin, Cornell, or M.I.T.; while another 31 individuals who could be identified in Who's Who in America had attended 28 other institutions. Had it been possible to obtain information on all the individuals engaged as trustees and governors of the 43 community trusts, without doubt our list of leading colleges or universities would have had to be enlarged, and the number of other colleges and universities substantially increased. This would hardly, however, challenge the top of the leadership list which shows H-Y-P contributing 79 workers out of a total listing of 268, or just under 30 per cent. Included would be the chairmen or directors of the following trusts:

California Community Foundation
Cambridge Foundation
Chicago Community Trust
Detroit Community Trust
Hartford Foundation for Public Giving
New Haven Foundation
New York Community Trust
Pittsburgh Foundation
Rochester Community Chest, Inc.
Waterbury Foundation
Winston-Salem Foundation.

OFFICERS OF COMMUNITY TRUSTS, 1948

Analysis of the trustees and governors of forty-three community trusts.

College or University	Undergraduate Degrees	Graduate or Professional Degrees	Net Total Individuals
HARVARD	24	23	41
YALE	30	8	31
PRINCETON	9		9
WISCONSIN	4	2	4
CORNELL	3		3
M.I.T.	2	1	3
	—	—	—
Total for 6 Leaders	73	34	87
Other Colleges and Universities	28	10	31

Omitted: Honorary degrees; trusts showing only institutional trustees; and 154 individuals who did not go to college or who did not graduate or whose college connections could not be ascertained.

Source: American Foundations and Their Fields, vol. 6, 1948.

G-3. RED FEATHER CHARITY DRIVE CHAIRMEN, 1955-57

Red Feather Campaign Chairmen are evidently more conspicuous, socially and politically, than the officers of Community Trusts; nevertheless, the leadership of the annual Red Feather Campaign represents a substantial effort and sacrifice on the part of the chairman, and no small confidence in his ability on the part of the responsible citizens of the community.

By correspondence, very full information was elicited on the college and university backgrounds of the 80 Red Feather Charity Drive Chairmen. So the information may be taken as reliable, though unfortunately the sample period was so short as to risk being unrepresentative. The returns showed Harvard and Princeton in the places of honor, with Michigan third, and with California, Dartmouth, Yale, and Johns Hopkins joined by Colorado, Oregon, Syracuse, Oberlin, Ohio State, Rutgers, and Tulane--universities which have appeared infrequently, if at all, in our previous tabulations. For the two years of the survey, Harvard, Princeton, and Yale together supplied 20 of the 80 chairmen, or 25 per cent; while Michigan and 5 other state universities for the state universities had generated 17, or 21 per cent.

RED FEATHER CHARITY DRIVE CHAIRMEN, 1955-57

Eighty volunteer Red Feather Campaign Chairmen in thirty cities each over 400,000 in population.

College or University	Undergraduate Connections	Graduate or Professional	Net Total Individuals
HARVARD	3	8	11
PRINCETON	8	-	8
MICHIGAN	4	1	4
CALIFORNIA	3	-	3
COLORADO	2	1	3
DARTMOUTH	3	1	3
OREGON	3	-	3
SYRACUSE	2	1	3
YALE	2	1	3
JOHNS HOPKINS	2	-	2
OBERLIN	2	-	2
OHIO STATE	2	-	2
RUTGERS (Graduate School of Banking)	-	2	2
TULANE	2	-	2
42 Other Colleges or Universities	37	6	36
Totals	75	21	70
No College Training			8
Unreported			2
Net Total Individuals			80

G-7. THE LEADERSHIP OF MAJOR AMERICAN FOUNDATIONS, 1957

Because of the passage of time and the emergence of some very wealthy foundations in the interval, it seemed of interest to analyze the educational backgrounds of the officers, directors, and trustees of thirty leading foundations as listed in the latest Foundation Directory (for 1960).

Nine foundations reappeared in the new list: Carnegie Corporation, Carnegie Institute of Washington, Commonwealth Fund, Field Foundation, John Simon Guggenheim Foundation, W. K. Kellogg Foundation, Macy Foundation, Mayo Foundation, and Rockefeller Foundation. For this new sampling, however, organizations like the General Education Board, the William C. Whitney Foundation, the Woodrow Wilson Foundation, the Carnegie Endowment for International Peace, etc., were dropped in favor of the Ford Foundation, the Hartford Foundation, Kresge Foundation, Samuel H. Kress Foundation, the Donner Foundation, the Old Dominion Foundation, and others.

In the interest of equity the names of all the officers and directors and trustees were looked up and tabulated on the basis of Who's Who in America for 1962-63, which tabulation credited Harvard with 55 individuals, Yale with 28, Princeton with 21, and no other institutions with more than 9. In the interest of a fuller accounting, the names were then read against the alumni directories of Harvard, Yale, Princeton, Columbia, and Cornell. This resulted in the addition of from 3 to 12 names per university. Had alumni directories been at hand for Dartmouth, Michigan, Minnesota, California, and M.I.T., no doubt some additional names could have been credited, though probably not in substantial numbers or in a way to alter the essential grouping of those institutions.

It may be noted that two state universities--Michigan and California-- appear in both foundation tables, and that Wisconsin, Virginia, and Minnesota represent the state universities in one table or the other. The preponderance of representatives from the private universities is nevertheless very great, with Harvard, Yale, and Princeton producing 118 out of 329 (or 36 per cent) of the total for 1957.

THE LEADERSHIP OF MAJOR AMERICAN FOUNDATIONS, 1957

An analysis of the educational backgrounds of the officers, directors, and trustees of thirty major foundations in the United States.

College or University	Undergraduate Connections	Graduate or Professional	Net Total Individuals
HARVARD	27 (30)	34 (46)	55 (67)
YALE	25 (31)	7 (10)	29 (37)
PRINCETON	18 (23)	5 (4)	21 (26)
MICHIGAN	7	7	11
MINNESOTA	2	8	10
DARTMOUTH	9	-	9
CALIFORNIA	5	5	8
COLUMBIA	3 (4)	6 (7)	8 (11)
CORNELL	5 (8)	4 (6)	8 (13)
PENNSYLVANIA	2	7	8
M.I.T.	7	3	7
Totals for 99 Other American Colleges and Universities	108	60	122
Foreign Colleges and Universities	16	16	16
Totals			
Number of Individuals with Some Known College or University Connection	212 (228)	126 (144)	219 (247)
No Institutional Connection			15
Not Listed in W.W. in Am. or Directories			66
Net Individuals			329

Note: Parenthetically enclosed numbers indicate the revised totals for five of the ten top universities as ascertained after checking the officers' names against their respective alumni registers.

Sources: The names were taken from The Foundation Directory, 1960. Only those officers appearing in Who's Who in America for 1962-63 and 1964-65 were classified.

In the field of medical philanthropy and in the leadership of particular medical crusades, the graduates of our colleges and universities have assumed great responsibility. In the late 1950's more than 80 per cent of the officers, directors, and trustees of 53 important foundations and associations (at least 271 out of 330 participants) had come from a college or university background.

No fewer than 149 institutions had contributed, though unequally, to the leadership of medical philanthropy. The table of educational connections in its first three places shows a familiar pattern, with Harvard leading as a university, Yale as a college, and Princeton very strong. Indeed Princeton (given its lesser enrollments) had achieved a distinctly higher ratio of production than either of its chief rivals. In the second flight Minnesota rises well above its level of expectation for most fields, both as a college and as a medical center, to achieve a tie with Columbia. Next in the list of leading contributors one finds Johns Hopkins, Chicago, N.Y.U., and Pennsylvania, all strong because of their professional medical interests. The ever reliable graduates of Michigan show up strongly here as on so many other tables, while the college men of old Dartmouth (without aid from their medical school) stand level with the rising power of the University of Texas.

A comparison of this table with the tables for big business leadership will signal the absence of M.I.T. and Cornell, California and Stanford, Wisconsin and Illinois, from the top leadership of the medical foundations in 1959. Readers will also find comparisons with the universities in medicine, and with our tables on other forms of philanthropy, illuminating.

THE LEADERSHIP OF MEDICAL FOUNDATIONS, 1959

An analysis of the educational backgrounds of the officers, directors, and trustees of fifty-three medical philanthropic foundations and associations in the United States (i.e., thirty-five foundations with assets of over $1,000,000 each, substantially concerned with medicine and health; and eighteen foundations devoted to particular medical objectives such as cancer, heart, diabetes, cerebral palsy, etc.).

College or University	Undergraduate Connections	Graduate or Professional	Net Total Individuals
HARVARD	22	33	46
YALE	26	7	29
PRINCETON	22	1	23
COLUMBIA	4	10	14
MINNESOTA	7	12	14
JOHNS HOPKINS	3	10	12
CHICAGO	6	8	10
N.Y.U.	2	8	9
PENNSYLVANIA	3	7	9
MICHIGAN	6	4	8
DARTMOUTH	7	0	7
TEXAS	6	2	7
Totals for 125 Other American Colleges and Universities	152	80	157
Foreign Colleges and Universities	12	18	23
Totals			
Number of Individuals with Some Known College or University Connection	256	154	271
No Institutional Connection	--	--	26
Unknown	--	--	33
Net Individuals			330

Sources: The Foundation Directory, 1960, and Encyclopedia of American Associations, 1959.

135

CHAPTER **H** SCIENCE AND
ENGINEERING

"It must be acknowledged that in few of the civilized nations of our time have the higher sciences made less progress than in the United States; and in few have great artists, distinguished poets, or celebrated writers been more rare. Many Europeans, struck by this fact, have looked upon it as a natural and inevitable result of equality. . . ." But Alexis de Tocqueville, that most discerning and friendly critic of Democracy in America, could not entirely agree. Writing in the 1830's, he thought that the "example of the Americans does not prove that a democratic people can have no aptitude and no taste for science, literature, or art." Rather the neglect of these higher aspects of civilization seemed to Tocqueville the result of special circumstances.

First, there was the fact that the Americans, "a very old and a very enlightened people," had come upon a new and unbounded country with every facility for making or increasing men's fortunes. The spirit of gain almost inevitably had led to the neglect or the commercialization of the higher arts. Out of the same circumstance had come the American tendency to emphasize the useful arts: The opportunity of individuals to better themselves, and the absence of preordained classes or inherited privileges, had naturally drawn attention to those means by which the poor and the underprivileged could succeed. Hence, a very widespread attention to the applications of science, with little interest in basic discoveries. In this classless but restless society the calm and the leisure essential for reflection were obviously missing. In any case Americans distrusted systems, or visionary speculation. Tocqueville thought also that the proximity to Europe and especially to England had freed us from the necessity of developing our own pure science. We could live on borrowed ideas and make the profitable applications. "In America the purely practical part of science is admirably understood, and careful attention is paid to the theoretical portion which is immediately requisite to application. On this head the Americans always display a clear, free, original, and inventive power of mind. But hardly anyone in the United States devotes himself to the essentially theoretical and abstract portion of human knowledge." In aristocratic societies all this might be cared for, but in a democracy the government might have to intervene. Those called upon to guide the

nations of our time should "understand that, possessing education and freedom, men living in democratic ages cannot fail
to improve the industrial part of science, and that hencefor-
ward all the efforts of the constituted authorities ought to
be directed to support the highest branches of learning and
to foster the nobler passion for science itself." (See Alexis
de Tocqueville, Democracy in America, ed. Phillips Bradley,
Knopf, 1945, 2:35-47.)

Tocqueville was writing in the 1830's--the age of Andrew
Jackson--and it would be many generations before the Americans
would care to follow such advice. The bequest of the English-
man, Smithson, was indeed finally accepted; and in 1862 the
Congress of the United States decided to come to the aid of
higher education in the West. But the Land Grant College Act
provided for colleges of agriculture and the mechanic arts,
not for the study or teaching of pure science. So it would
not be until many an ambitious young American had resorted to
the scientific laboratories of Germany and France that the
techniques and the attitudes of the higher scientific training could be introduced into our colleges. Institutionally,
it was not until after experiment with many a polytechnic
school--then the founding of the Yale and Harvard engineering
schools (called the Sheffield Scientific and Lawrence Scientific Schools)--and finally the development of true universities in this country with Cornell, Johns Hopkins, Harvard,
Chicago, Michigan, Columbia, and Yale--that our democratic
society began to provide opportunities and encouragement for
advances in the highest branches of the sciences. And such
has been the fever and restlessness of American life that
even then and in the years afterwards the leisure for contem-
plation and reflection has been hard to find and to protect.
Until the twentieth century the theoretical minds of the
first order, like J. Willard Gibbs, have been rare and un-
appreciated. Instead, American energies and money and attention have continued to go to the development of engineering
in all its branches and to the application of the sciences to
immediate human betterment. The national ethos which
Tocqueville so clearly described was still with us when we
had to import the theory and the theorists of nuclear fission--
and woke to find pure science deadly dangerous.

In America's great epoch of industrialization which followed the Civil War--with the generations of coal and iron and then the later generations of oil and electricity--among a people which owed so much to the steam railroad and which made heroes of Thomas A. Edison and Henry Ford--who were the outstanding American scientists? Our criteria were uncertain and our measurements inadequate. The lists we made were imperfect then. They are unmanageable now.

One thinks, however, first of the starred scientists, i.e., the scientists listed in <u>American Men of Science</u> who were honored by an asterisk after their names to indicate that they were distinguished beyond the others who were also recognized as practicing in this field. Eventually it became too difficult to attempt such distinctions and the asterisk or star was dropped. But for the years 1903 to 1943, the years in which the elite of American science were thus singled out, our outstanding scientists demonstrated a considerable range of origin. At the same time, their life histories indicated also a substantial concentration of experience at eight or ten of our leading colleges and universities. In this grouping the men from Harvard led quite decisively, both at the undergraduate and at the professional level. Johns Hopkins rated a strong second and Chicago a surprisingly strong third, considering that it had only been founded in 1890. Thanks to its production of Ph.D.'s Columbia ranked fourth, while Yale, second as an undergraduate producer, stood fifth at the graduate level and also over-all.

At the time of the compilation of this table manpower was lacking to calculate the undergraduate and graduate connections of all the starred scientists, or the contributions of other colleges and universities ranking below the ten largest producers. A study of Yale's scientists, who were probably not unrepresentative in this regard, revealed, however, some striking variations between the different fields of science. Thus Yale contributed only 2 per cent of the starred scientists in anthropology or astronomy or botany; 5 per cent in mathematics or zoology; 7 per cent in physics and chemistry; 11 per cent in anatomy and physiology; and 17 per cent in geology (the only field of science in which Yale outranked all other universities). Cumulatively, Yale's 172 out of 2,607 starred scientists represented 6.6 per cent of the total honor list, a showing considerably or greatly improved upon by Columbia, Chicago, Johns Hopkins, and especially Harvard. Which suggests that American scientists had been more concentrated at certain top institutions than had been the divines or the American businessmen. If representative, the record of the Yale contingent suggests also that the starred men of science had come about equally from the engineering and the liberal arts side in college but had gone on to considerable additional formal training. Thus, Yale's 172 graduates held 267 earned degrees from Yale distributed as follows: B.A. 63, Ph.B. 62, and B.S. 1; also M.A. 17, M.S. 4, Mus.B. 1, B.D. 1, M.D. 7, C.E. 4, and Ph.D. 107.

STARRED SCIENTISTS, 1903-43

The ten largest producers of starred scientists.

College or University	Undergraduate Degrees	Doctorates: Ph.D. or M.D.	Net Total Individuals
HARVARD	233	275	401
JOHNS HOPKINS	53	238	242
CHICAGO	64	194	215
COLUMBIA	65	175	201
YALE	109	114	172
CORNELL	89	89	155
MICHIGAN	82	44	108
CALIFORNIA	61	72	104
PRINCETON	46	57	85
PENNSYLVANIA	36	67	77

Source: Determined from Stephen Sargent Visher, Scientists Starred 1903-1943 in "American Men of Science," Johns Hopkins Press, 1947.

H-2. OFFICERS AND COUNCIL MEMBERS OF THE NATIONAL ACADEMY OF SCIENCES, 1863-1961

If we have known anything in this country comparable to the Royal Society in Great Britain, it has been the National Academy of Sciences--and the men of influence in the National Academy of Sciences over the past century make a fascinating study. To begin with one notes the high degree of concentration in a mere handful of universities, 82 out of 131 individuals having received all or part of their education at one or more of the 6 leading institutions: Harvard, Johns Hopkins, Yale, Columbia, M.I.T., and Chicago. After Chicago's production total of 10, our statistics uncovered a kind of break--the next American universities being Michigan and Cornell with 6, George Washington with 5, and Amherst, California, Princeton, and Minnesota with 4 each.

A second and not unexpected discovery was the large role played by foreign universities, especially those in Germany. After Berlin, with 10 individuals, came Göttingen and Leipzig each with 8, and Cambridge with 6.

A third discovery and one which perhaps flowed naturally from the preceding was the diversity and advanced character of the education reported for most of our leading scientists. Only 8 individuals out of 131 had attended no institution of higher learning; and comparatively few had taken but a single degree (e.g., Simon Newcomb, Harvard B.S. 1853, and James G. Dana, Yale B.A. 1833). Some distinguished individuals had obtained all their degrees at one institution, as had George W. Corner at Johns Hopkins, or W. B. Cannon and Alexander Agassiz at Harvard. More characteristic was the experience of Yale's great bone-digger Othniel C. Marsh, who took his B.A. at Yale, then studied at Berlin, Breslau, and Heidelberg before returning to head the Peabody Museum in New Haven as well as the National Academy of Sciences. Another two-continent man was Wolcott Gibbs, who earned his B.A., M.A., and M.D. at Columbia, then studied at Berlin and Paris, returned to teach at City College, and became a famous professor at Harvard. Most representative of all perhaps were men like Robert A. Millikan, who earned his B.A. and M.A. at Oberlin, then his Ph.D. at Columbia, then studied at the Universities of Berlin and Göttingen, returned to Oberlin to teach, and was drafted for a professorship at Chicago before winding up at the head of a great laboratory in Cal. Tech.

Even our rather selective investigation underscored the migratory habits of scientists--and the striking tendency of our major universities to borrow from and reinforce each other. Thus William H. Welch went from a B.A. at Yale, to an M.D. at Columbia, to study abroad, and then quickly to the building of the great new Johns Hopkins Medical School. General Francis A. Walker, graduate of Amherst, after a distinguished career in the Bureau of the Census and on the faculty of the Sheffield Scientific School at Yale, was called to direct and help build up the Massachusetts Institute of Technology. To our surprise, three Harvard bachelors took their Ph.D.'s at Yale; one of them, E. B. Wilson, returned to the Harvard faculty; while another, Isaiah Bowman, went on to become president of Johns Hopkins. In return, Ross G. Harrison, after an A.B. and A.M. at Johns Hopkins, an M.D. at Bonn, and some years again at the Hopkins, achieved an international reputation and a distinguished professorship

Education of the officers and council members of the National Academy of Sciences from its founding to 1961.

College or University	Undergraduate Connections		Grad., Prof'l. or Special		Net Total		Net Total Individuals
	Offic.	Coun.	Offic.	Coun.	Offic.	Coun.	
HARVARD	11	15	6	15	12	23	27
JOHNS HOPKINS	3	6	5	18	5	18	19
YALE	8	11	6	8	11	16	19
COLUMBIA	1	4	5	9	5	11	12
M.I.T.	4	6	4	5	6	9	12
CHICAGO	1	1	3	6	3	7	10
61 Other American Institutions	23	55	11	50	25	66	81
Foreign: BERLIN	-	-	4	9	4	9	10
29 Other Foreign Institutions	2	3	19	45	14	30	38
No Higher Education					5	6	8
Net Individuals					57	105	131

Source: Information from the Annual Reports of the Academy.

at Yale. Harlow Shapley, on the foundation of an A.B. at Missouri and a
Ph.D. at Princeton, rose finally to great eminence at Harvard. Alfred
Newton Richards, after earning his B.A. and M.A. at Yale, took a Ph.D. at
Columbia and was recognized by a professorship at Pennsylvania. To close
with one final example, the career of Detlev W. Bronk took him from an A.B.
at Swarthmore, study at Pennsylvania, and graduate degrees at Michigan,
through a professorial career to the presidency of Johns Hopkins, after
which came the presidency of the Rockefeller Institute for Medical Research.
Our scientists have been an inter-university and international breed.

H-3. MEDALISTS OF THE NATIONAL ACADEMY OF SCIENCES, 1886-1961

In default of any list of starred scientists since 1943--or any
equivalent of such a list--our office was driven to a pursuit of excellence through the award of medals of distinction by the National Academy
of Sciences. The results are interesting as a tribute to the originality
and vitality of men born, educated, and for the most part still working
in Europe. The role of Cambridge and the major German universities as
the laboratories for discoverers and discoveries is made unmistakable.

On this side of the water the same five universities head the list,
and in the same order, as in our table of starred scientists. Once again
Harvard College has led Yale College (and the Yale Scientific School) decisively in its stimulation of scientific interest and talent; but at the
graduate or professional level the alumni of Johns Hopkins, Chicago, and
Columbia have come close to matching the men from Cambridge. Of considerable interest as well is the appearance of California (Berkeley) in sixth
place, followed by M.I.T. and Princeton and Brown. Altogether 95 out of
213 individual medalists had received the whole or a part of their education and scientific training at one or the other of the nine leading
American universities, while 95 of all the medalists had lived or studied
abroad.

MEDALISTS OF THE NATIONAL ACADEMY OF SCIENCES, 1886-1961

Education of 213 individuals who received from the National Academy of Sciences one or more of the following medals: Barnard Medal for Meritorious Service to Science, John J. Carty Medal, Cyrus B. Comstock Prize Award, Henry Draper Medal, Daniel Giraud Elliot Medal, Public Welfare Medal, Kimber Genetics Award, Kovalenko Medal, Agassiz Medal, J. Lawrence Smith Medal, Mary Clark Thompson Medal, Charles Doolittle Walcott Medal, and James Craig Watson Medal.

College or University	Undergraduate Connections	Graduate Professional or Special Connections	Net Total Individuals
HARVARD	14	18	22
JOHNS HOPKINS	7	16	18
CHICAGO	4	15	16
COLUMBIA	5	13	14
YALE	5	6	9
CALIFORNIA (Berkeley)	4	6	8
M.I.T.	5	3	7
PRINCETON	4	6	6
BROWN	5	3	5
69 Other American Institutions	80	50	83
Foreign: CAMBRIDGE	7	7	12
GÖTTINGEN	1	9	10
BERLIN	-	9	9
MUNICH	1	7	8
LEIPZIG	1	5	6
OXFORD	1	5	6
COPENHAGEN	1	4	5
57 Other Foreign Institutions	44	54	63
None or Unknown			28

Source: List of names taken from the Annual Report of the National Academy of Sciences for 1960-61.

A few of our scientific museums date back to the early national period, notably the Academy of Natural Sciences in Philadelphia (estab. 1812), the Smithsonian (1849), and the New York State Museum (1836, first curator-director 1847). The youngest here studied are the University of Michigan Museum of Anthropology (1925), the Chicago Museum of Science and Industry (1926), Cranbrook (1930), and the Adler Planetarium (1930).

Our tabulation of directors reflects the strong scientific and museum interest in Chicago and a quite striking contribution by the University of Kansas. Next after the 7 leaders named in our table came the University of Berlin with 4 directors, and Dartmouth, Iowa, and Northwestern, each with 3. Over-all, 1 in every 5 directors with a college or university connection had studied at Harvard.

DIRECTORS OF SCIENTIFIC MUSEUMS, 1812-1965

Directors of the following scientific museums from their founding to 1965: Academy of Natural Sciences, Philadelphia; Adler Planetarium, Chicago; American Museum of Natural History, New York; Bernice P. Bishop Museum, Honolulu; Chicago Natural History Museum; Cranbrook Institute of Science, Bloomfield Hills, Michigan; Denver Museum of Natural History; Harvard University Museum of Comparative Zoology; Museum of Science and Industry, Chicago; New York State Museum and Science Service; Peabody Museum of Archaeology and Ethnology, Harvard University; Peabody Museum of Natural History, Yale University; Smithsonian Museum, Washington, D.C.; U.S. National Museum, Museum of Natural History, a part of the Smithsonian; University of Kansas Museum of Natural History; University of Michigan Museum of Anthropology; University of Pennsylvania University Museum.

College or University	Undergraduate Connections	Graduate or Professional	Net Total Individuals
HARVARD	12	11	17
CHICAGO	5	9	11
YALE	4	8	10
PENNSYLVANIA	2	7	8
MICHIGAN	4	4	7
COLUMBIA	1	6	6
KANSAS	5	2	5
43 Other American Institutions	47	23	47
19 Foreign Institutions	4	20	12
No Higher Education			11
Unknown			12
Net Total Individuals			109

Sources: <u>Museums Directory of the United States and Canada</u>, 1961, publications of the museums and correspondence with the directors' offices.

A comparison of this Knapp and Goodrich table with our first table on starred scientists (H-1) is instructive on several counts. The quantitative and the qualitative measurements are not the same. By their method of conflating the Ph.D. with the asterisks of the starred scientists, Knapp and Goodrich greatly enlarge the number of trained scientists who may be counted. As a consequence we are enabled to recognize the contribution of the Universities of California, Wisconsin, Cornell, Illinois, Michigan, Minnesota, and Ohio State at both the undergraduate and graduate levels: a suggestive reminder of the emphasis on the sciences at our major state universities. The tabular division between disciplines also makes possible identification of the numerical leader in each of the sciences at the college level, with Cornell the only university to produce more bachelors than any other for as many as two separate fields of science. On the other hand, the preponderance of the Ph.D. degree obscures the qualitative achievement of some of these university constituencies, e.g., one would never suspect from this table that Yale had produced the most starred geologists or that Harvard had had something to do with almost as many starred scientists as California, Chicago, and Michigan put together.

The gross totals on the undergraduate production of future Ph.D.'s are interesting in a second way as suggesting the high productivity of Johns Hopkins as a college and of Haverford and Wesleyan as well--and the very high productivity indeed of Reed College, Cal. Tech., Kalamazoo, Earlham, Oberlin, Hope, DePauw, and Antioch. How decisively the 40 trained scientists who started at Reed College will be able to contribute to a society which contains 496 scientists from both Illinois and Michigan, and more than 500 from each of 5 other universities, will be an interesting question. What seems clear is that certain of our good smaller colleges place a great deal more emphasis on science than do others well known for their production of men of affairs and humanists.

COLLEGIATE ORIGINS OF AMERICAN SCIENTISTS, 1880-1938

Collegiate origins of American scientists, graduating between the years 1880 and 1938, who earned their bachelor's degree from an American college and also either earned the Ph.D. degree (or its equivalent) or were starred in _American Men of Science_, vols. 3 and 7, 1921 and 1944.

College or University	Chemistry	Biology	Physics	Geology	Mathematics	Psychology	Astronomy	Total	Index of Productivity[c]
CALIFORNIA	149	228	55	52	38	39	23[a]	584	21.5
HARVARD	141	159	52	63	72[a]	43	13	543	18.4
WISCONSIN	183	211	45	44	21	24	7	535	26.2
CORNELL	131	238[a]	61[a]	42[a]	29	26	3	530	21.8
CHICAGO	154	161	44	67[a]	46	38	8	518	39.9
ILLINOIS	243[a]	144	31	27	23	28	-[b]	496	16.5
MICHIGAN	156	151	57	46	31	39	16	496	14.4
COLUMBIA	137	94	33	25	26	57[a]	4	376	15.9
MINNESOTA	124	131	22	29	21	26	5	358	19.7
OHIO STATE	123	126	30	17	12	35	-[b]	343	11.1
YALE	117	86	40	34	31	17	2	327	10.3
Smaller Colleges:									
JOHNS HOPKINS	81	44	40	31	14	10	-[b]	220	37.3
OBERLIN	72	69	37	14	8	16	2	218	55.8
WESLEYAN	37	42	15	5	9	17	5	130	34.3
DePAUW	41	46	18	7	1	8	0	121	47.6
CAL. TECH.	40	9	32	11	7	-[b]	-[b]	99	70.1
HAVERFORD	20	14	9	4	10	7	0	64	39.4
EARLHAM	16	25	7	1	4	6	2	61	57.5
HOPE	33	18	2	0	2	1	0	56	51.1
KALAMAZOO	30	9	8	1	4	1	1	54	66.3
REED	11	6	16	0	3	4	0	40	131.8
ANTIOCH	15	4	2	2	1	4	0	28	45.1

[a] Indicates leader in each field. [b] No figure given in tables. [c] Index of Productivity of Male Graduates 1924-34.

Source: Table adapted by permission from R. H. Knapp and H. B. Goodrich, Origins of American Scientists (University of Chicago Press, 1952. Cf. pp. 299-323, 371-418).

Trying to find accepted or acceptable lists of leaders in the various branches of engineering in this country proved extraordinarily difficult, in fact finally impossible. The biographical dictionary Who's Who in Engineering seemed too inclusive, insufficiently selective, and in any case much too bulky. No doubt there must be briefer and more manageable indexes to engineering personnel distinguished for their achievements or professional offices in particular engineering specialties, e.g., chemical engineering, electrical engineering, metallurgy, etc. Unfortunately we failed to turn them up.

In the circumstances our tabulation of the winners of certain distinguished engineering medals should be regarded merely as an interesting sample of what an adequate survey might produce. So far as it goes it suggests the great strength of M.I.T. at both college and professional levels. Evidently the graduates of Cornell and the U.S. Naval Academy have distinguished themselves in this line. And it is interesting to see that the traditionally strong state universities of California, Illinois, Michigan, and Wisconsin have been surpassed in this instance by Ohio State. The absence of California Institute of Technology from the top twenty engineering institutions came to the compiler as a surprise, until he realized that many of the medalists had been educated before 1920, most even before 1910 (in the days when Cal. Tech. did not exist save in its prenatal form as Throop Polytechnic Institute).

It may be of some interest to note that a number of engineers won more than one medal. The list follows:

Winners of Three Engineering Medals

W. F. Durand--Fritz, Guggenheim, ASME--U.S. Naval Acad. '80; Lafayette
    Ph.D. '88
Frank B. Jewett--Edison, Fritz, Hoover--Throop (now Cal. Tech.) A.B. '98;
    Chicago Ph.D. '02
Charles F. Kettering--NSPE, ASME, Hoover--Ohio State E.E. in M.E. '04
Philip Sporn--ASME, Fritz, Edison--Columbia E.E. '17, post grad. '17-18
Ambrose Swasey--ASME, Fritz, Hoover--no higher education
Theodor von Karman--ASME, Fritz, Guggenheim--Royal Tech. U. Budapest M.E.
    '02; Göttingen Ph.D. '08

Winners of Two Engineering Medals

Comfort A. Adams--Edison, Lamme--Case Sch. of Applied Sci. S.B. 1890,
    E.E. 1905
Alexander Graham Bell--Fritz, Edison--Edinburgh, London U.
Vannevar Bush--Edison, Lamme--Tufts B.S., M.S. '13; M.I.T. and Harvard
    Eng. D. '16
John Joseph Carty--Fritz, Edison--no higher education
Walker Lee Cisler--NSPE, Hoover--Cornell '22
Frank Conrad--Edison, Lamme--no higher education
Hugh L. Dryden--Fritz, Guggenheim--Johns Hopkins A.B. '16, A.M. '17,
    Ph.D. '19

MEDALISTS OF CERTAIN PROFESSIONAL ENGINEERING SOCIETIES, 1902-64

Educational backgrounds of the individuals who have received the following medals: John Fritz (1902-64) and Hoover (1930-63) Medals, both offered jointly by the American Society of Civil Engineers, American Institute of Mining, Metallurgical and Petroleum Engineers, American Society of Mechanical Engineers, and the American Institute of Electrical Engineers; the Edison (1902-61) and Lamme (1928-61) Medals, both presented by the American Institute of Electrical Engineers; the Daniel Guggenheim Medal (1928 to 1962 with six years unidentified) presented by the American Society of Mechanical Engineers, the Society of Automotive Engineers, and the Institute of Aeronautical Sciences; American Society of Mechanical Engineers Award (1921-62); National Society of Professional Engineers Award (1949-64); and American Society of Naval Engineers Award (1958-63).

College or University	Undergraduate Connections	Graduate or Professional	Net Total Individuals
M.I.T.	27	10	33
CORNELL	8	6	14
COLUMBIA	6	9	13
HARVARD	6	8	12
U.S. NAVAL ACAD.	9	-	9
YALE	8	2	8
OHIO STATE	6	1	7
CALIFORNIA	5	1	5
ILLINOIS	4	3	5
MICHIGAN	5	1	5
WISCONSIN	5	-	5
C.C.N.Y.	4	1	4
CHICAGO	-	4	4
PITTSBURGH	-	4	4
STANFORD	4	-	4
U.S. MILITARY ACAD.	4	-	4
UNION	1	3	4
BROOKLYN POLY. INST.	3	1	3
CARNEGIE INST. TECH.	3	-	3
JOHNS HOPKINS	2	3	3
66 Other American Institutions	68	22	67
Foreign:			
BERLIN	-	4	4
GÖTTINGEN	-	4	4
30 Other Foreign Institutions	23	15	31
No Higher Education			17
Unknown			14
Net Total Individuals			203

Gano Dunn--Edison, Hoover--C.C.N.Y. B.S. '89, M.S. '97; Columbia E.E. '91
William LeRoy Emmet--ASME, Edison--U.S. Naval Acad. '81
James F. Fairman--NSPE, Edison--Michigan B.S.E.E. '18, M.S. '21
John R. Freeman--ASME, Fritz--M.I.T. B.S. '76
Herbert Hoover--NSPE, Hoover--Stanford B.A. '95
Morris E. Leeds--Edison, ASME--Haverford B.S. '88; Berlin '92-93
Robert Andrews Millikan--ASME, Edison--Oberlin A.B. '91, A.M. '93;
    Columbia Ph.D. '95; Berlin; Göttingen
A. A. Potter--NSPE, Lamme--M.I.T. B.S. in Eng. '03
Granville M. Read--NSPE, ASME--no information found
Charles F. Scott--Edison, Lamme--Ohio State A.B. '85; Johns Hopkins
Joseph Slepian--Edison, Lamme--Harvard A.B. '11, A.M. '12, Ph.D. '13;
    Göttingen '13-14; Sorbonne '14
John F. Stevens--Fritz, Hoover--Pennsylvania B.Sc. '90, M.E. '91
Lewis B. Stillwell--Edison, Lamme--Wesleyan '82-84; Lehigh E.E. '85
Elihu Thomson--Fritz, Edison--Central High School, Philadelphia A.B. '70
George Westinghouse--Fritz, Edison--Union
Harry A. Winne--NSPE, Fritz--Syracuse E.E. '10
V. K. Zworykin--Edison, Lamme--Petrograd Inst. of Tech. E.E. '12; College
    de France '14-16; Pittsburgh Ph.D. '26

CHAPTER J LITERATURE
AND THE ARTS

In the various branches of literature and the fine arts it has proved extraordinarily difficult to find or to devise genuine measurements of distinction. These areas of achievement seem to lend themselves awkwardly or not at all to statistical analysis. Some notion of what the record has been, however, may be obtained from the occasional glimpses which are provided by the tables here assembled.

Our third table, for example, analyzes the award of Pulitzer Prizes, over a forty-year period, in history, biography, drama, novels, poetry, and music (the many awards in journalism were deliberately omitted). The results of that investigation will speak for themselves. Quite limited samplings from the worlds of history, creative writing, music, and the theatre all carry their messages. The tables on architecture, more substantial in their way, suggest the quite unusual contributions to American architectural education made over a long period of years by M.I.T., with Pennsylvania and Harvard not far behind. Yet over-all in the arts and letters, and most strikingly in literature, Harvard ranks first and the rest come nowhere. Unquestionably the sons of John Harvard have benefited from the strong literary traditions of the Puritans, the neighborhood of Boston, and the cultural atmosphere of the Massachusetts Bay region. As is well known, New Englanders, at least from that section of their rock-bound wilderness, have had a way with words from the very beginning. The record shows that the men of Yale did compose the theologies and create the dictionaries for our nation; but in literary and artistic matters generally New Haven has shone only fitfully, if at all. As Secretary Anson Phelps Stokes once remarked, "Yale has been more fortiter in re than suaviter in modo."

Columbia, in part because of the rich variety of its special faculties, in part perhaps also because of its location in the publishing capital of the nation, has exercised in recent years increasing attraction for ambitious young writers (although many of them have attended merely for a time rather than for a regular course and degree). Indeed our tables confirm the impression that writers and artists generally have been slow to accept an academic preparation for their vocations--or perhaps, like James Fenimore Cooper,

they have been rebellious when they tried it and got themselves dismissed for their pains. As the biographical data
make clear, among the writers who won two or more Pulitzer
Prizes, the five most successful authors between them managed
to earn exactly one degree.

By contrast, our colleges have been rich producers of a
clientele for literature and the arts, as can be illustrated
by such an organization as the Century Association, or by
membership in the American Academy and the National Institute
of Arts and Letters.

J-1. FORMER MEMBERS OF THE AMERICAN ACADEMY AND THE NATIONAL INSTITUTE OF ARTS AND LETTERS

The distinction of both Harvard College and the Harvard graduate and professional schools as centers for literature and the arts and as producers of men of literary originality and cultivation has been underscored again and again by the elections to the National Institute of Arts and Letters and by the coopting of some of its members by the still more highly selective American Academy. Among the former members, who were deceased in 1963, the graduates of Yale at both levels had constituted a large company, with the men of Columbia and Princeton next in numbers. The fact that Johns Hopkins had been a distinguished university as well as a center for medicine and the sciences is reflected in its fifth-place position among the producers of candidates for these two societies.

It may be observed that a considerable number of Academy and Institute members had risen to distinction in the arts with no formal higher education, or with a professional training but no academic background. Our artists, like our men of business, have been slower than the learned professions or the career services to see the value of the college or university experience.

Between them Harvard, Yale, Columbia, and Princeton had produced as many former members as all the other American colleges and universities, or as all the art institutes and foreign universities together.

FORMER MEMBERS OF THE AMERICAN ACADEMY AND THE NATIONAL
INSTITUTE OF ARTS AND LETTERS

Educational backgrounds of all the deceased members of either the
American Academy or the larger National Institute of Arts and Letters from
whose membership the more restricted Academy was drawn, tabulated in 1963.
Individuals attending only an art institute, music conservatory, or other
institution designed specifically to prepare for professional degrees were
tabulated in the column of Graduate or Professional Connections.

College or University	Undergraduate Connections	Graduate or Professional	Net Total Individuals
HARVARD	78	42	96
YALE	36	21	41
COLUMBIA	19	27	37
PRINCETON	25	10	26
JOHNS HOPKINS	0	10	10
Art Institutes			
ART STUDENTS' LEAGUE	0	28	28
PENNSYLVANIA ACAD. OF F. A.	0	15	15
NATIONAL ACADEMY OF DESIGN	0	11	11
All Other American Colleges, Universities, and Institutes	149	81	191
Foreign Colleges, Universities, and Institutes	23	199	145
No Connections or Unknown	-	-	151
Net Totals	311	288	567

Sources: National Institute of Arts and Letters--American Academy of Arts
and Letters, 1963, Who's Who in America, 1962-63, and Who Was
Who in America, vols. I, II, III.

J-2. 1963 MEMBERS OF THE AMERICAN ACADEMY AND THE
NATIONAL INSTITUTE OF ARTS AND LETTERS

Among the current members in 1963 the graduates of Harvard once again
outnumbered those of any other two institutions. Columbia had passed Yale
through the greater participation of its alumni both academic and professional. And Chicago, M.I.T., and N.Y.U. had replaced Princeton and Johns
Hopkins among the top producers.

It may be noted that the percentage of members educated abroad remained about the same, but the proportion of those without academic connection (or unknown) had substantially decreased. In the professional
category, the Art Institute of Chicago had joined the Art Students'
League, the Pennsylvania Academy of Fine Arts, and the National Academy
of Design as an effective producer. In spite of a wider dissemination of
academic experience among American colleges and art institutes, Harvard,
Columbia, and Yale between them had increased their share.

1963 MEMBERS OF THE AMERICAN ACADEMY AND THE NATIONAL INSTITUTE OF ARTS AND LETTERS

Educational backgrounds of all living members of either the American Academy or the larger National Institute of Arts and Letters from whose membership the more restricted Academy was drawn, tabulated in 1963. Individuals attending only an art institute, music conservatory, or other institution designed specifically to prepare for professional degrees were tabulated in the column of Graduate or Professional Connections.

College or University	Undergraduate Connections	Graduate or Professional	Net Total Individuals
HARVARD	38	17	45
COLUMBIA	13	13	22
YALE	7	11	13
CHICAGO	8	1	8
M.I.T.	5	3	7
N.Y.U.	5	2	7
Art Institutes			
ART STUDENTS' LEAGUE	0	24	24
PENNSYLVANIA ACAD. OF F. A.	0	10	10
ART INSTITUTE OF CHICAGO	0	8	8
NATIONAL ACADEMY OF DESIGN	0	7	7
89 Other American Colleges, Universities, and Institutes	92	63	112
Foreign Colleges, Universities, and Institutes	14	69	55
No Connections or Unknown	-	-	32
Net Totals	150	134	232

Sources: National Institute of Arts and Letters--American Academy of Arts and Letters, 1963, and Who's Who in America, 1962-63.

159

J-3. THE UNIVERSITIES AND THE PULITZER PRIZES, 1917-57

The Pulitzer Prizes will not be accepted as the ultimate measure of creative art, but the division of awards between the major universities and between the undergraduate and professional schools of the several leaders shows the outstanding pre-eminence of Harvard and the relative weakness of the Yale Graduate Schools.

	HARVARD					YALE					PRINCETON					OTHER LEADING UNIVS. IN EACH FIELD			ALL OTHER COLLEGES AND UNIVERSITIES					
	No. of Awards	No. of Individuals	Studied at	Higher Degree	College Degree	No. of Awards	No. of Individuals	Studied at	Higher Degree	College Degree	No. of Awards	No. of Individuals	Studied at	Higher Degree	College Degree	No. of Awards	No. of Individuals		No. of Awards	No. of Individuals	Studied at	Higher Degree	College Degree	
History	15	15	-	11	8	1	1	-	-	-	3	3	-	1	2	3, 3	3, 3	Chicago, Columbia	26	26	9	5	21	History
Biography	10	10	1	5	5	3	2	-	-	2	1	1	-	-	1	5	5	Columbia	27	26	8	4	19	Biography
Drama	9	4	4	-	-	2	1	-	-	1	6	3	1	-	2	2, 2	2, 2	Columbia, N. Carolina	16	15	1	4	13	Drama
Novels	3	3	1	-	2	4	4	-	1	3	3	2	-	1	1	3	3	Columbia	19	18	2	8	10	Novels
Poetry	17	10	6	3	3	6	4	-	1	4	-	-	-	-	-	4, 2	1, 2	Dartmouth, Vassar	10	10	3	2	8	Poetry
Music*	3	3	1	-	2	4	3	2	2	2	-	-	-	-	-	2	2	Am. Conserv. of Music	7	6	1	2	4	Music*
Totals	57	43	12	18	20	20	15	2	4	12	13	9	1	2	6	13	13	Columbia	105	100	24	24	75	Totals

*Awarded only since 1943.

Note: Apparent discrepancies in this table are accounted for by the fact that certain outstanding writers won more than one Pulitzer Prize, or won prizes in more than one category, and sometimes studied at more than one institution. The winners of more than one award have been the following:

J-4. WINNERS OF TWO OR MORE PULITZER PRIZES, 1917-57

No. of Awards	Field	Name	Educational Background
4	Drama (3) Biography (1)	R. E. Sherwood	Studied at Harvard 1914-17
4	Drama	Eugene O'Neill	Studied at Princeton 1906-07 at Harvard under Baker 1914-15
4	Poetry	Robert Frost	Studied at Dartmouth 1892 and Harvard 1897-99 Professor and lecturer at Amherst and other colleges and universities
3	Poetry	E. A. Robinson	Studied at Harvard 1890-93
3	Drama (2) Novels (1)	Thornton Wilder	Yale B.A. 1920
2	History (1) Biography (1)	S. F. Bemis	Clark B.A. 1912, A.M. 1913 Harvard M.A. 1915, Ph.D. 1916 Professor at Yale
2	Poetry	S. V. Benet	Yale B.A. 1919, M.A. 1920
2	Biography	Marquis James	Studied at Oklahoma Christian College 1910
2	Biography	B . J. Hendrick	Yale B.A. 1895
2	Poetry	A. MacLeish	Yale B.A. 1915, Harvard LL.B. 1919 Professor at Harvard
2	Music	Gian-Carlo Menotti	Grad. Curtis 1933 Teacher at Curtis
2	Biography	Allan Nevins	Illinois B.A. 1912, M.A. 1913 Professor at Columbia
2	History (1) Poetry (1)	Carl Sandburg	Studied at Lombard College, 1898-1902
2	Novels	Booth Tarkington	Studied at Purdue and Princeton (class of 1893)
2	Drama	Tennessee Williams	Studied at Missouri 1931-33 and at Washington U. (St. L.) 1936-37 U. of Iowa B.A. 1938

The celebrated and continuing preeminence of Harvard as the alma mater of authors was emphatically confirmed by our study of the works selected for the permanent reference collection in the White House Library. These works represented many fields: beginning with literature, literary history, and criticism, and covering geography, ethnology, biography, journalism, travel, science and technology, medicine and public health, entertainment, sports, education, philosophy and psychology, religion, folklore, and music. Approximately 20 per cent of the authors had not attended college or could not be located, but almost 11 per cent had studied at Harvard College. When graduate connections and faculty affiliations were added, it developed that Harvard had had a connection with one quarter of all the authors for the White House Library. Outside the Harvard Yard the concentration of literary production in certain leading colleges and universities was confirmed, at the college level in favor of Yale, Princeton, Columbia, and Wisconsin, at the graduate and professional level in favor of Columbia, Yale, Chicago, and Wisconsin. Altogether, out of the 767 individuals with some known college or university connection, 601 had had a connection with one or more of the top 16 colleges or universities, while only 538 had had a connection at one or another of the many hundreds of institutions of higher learning elsewhere in the United States.

Analysis of the past or present employment of the authors as members of the faculty at one or the other of our colleges and universities showed almost the same concentration or emphasis: Harvard, Columbia, Yale, Chicago, Princeton, and California leading the field, with Pennsylvania, Johns Hopkins, and Stanford joining Wisconsin in the second flight. On the whole, however, the older and more famous institutions proved less dependent on their faculties for their literary connections. To put this matter in another way, 35 per cent of Harvard's total author list had or had had a faculty connection with Harvard and the same had been true for Chicago and Wisconsin. Half of the Columbia-connected authors were teaching or had taught at that university and the same proved true for Yale, Princeton, Johns Hopkins, Pennsylvania, Michigan, Cornell, and North Carolina. On the other hand, thirty out of California's thirty-nine had or had had a faculty appointment and more than half of the authors connected with Stanford, Illinois, N.Y.U., and Minnesota had taught on their faculties. In reaching these estimates the lumping of the past and present faculty connections together made it impossible to ascertain where living authors were now connected or where deceased authors had done their last and most advanced teaching. On the face of the returns it looked as if faculty authors had been more widely distributed than graduate authors. On the other hand, it may be that an investigation of last or major appointments would show the same concentration of talent toward the top of the list.

AUTHORS IN THE WHITE HOUSE LIBRARY, 1963

The educational connections of the 960 authors whose works were selected for the permanent reference collection in the White House Library, 1963. Some 2,600 volumes in 1,780 titles were finally selected after nomination by the reference department of the Library of Congress, review and modification by three distinguished editors and historians, and a third systematic sifting by a national committee under James T. Babb, Librarian of Yale, with the aid of scholars in certain departmental fields at Yale. The individual authors were then checked in Who's Who in America, Who Was Who in America, Dictionary of American Biography, Dictionary of National Biography, and certain other biographical dictionaries and newspaper obituaries.

College or University	Undergraduate Connections	Graduate Connections	Faculty Affiliations	Net Total Individuals
HARVARD	104	149	81	229
COLUMBIA	28	94	67	135
YALE	43	57	49	101
CHICAGO	16	56	32	83
PRINCETON	31	17	32	61
WISCONSIN	19	37	22	55
JOHNS HOPKINS	6	26	23	44
PENNSYLVANIA	9	28	24	41
CALIFORNIA	11	12	30	39
STANFORD	9	7	22	31
MICHIGAN	12	10	17	30
ILLINOIS	8	9	19	29
N.Y.U.	5	8	17	29
CORNELL	6	11	15	27
MINNESOTA	3	12	18	26
NORTH CAROLINA	9	9	13	25
Totals for All Other American Colleges and Universities	431	201	647	468
Totals for All Foreign Colleges and Universities	62	161	65	153
None or Unknown	-	-	-	193
Individuals with Known College or University Connections	-	-	-	767
Net Totals	812	904	1,128	960

The table on PRIZES IN HISTORY confirms and emphasizes Harvard's distinction in this field of intellectual activity (cf. Pulitzer Prize table). It also shows a large graduate effort at Columbia and the long-range distinction of Columbia's faculty. For a university with a small graduate school Princeton makes a strong showing; Cornell, we thought, should have ranked higher. The contributions of Oxford, Berlin, and the Sorbonne are what might have been expected. That a great deal of migration takes place between college and graduate school, and between graduate school and faculty appointment, is evident; if there had been no overlaps or transfers or multiple connections, the first seven universities alone would have accounted for the total number of prize winners.

An interesting way of judging the competitive production of prize winners is to ask how many undergraduates ever went into history from each of the leading institutions, and how many received their graduate training at each. On these points the tables in Doctorate Production in United States Universities, 1920-1962, with Baccalaureate Origins of Doctorates in Sciences, Arts and Professions published by the National Academy of Sciences and National Research Council, 1963, yield some pertinent statistics. The major undergraduate producers of future Ph.D.'s in history for the years 1920-62 were: Harvard 246, California (Berkeley) 194, Yale 158, Chicago 127, C.C.N.Y., Columbia, and Wisconsin 120, Princeton 101, Michigan 99, and U.C.L.A. 97. One way of translating these figures is to note that 15 of Harvard's 24 college men had graduated before 1920: i.e., 9 of the 246 future Ph.D. students, who had graduated from Harvard College in the years 1920-62, would finally win one of these history prizes. Similarly, 3 of Columbia's future winners had graduated before 1920, as had 2 from Chicago, 1 each from Princeton and Pennsylvania, and all 4 from Wisconsin. The ratios of achievement had therefore been: Harvard, 9 out of 246 or 3.7 per cent; Columbia, 4 out of 120 or 3.3 per cent; Chicago, 3 out of 127 or 2.4 per cent; Yale, 5 out of 158 or 3.2 per cent; Princeton, 5 out of 101 or almost 5 per cent--whereas California (Berkeley) would produce 1 prize winner out of a crop of 194 intending historians.

The same source on the production of Ph.D.'s gives the following figures: Harvard 725 Ph.D.'s, Columbia 694, California (Berkeley) 417, Wisconsin 405, Chicago 391, Yale 270, Pennsylvania 269, Michigan 210, Illinois 205, and Princeton 103. With subtraction for prize winners who had graduated before 1920, this means that 30 of Harvard's 725 Ph.D. students, 18 of Columbia's 694, 8 of Chicago's 391, 3 of Princeton's 103, 6 of Yale's 270, 5 of Wisconsin's 405, 8 of Pennsylvania's 269, and 1 of California's 417 would win a prize in history by 1961.

The count of faculty connections is interesting as indicating a wider distribution of prize winners among the universities. There is some risk, however, that the distribution may seem wider than it actually has been, for a number of the prize winners may have moved from a smaller college or a lesser university to a greater university just before or just after making their mark in the profession.

164

PRIZES IN HISTORY, 1893-1961

College education, graduate training, and faculty connections of the 165 winners of following national Honors or Prize competitions for works in history (1893-1961): d Medal of the National Institute of Arts and Letters; the H. B. Adams, G. L. Beers, J. Beveridge, J. H. Dunning, and R. H. Schuyler Prizes of the American Historical ociation; the Bancroft, Loubat, Parkman, and Pulitzer Prizes.

lege or University	Undergraduate Connections	Graduate Connections	Faculty Connections	Prize-winning Individuals
VARD	24	43	30	52
UMBIA	7	24	19	33
CAGO	5	12	7	22
E	5	9	8	17
NCETON	6	4	10	15
CONSIN	4	8	9	15
NSYLVANIA	1	11	9	12
NFORD	1	4	9	11
INOIS	2	4	7	10
NS HOPKINS	3	4	6	10
HIGAN	3	3	8	10
NELL	2	4	3	7
GERS	1	1	6	7
AS	2	3	5	7
IFORNIA (Berkeley)	1	1	5	6
IANA	2	4	3	6
THWESTERN	1	1	5	6
REMONT COLLEGES	1	1	5	5
TH	-	-	5	5
LIAMS	4	1	3	5
OKLYN	1	-	3	4
WN	1	1	4	4
.N.Y.	2	-	2	4
IFORNIA (L.A.)	1	2	3	4
E	-	1	4	4
RY	3	1	2	4
NESOTA	-	1	3	4
.U.	2	1	1	4
TH CAROLINA	1	3	2	4
O STATE	1	1	2	4
DERBILT	-	2	3	4
HINGTON (Seattle)	1	-	3	4
Other American titutions	63	22	149	91
eign:				
XFORD	1	6	-	7
ERLIN	-	3	1	4
ORBONNE	-	4	-	4
4 Others	12	9	4	18
nown				5
Total Individuals				165

rce: Basic data taken from Literary and Library Prizes published by the R. R. Bowker Company, 1963.

Perhaps this table belongs in an appendix, for it is as much a measure of promise as of achievement. The fellowship awards presumably were given to writers of some demonstrated capacity or power, yet for the purpose of helping rather than rewarding creative writing. The awards, therefore, constitute a kind of prophecy of achievement and are interesting in their own right. They suggest, for example, that growing literary interests in Columbia College (already hinted at in Tables J-1 and J-2) had attracted unusual numbers of young men and women, of ambition and promise in writing, to the university on Morningside Heights. Chicago and California also seemed to rank high as producers of potential writers. An impressive number of Guggenheim Fellows derived from the undergraduate schools at Wisconsin, North Carolina, and Vanderbilt, and from the graduate school at Iowa.

Out of curiosity as to how many of these promising creative writers had been serious about their college educations, and how many had merely attended an institution for a short interval, our statistics were re-examined for earned degrees. Tabulation showed that 5 of the 20 men who had attended Columbia College had earned a bachelor's degree, and 11 of the 27 who had taken graduate or professional work had achieved a graduate or professional degree. The Harvard writers proved somewhat more stable, with 12 of the 13 undergraduates and 14 of the 21 graduate students staying to earn their credentials. For Chicago the comparable figures were 6 out of 12 and 5 out of 9. Yale's 3 undergraduates all achieved the B.A., but only 4 out of its 12 graduate students earned graduate degrees. And for California the figures were 6 out of 7 and 6 out of 9.

It should be noted that Radcliffe (1 B.A. and 1 M.A.) and Barnard (2 B.A.'s) were counted separately, whereas in most tables they have been credited to Harvard and Columbia. If they were so credited here, the effect would be to increase the net total figures for Harvard and Columbia by 2 each. Either way, the eager writers from Columbia seemed to outnumber their counterparts from Cambridge about 5 to 3. It will be interesting to see if they can maintain this advantage and prove it in performance in the years to come.

GUGGENHEIM FELLOWSHIPS FOR CREATIVE WRITING, 1926-62

The educational backgrounds of the John Simon Guggenheim Fellows, who received grants for creative writing in fiction, drama, and poetry (1926-62).

College or University	Undergraduate Connections	Graduate or Professional	Net Total Individuals
COLUMBIA	20	27	45
HARVARD	13	21	28
CHICAGO	12	9	17
CALIFORNIA	7	9	13
YALE	3	12	13
STANFORD	6	6	10
VANDERBILT	7	4	10
WISCONSIN	9	1	10
IOWA	1	8	9
NORTH CAROLINA	7	2	8
Totals for 116 Other American Colleges and Universities	169	37	144
Foreign Colleges and Universities	41	30	55
Totals			
Number of Individuals with Some Known College or University Connection	224	121	227
No College or University Connection or Unknown	-	-	28
Net Individuals			255

The implausibility of expecting actors and actresses to have gone to college at first deterred investigation of the world of the theatre. A number of our playwrights--as the Pulitzer Prizes made clear--had at least attended college for a while. Instead of attempting to expand that investigation, however, it seemed interesting to ask about the university connections of still a third group, those who had been directing the dramatic productions on Broadway. Even here the difficulty of ascertaining the life histories of men in the world of the theatre, many of whom had just started to achieve reputations, reduced our analysis to a somewhat imperfect sampling. This sampling showed that higher education had not yet become indispensable to success in directing: 40 of the 170 individuals on whom adequate information could be obtained were self-made men. However, 130 had gone to college or taken professional training, and the results of our analysis of these educational connections may be of more than casual significance. On the undergraduate level, it becomes clear that there must have been a strong interest in the theatre in Yale College, N.Y.U., and Columbia. At the graduate or professional level the role played by the Yale Department (later School) of Drama is also unmistakable.

Perhaps even more emphatic, however, is the indebtedness of Broadway to Europe, with no fewer than 47 individuals educated abroad in one or another of 35 colleges, universities, or professional schools. Had Oxford and Cambridge been listed separately from the others, Oxford would have ranked in second place, between Yale and N.Y.U., with 12 individuals. Cambridge would have come just after Princeton, with a net contribution of 4. In many a vocation the leaders produced by Harvard, Yale, and Princeton have outnumbered those educated in Europe, but apparently this does not hold for the theatre.

DIRECTORS ON BROADWAY, 1952-61

An analysis of the educational backgrounds of the Broadway directors listed in the New York Theatre Critics' Reviews.

College or University	Undergraduate Connections	Graduate or Professional	Net Total Individuals
YALE	11	7	18
N.Y.U.	7	2	9
COLUMBIA	7	-	7
HARVARD	5	1	6
PRINCETON	4	1	5
CARNEGIE TECH.	3	-	3
C.C.N.Y.	3	-	3
PENNSYLVANIA	2	1	3
Net Total Individuals for 37 Other Colleges, Universities, and Professional Schools	43	3	45
Net Total Individuals for 35 Foreign Colleges, Universities and Professional Schools	41	20	47
American Academy of Dramatic Arts	4	-	4
Royal Academy of Dramatic Arts	9	-	9
Totals			
Individuals with Known College, University or Professional School Connection			130
No College			40
Unknown			98
Net Individuals			268

Our society has not been noted until very recently for its music or
for its musicians, and we have produced only a small handful of composers
of international reputation. To complicate the problem for statistical
analysis, quite a number of our composers did not let their ancestors "do
the immigrating" to this country for they were immigrants themselves, some
of them after making an international reputation. To discriminate, John
Tasker Howard adopted the following definition: "A composer is an American if, by birth or choice of permanent residence, he becomes identified
with American life and institutions before his talents have had their
greatest outlet; and through his associations and sympathies he makes a
genuine contribution to our cultural development." (p. xx, Introduction,
Our American Music, 1965). Howard's selection and identification of composers comprises accordingly a rather generous list of all those Americans
(by birth or adoption) who may be recognized as having written and published at least a few pieces in this country, and had their works per-
formed.

As might have been anticipated, our efforts to identify the higher
education of many individuals proved unavailing: One third of Howard's
table of 783 composers could not be satisfactorily classified, while another fifth proved to have attended no conservatory or institution of
higher learning.

The education of the composers for whom our information was adequate
turns out to have been obtained from a wide range of academic and technical institutions, with altogether 194 contributing to the education and
training of the 373 individuals involved. Among the professional institutions the Juilliard School has evidently been the most productive, followed by the New England Conservatory and the Curtis Institute. Among the
academic institutions Harvard has been by all odds the greatest nursery of
musicians (the Radcliffe component in our figures being 1). One notes the
distinction of Rochester; the considerable contributions of Northwestern,
Oberlin, Chicago College of Music, and Pennsylvania; the participation of
a number of well-known colleges and city or state universities; finally
also the rare appearance of such institutions as Arizona, Mills College,
Nebraska, and Western Reserve.

It may be anticipated that in the future our musicians, like our
businessmen, will find the road of achievement taking them more frequently
through college.

AMERICAN COMPOSERS, 1620-1965

The education of American composers from the first colonial days to the present. Composers are those identified by John Tasker Howard and considered of sufficient importance to have their names italicized in the text of the fourth edition of Howard's Our American Music, 1965.

College or University	Undergrad. Connects.	Grad. or Prof'l.	Net Total Individuals	Professional Institutions and Foreign Universities Institution	Connects.
HARVARD-RADCLIFFE	43	15	50	JUILLIARD-INST. MUS. ART	30
ROCHESTER-EASTMAN	15	15	25	NEW ENGLAND CONSERV.	17
YALE	15	12	24	CURTIS INSTITUTE	13
COLUMBIA	14	10	21	STAATLICHE HOCHSCHULE FÜR MUSIK--MUNICH	9
NORTHWESTERN	7	4	11	ROYAL CONSERV.--LEIPZIG	8
CHICAGO COLL. MUS. (ROOSEVELT U.)	-	10	10	STATE CONSERV.--ST. PETERSBURG	8
OBERLIN COLL.-CONSERV.	2	8	10	AMERICAN CONSERV.-CHICAGO	7
				CINCINNATI COLL.-CONSERV.	7
PENNSYLVANIA	6	3	9	PARIS CONSERV.	7
C.C.N.Y.	7	-	7	NATIONAL CONSERV. MUSIC	6
N.Y.U.	6	2	7	PEABODY CONSERV.	6
SYRACUSE	6	1	6	LEIPZIG	4
				ROYAL ACAD. MUSIC-LONDON	4
CALIFORNIA	3	1	4		
CHICAGO	4	-	4	CLEVELAND INST. MUSIC	3
PRINCETON	3	2	4	DAVID MANNES COLL. MUSIC	3
SOUTHERN CALIF.	3	1	4	HOCHSCHULE FÜR MUSIK-BERLIN	3
MICHIGAN	2	1	3	MOSCOW CONSERV.	3
MINNESOTA	2	1	3	MUNICH	3
WISCONSIN	3	-	3	PARIS	3
				SCHOLA CANTORUM	3
ARIZONA	2	1	2	STUTTGART CONSERV.	3
BROWN	2	-	2	VIENNA CONSERV.	3
BROOKLYN POLY. INST.	-	2	2	ZURICH CONSERV.	3
CORNELL	1	1	2		
DARTMOUTH	2	-	2	ACAD. OF ST. CECILIA	2
GEORGE WASHINGTON	1	1	2	BERLIN	2
M.I.T.	2	-	2	BRUSSELS CONSERV.	2
MILLS	2	-	2	COLOGNE CONSERV.	2
NEBRASKA	1	1	2	LISZT CONSERV.-BUDAPEST	2
STANFORD	2	-	2	MANHATTAN SCH. MUSIC	2
U.C.L.A.	2	1	2	PHILADELPHIA CONSERV.	2
WASHINGTON	2	-	2	WESTMINSTER CHOIR COLL.	2
WESTERN RESERVE	2	1	2		
WILLIAMS	2	-	2	58 Others	55
62 Others	53	11	58		

Composers with College Connections   373
Composers with No Higher Education   152
No Information   258
Net Total Individuals   783

In several of the fine arts--notably sculpture, painting, acting, and
musical performance--we attempted no statistical measurements. This was
fundamentally because of the difficulty of finding adequate or representative honor lists, but also in part because so many of the artists would
have had to be classified "No College or Unknown." Even in the most
learned of the fine arts, the profession of architecture, considerable uncertainties were quickly encountered. It appeared, however, that the
American Institute of Architects might serve in a representative capacity.

In a little more than a century the American Institute of Architects
has known forty-one presidents, and has awarded its Gold Medal to twenty-
one outstanding practitioners of this old but ever-living art. It is perhaps no surprise to discover that American architecture has owed much to
the tutelage of France: Eight of the presidents and seven of the Gold
Medalists, thus honored, had studied at the Ecole des Beaux Arts, Paris.
For the United States the Massachusetts Institute of Technology has been
the outstanding producer, with Cornell, Harvard, Pennsylvania, and Yale
grouped behind it, and with Columbia and Michigan following. Among the
nineteen other American institutions, contributing one president or Gold
Medalist each, were N.Y.U., Princeton, Chicago, Nebraska, and Washington
University. Five individuals achieved both the presidency of the A.I.A.
and its Gold Medal:

Charles Follen McKim, Lawrence Scientific School at Harvard, and
    École des Beaux Arts
    (Pres. 1901-02, G.M. 1909)

George Browne Post, Civil Engineer, N.Y.U.
    (Pres. 1895-97, G.M. 1911)

Milton Bennett Medary, B.A. at Pennsylvania
    (Pres. 1926-27, G.M. 1929)

Charles Donagh Maginnis, Cusack's Academy, Dublin, Ireland
    (Pres. 1937-38, G.M. 1948)

Ralph Walker, studied at M.I.T.
    (Pres. 1949-50, G.M. 1957)

PRESIDENTS AND GOLD MEDALISTS OF THE AMERICAN INSTITUTE OF ARCHITECTS

Academic and professional connections of the presidents (1857-1964) and the Gold Medalists (1909-62) of the American Institute of Architects.

College or University	College Degree or Attendance		B.F.A. B. Arch. B.S. Arch.		M.F.A. M. Arch. M.S. Arch.		Other Graduate, Professional or Special Studs.		Net		Net Total Individuals
	Pres.	GM	Pres.	GM	Pres.	GM	Pres.	GM	Pres.	GM	
M.I.T.	3	1	1	-	-	-	4	3	8	4	11
CORNELL	-	-	3	1	-	-	1	-	4	1	5
HARVARD	5	1	-	-	-	-	-	-	5	1	5
PENNSYLVANIA	3	1	2	-	1	-	-		5	1	5
YALE	1	2	1	2	1	-	-	-	2	3	5
COLUMBIA	-	-	1	-	-	-	1	1	2	1	3
MICHIGAN	2	-	1	-	-	-	-	-	2	-	2
19 Other American Institutions	13	4	2			-	2		15	4	18
Foreign:											
ÉCOLE DES BEAUX ARTS, PARIS	-	-	-	-	-	-	8	7	8	7	14
4 Others	1	1	-	-	-	-	1	2	2	3	4
No Connections											2
Net Total Individuals											57

Sources: American Directory of Architects, 1962, and information supplied by the Executive Director, the American Institute of Architects.

In a further effort to locate the breeding grounds of American architects, a study was made of some 604 individuals elected Fellows of the
American Institute of Architects over a substantial span of time. For
purposes of analysis and comparison the Fellows were divided into those
elected in the years 1913-52, and a larger but younger group elected in
the years 1953-64.

The first of these analyses surprised us by its pattern. Evidently,
M.I.T. and Pennsylvania had stood head and shoulders above the field in
this country and had each done as much for the professional training of
architects as had the celebrated École des Beaux Arts in Paris.

In third and fourth places came the graduates of Columbia and Harvard, with Harvard stronger as a college and Columbia as a professional
school. In sixth place, very honorably, came the American Academy in
Rome, followed by Illinois, Cornell, and Michigan. Outnumbered and
located toward the bottom of the third flight of producing institutions
we found the graduates of Yale and Princeton and the Beaux Arts of New
York.

FELLOWS OF THE AMERICAN INSTITUTE OF ARCHITECTS, 1913-52

Educational backgrounds of the architects elected to the College of Fellows of the American Institute of Architects: 1913-52.

College or University	College Degree or Attendance	B.F.A. B. Arch. B.S. Arch.	M.F.A. M. Arch. M.S. Arch.	Other Graduate Professional or Special Connects.	Net Total Individuals
M.I.T.	14	18	5	14	46
PENNSYLVANIA	8	29	18	6	43
COLUMBIA	10	15	1	7	28
HARVARD	14	4	2	8	21
ILLINOIS	7	6	3	-	13
CORNELL	3	9	1	-	12
MICHIGAN	3	8	2	1	12
CALIFORNIA	4	3	-	2	9
ARMOUR INSTITUTE	5	3	-	1	8
CARNEGIE TECH	5	3	-	1	8
YALE	5	2	1	3	8
PRINCETON	6	-	3	1	7
BEAUX ARTS, N.Y.	-	-	-	6	6
70 Other American Colleges and Universities, Art and Archit. Schools	61	21	4	19	91
Foreign:					
ÉCOLE DES BEAUX ARTS, PARIS	-	-	-	43	43
AMERICAN ACADEMY IN ROME	-	-	-	15	15
17 Other Foreign Colleges, Universities, Academies, Art Schools	3	1	1	17	19
None or Unknown					16
Net Individuals					256

Sources: Biographical information from Who's Who in America and American Directory of Architects.

J-12. FELLOWS OF THE AMERICAN INSTITUTE OF ARCHITECTS, 1953-64

Our study of the rising generation of American architects, as represented by the Fellows elected to the American Institute of Architects in the years 1953-64, revealed a widening institutional participation in this country and some decline in the influence of Europe. The École des Beaux Arts could no longer match the three leading American universities, and the total attendance abroad had shrunk from about 30 per cent to about 20 per cent of the architects of the A.I.A. It should be said on behalf of the École des Beaux Arts, once the goal of so many aspiring architects, that it came to be regarded as too classical and old-fashioned and for a time fell quite out of favor; but more recent evidence suggests that it has not altogether lost its magnetic powers.

The distribution of Fellows between American schools and universities showed the continued and growing distinction of M.I.T. in this field of design, with Pennsylvania still very strong and Harvard moving up. While Yale was still generating less than its usual share of leaders in the college, the returns were beginning to show the effects of its new professional program in architecture.

Geographically, five or six of the strongest schools of architecture have been attached to Eastern universities, but recently the South and California have each developed a pair, while the University of Illinois, Armour Institute of Technology, and Illinois Institute of Technology separately or together have served the Middle West. From this and other indications it is clear that the wider distribution of architectural opportunity has been developing steadily.

Beneath the statistical surface of the most recent elections one may be tempted also to detect the presence of famous masters in architecture (e.g., Walter Gropius at Harvard) and their effect in drawing ambitious young architects to particular institutions.

Educational backgrounds of the architects elected to the College of Fellows of the American Institute of Architects: 1953-64.

College or University	College Degree or Attendance	B.F.A. B. Arch. B.S. Arch.	M.F.A. M. Arch. M.S. Arch.	Other Graduate Professional or Special Connects.	Net Total Individuals
M.I.T.	20	9	21	19	58
HARVARD	16	10	23	11	48
PENNSYLVANIA	17	25	10	4	47
ILLINOIS	25	6	1	2	32
COLUMBIA	9	12	3	10	29
CORNELL	6	18	1	3	26
CALIFORNIA	23	1	-	8	25
YALE	9	15	2	1	20
GEORGIA TECH	12	6	-	-	17
SOUTHERN CALIFORNIA	8	8	-	1	17
PRINCETON	12	1	7	3	15
MINNESOTA	8	5	-	1	14
MICHIGAN	8	3	1	-	11
TEXAS	4	6	-	1	11
111 Other American Colleges and Universities, Art and Archit. Schools	159	68	9	28	208
Foreign: ECOLE DES BEAUX ARTS, PARIS	-	-	-	34	34
38 Other Foreign Colleges, Universities, Academies, Art Schools					50
Unknown					29
Net Individuals					442

Sources: Biographical information from Who's Who in America and American Directory of Architects.

In a further effort to identify the major sources for the supply and
training of promising young architects in twentieth-century America, the
145 winners of three major prize fellowships for architectural students
were studied. The resulting tabulation showed seven institutions grouped
very closely together--with Illinois, Pennsylvania, and M.I.T. joining
Yale, Harvard, Princeton, and Columbia in the effective production of
92 out of the 145 winners.

A special effort was made to distinguish the degrees or level of instruction, but not always with entire success. The large numbers in the
fourth column (other graduates, professional or special connections) reflect our inability to determine the exact status of the prize winners at
certain institutions. However, the table makes it clear that Yale and
Columbia had produced the greatest number of bachelor degrees in architecture, while Harvard, M.I.T., and Princeton led at the master's level, and
Pennsylvania, Princeton, and N.Y.U. had been the most productive liberal
arts colleges.

This table is unusual in the sense that it does not measure the total
formal training in architecture of the individuals under study. All of
these prize winners (and presumably many of their unsuccessful competitors)
then went abroad for further instruction at the American Academy in Rome,
the Beaux Arts in Paris, etc.--after which they would still have to survive the hazards of life and the risks of their profession before some
outstanding success could justify their recognition as leaders in architecture.

Note: I should like to thank particularly, for their interest and gener-
ous help in this investigation, Mr. William H. Scheick, Executive Director,
American Institute of Architects; Margot A. Henkel, Executive Secretary,
New York Chapter, American Institute of Architects; Mary T. Williams,
Executive Secretary, American Academy in Rome; Cecylia B. Rother, Execu-
tive Secretary, National Institute for Architectural Education.

PRIZE FELLOWSHIPS IN ARCHITECTURE

Education and professional training of the 145 winners of three major prize fellowships for architectural students: 65 winners of Fellowships in Architecture to the School of Fine Arts, American Academy in Rome, 1909-64; 50 winners of Lloyd Warren Fellowships (Paris Prize in Architecture), 1904-63; 30 winners of the Le Brun Traveling Scholarship, 1912-62.

College or University	College Degree or Attendance	B.F.A. B. Arch. B.S. Arch.	M.F.A. M. Arch. M.S. Arch.	Other Graduate, Professional or Special Connects.	Net Total Individuals
YALE	2	14	4	-	16
ILLINOIS	1	6	4	8	15
PENNSYLVANIA	5	7	3	7	15
HARVARD	2	5	7	2	13
M.I.T.	1	1	6	6	13
PRINCETON	4	-	6	6	13
COLUMBIA	2	11	2	1	12
CORNELL	-	5	2	1	8
N.Y.U.	3	1	-	3	7
MINNESOTA	2	4	-	-	5
NORTH CAROLINA STATE COLL.	-	1	-	4	5
OKLAHOMA STATE COLL.	1	3	-	2	5
BEAUX ARTS, N.Y.	-	-	-	4	4
CATHOLIC UNIVERSITY	-	2	-	2	4
ILLINOIS TECH	2	1	-	1	4
PRATT INSTITUTE	1	3	1	-	4
COOPER UNION	2	-	-	1	3
CRANBROOK ACADEMY	-	-	1	2	3
WASHINGTON U. (St. Louis)	-	2	-	1	3
41 Other American Institutions	28	16	2	7	48
4 Foreign Institutions	1	-	-	4	5
Unknown or Private Apprenticeship					20

Sources: American Academy in Rome Report, 1955-1959, National Institute for Architectural Education, Membership Directory of the American Institute of Architects, Architects Directory.

CHAPTER K   EDUCATION AND
             SCHOLARSHIP

To turn from literature and the arts to education and scholarship is to enter a more solemn world, yet one that in its special way reflects the American character. Scholarship--in almost everything until 1861 and in all too many things until our involvement in the great World Wars--scholarship was something which we seemed as a people determined to leave to others: to the English, to the Germans, to Europeans generally. Only recently has the American professor even begun to come into his own. And if today the word "scientist" has acquired unprecedented luster, one must still allow that too often our great new armies of Ph.D.'s seem more notable for their numbers than for originality or for personal distinction.

All this notwithstanding, education in the sense of the general enlightenment--the teaching of literacy and a knowledge of good and evil--the little red schoolhouse and the requirement that all children should be sent to school--these were built into the foundations of our republic. A people must educate themselves to be able to govern themselves: Such was the theory, or rather (since we have always been doggedly untheoretical) the profound assumption of our Jeffersonian inheritance: an assumption equivalent to fierce belief.

It followed that the challenges and rewards of careers in education and scholarship remained long most uneven. With universal education the goal but the emphasis upon elementary and secondary instruction, school teaching became necessary but somehow hardly worthy of a full-blooded man--and the men's colleges were driven out of the business of supplying the school teachers of the nation. When a number of these colleges with great pains achieved a certain academic excellence and intellectual ambition, it still seemed to both graduates and parents that opportunity and character were what mattered, that the student was more important than the instructor, and that the college life should not be sacrificed to intellectual pursuits or research in library or chemical lab. The Ph.D. was first offered in this country at Yale in 1860-61, but until almost the turn of the century few ventured to expose themselves to the rigors of this scholarly apprenticeship. From all this it also followed that throughout most of our educational system, from high school principal to university president, the administrator overshadowed the teacher or scholar-professor, just as the organizer of an educational idea or reform automatically became more notable than its inventor.

In recent years much of this has been changing. Yet the world of scholarship and education is often still a strange and lopsided place, divided against itself and difficult to appraise. It would have been most interesting to study the principals of the larger state and city public school systems for these have assuredly become the directors of big business in contemporary education. Unfortunately, we could not find the tools to measure the mass movements in education or discover the numerical contributions of the state normal schools and more notable teachers' colleges to the leadership of the public school systems of our major cities and states. Our study is the poorer on that account. Failing such data we have focused instead on the common ground of education and scholarship, that is, on higher education. And in this broad field we have tried to scan a variety of contributions and concerns: from the staffing of the better college preparatory schools, to Rhodes Scholarships, to college presidencies; and from fellowships for promising younger scholars in the major divisions of learning to prizes for distinguished humanistic achievement. Finally, we have assayed just a glimpse or two of the juggernaut Ph.D., or the manufacture of scholars for the generations to come.

Before undertaking a detailed study of categories of achievement in higher education, our office searched, and searched in vain, for some Hall of Fame or adequate honor roll for all the fields of American education from the earliest settlements to the present. Finally, on the initiative and with the imaginative aid of Barbara Simison, Senior Assistant Reference Librarian in the Yale University Library, an attempt was made to create our own list--and a considerable roster of notable educators was painstakingly assembled. Miss Simison started with a nucleus of thirty-three outstanding names as given in the biographical section of the Lincoln Library of Essential Information. From that small group John Harvard and Elihu Yale were promptly subtracted. But to the remainder we then added the names of those educators (at whatever level or in whatever fields of effort) who are recorded as having made contributions of considerable importance to the educational development of this country. The resulting list of 236 individuals, somewhat arbitrarily labeled "Great Educators," was then analyzed with the results here given.

In our table, after the outstanding contributions of the alumni of Harvard and Yale, of Columbia and Princeton, one notes particularly the by no means inconsiderable record of the graduates of Brown, Johns Hopkins, Williams, and Andover Theological Seminary--and the significant role played also by certain major German universities, by Oxford, and by Paris.

A review of the individual graduates of the leading colleges and universities made plain to us not only the distinction, but the variety and interest of their achievements. Among the Columbia names, for example, we found Mortimer J. Adler, Charles A. Beard, Nicholas Murray Butler, John Erskine, Frederick Keppel, J. Brander Matthews, A. J. Nock, and Edward Thorndike. Princeton's list started chronologically with Benjamin Rush and Tapping Reeve and concluded with Andrew F. West, Woodrow Wilson, and Harold Willis Dodds. Brown proved to have produced not only Horace Mann but a cluster of notable college presidents: Eliphalet Nott (president of Union), James Burrill Angell (Michigan), Benjamin Ide Wheeler (California), Mary Emma Woolley (Mount Holyoke), and Alexander Meiklejohn (Amherst).

Among the Harvard-educated presidents of interest to our historians of higher education were Thomas Clap (president of Yale), Josiah Quincy, Edward Everett, Charles W. Eliot, and James Bryant Conant (all of Harvard), with Frank Aydelotte (Swarthmore) and Henry N. McCracken (Vassar). From Harvard had come also such educators or intellectual innovators as Joseph Cogswell, Ralph Waldo Emerson, Oliver Wendell Holmes, Charles Eliot Norton, William James, Arthur O. Lovejoy, Paul Elmer More, and Irving Babbitt. By reason of their professional distinction and educational influence the Harvard list included also such men of the law as Joseph Story, Felix Frankfurter, and Roscoe Pound, and a great cluster of nineteenth-century historians: Bancroft, Motley, Parkman, and Prescott, with Albert Bushnell Hart and James Harvey Robinson for more recent times.

Hopkins proved to be strongly represented for its college by Abraham Flexner and as a university by John Dewey, Josiah Royce, Frederick Jackson Turner, and Woodrow Wilson. Finally, Yale's list of noteworthy presidents

"GREAT EDUCATORS," FROM THE EARLIEST SETTLEMENTS

College or University	Undergraduate Connections	Graduate or Professional	Net Total Individuals
HARVARD	36 (21)*	22 (6)	48 (22)
YALE	34 (18)	9 (2)	35 (38)
COLUMBIA	9 (1)	12	16 (1)
PRINCETON	10 (6)	4	11 (6)
BROWN	7 (3)	3	7 (3)
JOHNS HOPKINS	1	6	7
WILLIAMS	7 (2)	1	7 (2)
ANDOVER THEO. SEM.	-	6 (3)	6 (3)
DARTMOUTH	6 (3)	1	6 (3)
CALIFORNIA (Berkeley)	5	-	5
MICHIGAN	5	1	5
UNION	5 (4)	-	5 (4)
N.Y.U.	3	3	4
<u>60 Other American Institutions</u>	64	37	75
<u>Foreign:</u>			
BERLIN	-	8	8
OXFORD	3	5	7
LEIPZIG	-	6	6
HEIDELBURG	-	5	5
MUNICH	-	4	4
PARIS	-	4	4
<u>25 Other Foreign Institutions</u>	4	30	26
None or Unknown			42
Net Total Individuals			236

*Figures in parentheses indicate the number of those important in education before the Civil War.

Sources: Educators listed in <u>The Lincoln Library of Essential Information</u> (Buffalo, 1956) in the biography section, and those educators considered significant in John S. Brubacker and Willis Rudy, <u>Higher Education in Transition, an American History, 1936-1956</u> (New York: Harpers, 1958); R. Freeman Butts and Lawrence A. Cremin, <u>A History of Education in American Culture</u> (New York: Holt, 1961); Adolphe E. Meyer, <u>An Educational History of the American People</u> (New York: McGraw-Hill, 1957); Stuart G. Noble, <u>A History of American Education</u> . . . Rev. ed. (New York: Rinehart, c. 1954); or Frederick Rudolph, <u>The American College and University, a History</u> (New York: Knopf, 1962).

ranged from Samuel Johnson (Columbia) and Eleazar Wheelock (Dartmouth) to Andrew D. White (Cornell), D. C. Gilman (Johns Hopkins), William Rainey Harper and Robert M. Hutchins (Chicago)--not to mention Yale's own Ezra Stiles, the Timothy Dwights, and A. Whitney Griswold. Out of Yale College had also come a legal educator, James Kent; such influential religious leaders as Lyman Beecher and Horace Bushnell; the dictionary and textbook pioneers, Noah Webster and Jedidiah Morse; and such notable professors as Benjamin Silliman, Thomas R. Lounsbury, and William Graham Sumner.

K-2. HEADMASTERS AND PRINCIPALS OF 66 PREPARATORY SCHOOLS, TO 1955

The measurement of college and university influence in secondary education was not without its difficulties. To begin with, no ready-made list of "notable preparatory and secondary schools" was available. In the second place, the requirement of distinction over a reasonable span of years would necessarily weight the table heavily on the side of the private preparatory schools. Finally, however, a list of 100 institutions, including a small number of distinguished high schools, was put together with the help of Yale admissions officers. In all probability no other university constituency or group of educational experts would have selected the identical 100 schools, but the presumption is strong that 80 or 90 of these institutions would have appeared in almost any list of notable schools.

This first table, on headmasters and principals from school founding until 1955, was inevitably weighted in favor of the older schools. It showed that, for the sixty-six schools which supplied the required information (at least for their current headmasters and in many cases for their entire list since date of establishment), the colleges of Yale, Harvard, and Princeton had been the big suppliers of school heads--while the smaller colleges of Amherst, Williams, Dartmouth, and Haverford had made notable contributions. Since a majority of these schools were located on or near the Atlantic seaboard, and many of them were older than the state and city universities, the absence of Michigan, Illinois, Wisconsin, and California from the list of leaders was to have been expected. The failure, however, of Brown, Wesleyan, Bowdoin, Union, Hamilton, Swarthmore, and Cornell to contribute substantially seemed more worthy of remark.

HEADMASTERS AND PRINCIPALS OF 66 PREPARATORY SCHOOLS, TO 1955

The college and university backgrounds of 391 headmasters and principals, past and present, of 66 notable preparatory and secondary schools. In 1955 a list was compiled of 100 well known and productive schools, both private and public. Of these schools, 76 were successfully reached.

College or University	Undergraduate Bachelors, etc.	Graduate Masters	Graduate Ph.D. or Profess.	Studied at	Net Total Individuals
HARVARD	43	28	8	14	77
YALE	59	13	6	4	63
PRINCETON	28	8	5	4	35
COLUMBIA	4	15	5	6	26
PENNSYLVANIA	7	5	4	3	15
AMHERST	12	2	-	-	14
WILLIAMS	12	-	-	1	13
DARTMOUTH	9	2	1	-	11
HAVERFORD	9	2	1	-	10
12 Theological Schools	-	1	20	13	32
Foreign Institutions	8	8	3	19	23
76 Other Institutions with Less Than 10 Connections	104	32	23	24	136
None or Unknown					67

Sources: Information on the heads (active, retired, or dead) was obtained for 66 of these institutions, either through correspondence or through school histories or through Porter Sargeant's annual A Handbook of Private Schools for American Boys and Girls. For Harvard, Yale, and Princeton the attributions were then checked against the respective alumni registers.

Our second analysis of secondary schools consisted of an attempt to analyze the educational preparation of the faculties as they were constituted in the year 1955. In this tabulation the good small New England colleges made a notable showing. After Harvard, Yale, Princeton, Columbia, and Pennsylvania, it was by graduates of Williams, Bowdoin, Wesleyan, Dartmouth, Haverford, Brown, and Trinity, that our notable secondary schools had been staffed.

At the university level the five major contributors presented an interesting contrast: 97 per cent of those who held degrees from Princeton had graduated from its college, compared to 85 per cent for Yale, 61 per cent for Harvard, 45 per cent for Pennsylvania, and 23 per cent for Columbia. Evidently Columbia and Harvard, and Pennsylvania and Middlebury too, were making use of the M.A. degree in a way that Yale and Princeton were not. Where faculties holding masters degrees from Columbia and Harvard were advising their best students to go to college, we neglected to inquire.

FACULTIES OF 69 PREPARATORY SCHOOLS, 1955

Earned degrees for 2,339 individuals comprising the faculties of the 69 notable preparatory or secondary schools as of the year 1955. Only the 15 most productive colleges and universities were finally tabulated.

College or University	Degrees			Net Total Individuals
	Bachelors	Masters	Advanced	
HARVARD	159	135	18	262
YALE	159	40	21	187
COLUMBIA	41	147	12	176
PRINCETON	117	16	8	121
PENNSYLVANIA	38	54		84
WILLIAMS	69	4		70
MIDDLEBURY	18	53		68
WESLEYAN	48	16		58
BOWDOIN	54	1		54
BROWN	36	13		44
TRINITY	29	14		41
DARTMOUTH	38	3		40
HAVERFORD	38	5		38
SPRINGFIELD	29	9		33
BOSTON UNIVERSITY	17	17		32

Sources: Information on educational backgrounds was obtained directly from the schools and was checked against alumni registers when necessary and possible.

With few exceptions our older colleges and universities have taken
pride in the colleges they have founded or the college presidents they
have produced. For more than two centuries, it is true, the graduates of
Harvard took little part in the movement; having established one Collegiate
School (now Yale) in Connecticut, they perhaps felt they had done enough,
or even too much. The graduates of Yale, by contrast, almost from its beginnings showed a lively interest in college founding; and by 1905 Yale's
sons had first presided, or played a decisive role in the founding of,
some forty-one colleges and universities in this country. Beginning with
the College of New Jersey (Princeton 1746), King's College (Columbia 1754),
and Dartmouth College (1769), they were interrupted by the Revolution but
resumed their educational mission with the University of Georgia in 1785.
Thereafter Yale graduates became the first presidents of Williams and
Middlebury in New England; of Hamilton, Kenyon, and Western Reserve; of
Illinois and of Wabash; of Tulane and Missouri and Atlanta in the South;
of Beloit, the University of Wisconsin, and Washington in St. Louis.
When Cornell and Johns Hopkins and Chicago then pioneered the new univer-
sity movement, their first great building presidents proved to be gradu-
ates of Yale--as were also the first presidents of the Universities of
California, Oregon, and Arkansas, of Pomona and the University of Florida.

In its turn Yale's first offshoot, the College of New Jersey, became
the mother of colleges in the Midwest and the mid-South, many of them
with Presbyterian affiliation; and by 1896 Princeton could claim to have
supplied no fewer than seven founders and sixty-five college presidents
among its sons.

But now who presides over the nation's colleges and universities? In
an effort to take a representative sampling, 150 well-known colleges and
universities in the United States were listed and grouped in seven balanced categories so as to give adequate representation to the great private and public institutions, the state and city universities, the technological schools and Catholic colleges, and women's colleges as well.

Analysis of the presidents of these 150 institutions in 1961-62 showed
a wider distribution of undergraduate origins than had been expected, but a
very marked degree of graduate school concentration at Harvard, Columbia,
and Chicago. Yale College ranked second as a producer of presidents, and
Princeton tied for third, but on an over-all basis of university degrees
or connections their record was much less impressive. Examination of
Harvard's 28 graduate or professional connections identified 4 presidents
who had studied in Cambridge but taken no degree, 1 LL.B., 1 S.J.D., 2
M.B.A.'s, 2 M.D.'s, and 14 Ph.D.'s. Columbia's 17 graduate or professional
school alumni divided into 1 Med.Sci.D., 1 M.S., 4 M.A.'s, 5 Ph.D.'s, and
6 with both masters and doctors degrees. Of the 150 presidents of prominent colleges and universities in 1961-62, 20 per cent had studied at Harvard and almost 50 per cent at one or another of the first 5: Harvard,
Columbia, Chicago, Yale, and Michigan.

It might be added that, had a wider sampling of institutions been
taken, each of the leading universities could have improved its score.
Thus, in 1963 a count of living college presidents holding earned degrees

COLLEGE AND UNIVERSITY PRESIDENTS, 1961-62

Education of the presidents of 150 prominent colleges and universities in the United States. This quality sampling includes 20 private universities, 33 public (state and city) universities, 20 men's colleges, 25 co-educational colleges, 20 women's colleges, 16 technological institutions, 12 Catholic institutions, and 4 unclassified.

College or University	Undergraduate	Graduate or Professional	Net Total Individuals
HARVARD	7	28	30
COLUMBIA	3	17	18
CHICAGO	1	11	11
YALE	6	8	9
MICHIGAN	4	6	7
CALIFORNIA	2	6	6
NORTH CAROLINA	1	5	6
PRINCETON	4	4	6
WISCONSIN	1	6	6
JOHNS HOPKINS	1	5	5
Totals for 109 Other American Colleges and Universities	118	80	120
Foreign Colleges and Universities	17	29	30
Totals			
Individuals with Some Known College or University Connection	149	143	149
Unknown	-	-	1
Net Individuals			150

Sources: A list of institutions provided by Who's Who in America (60 top universities determined by the educational analysis of new names in volume 32 of Who's Who in America), and Lovejoy's Complete Guide to American Colleges and Universities, 1961-62.

from Yale showed 72 names; while, for the whole group of accredited institutions in the United States, a Harvard survey (cited in the May 17, 1965 <u>Newsletter</u> of the Harvard Graduate Society for Advanced Study and Research) identified 10 per cent of the presidents as Harvard graduates, many of them Harvard Ph.D.'s.

K-5. THE UNIVERSITIES AND THE LEARNED SOCIETIES, 1948, 1954, 1960

Some 17 universities and colleges seem to have contributed at least 10 officers or directors each to the 3 major learned societies--the National Research Council, S.S.R.C., and A.C.L.S.--and to their member societies for the years 1948, 1954, and 1960. However, only 7 institutions contributed as many as 20 officers, and the first 5 universities between them could claim a share in the education or teaching services of 166 out of the 211 individuals in this sampling.

A major factor in the imbalance had unquestionably been the concentration of graduate study at a very few universities, in particular at Harvard, Columbia, and Chicago. The faculty connections of the learned society officers were obviously much more widely distributed. Thus N.Y.U. at one time or another appointed 9 individuals to its faculty who had been, were, or would be officers of a learned society, but generated no such future office holders from its college. In the same way Smith College would achieve 6 connections with learned society leadership through its faculty, none through its alumnae. Calculations carried below the level of itemization in our table showed that U.C.L.A. and Washington University of St. Louis each employed or had employed 4 professors who also were or would be officers of the learned societies, while generating no such officers through either undergraduate or graduate instruction. Finally, the 145 other American institutions could claim 132 faculty connections but only 84 undergraduate connections, a difference of some 36 per cent.

At the undergraduate level the order of achievement was Harvard, Chicago and Yale, Princeton, Columbia and Cornell, Northwestern, Oberlin, and Minnesota--distinguished achievements for both Northwestern and the coeducational college of Oberlin.

192

THE UNIVERSITIES AND THE LEARNED SOCIETIES, 1948, 1954, 1960

The undergraduate and graduate education and faculty connections of the chief officers and directors of the National Research Council, Social Science Research Council, and American Council of Learned Societies for the years 1948, 1954, and 1960—together with the presidents of the member societies of the American Council of Learned Societies (24 in 1948, 28 in 1960) and the Social Science Research Council (7 throughout but 5 of these also in A.C.L.S.).

College or University	Undergraduate Connections	Graduate Connections	Faculty Connections	Net Total Individuals
HARVARD	18	52	34	67
COLUMBIA	8	30	28	46
CHICAGO	10	32	24	42
YALE	10	20	27	36
PRINCETON	9	11	21	29
WISCONSIN	4	7	13	22
CORNELL	8	8	16	21
JOHNS HOPKINS	2	9	11	18
NORTHWESTERN	7	7	9	17
PENNSYLVANIA	4	9	11	15
STANFORD	4	5	8	15
MICHIGAN	4	7	10	14
CALIFORNIA (Berkeley)	4	6	10	13
MINNESOTA	5	4	8	13
OHIO STATE	2	2	12	13
ILLINOIS	2	2	7	11
TEXAS	4	3	7	10
N.Y.U.	-	2	9	9
OBERLIN	6	4	2	8
INDIANA	1	2	6	7
IOWA STATE	3	1	4	7
NORTH CAROLINA	-	3	6	7
CLARK	1	3	2	6
M.I.T.	2	3	4	6
SMITH	-	-	6	6
VANDERBILT	1	1	5	6
AMHERST	3	-	4	5
BROWN	-	2	3	5
DARTMOUTH	3	-	2	5
IOWA	-	1	4	5
145 Other American Institutions	84	26	132	133
Foreign:				
OXFORD	7	9	4	13
PARIS	1	10	-	10
BERLIN	-	8	1	8
CAMBRIDGE	-	6	1	7
LONDON	1	6	2	7
TORONTO	3	3	4	7
45 Other Foreign Institutions	6	29	26	36
Unknown				1
Total Individuals				211

Among the American academies or societies which have honored distinction in learning, the American Philosophical Society may be regarded as not only the oldest but perhaps the most national in its horizons and impartial in its elections. The Academy of Arts and Sciences in Boston enrolls a great number of distinguished scholars and engineers, but the major emphasis on men living in the vicinity of Cambridge disqualifies it in some degree as a national register of talent. In New York, the National Institute of Arts and Letters and the Century Association focus on writers and artists, or on the practitioners and the amateurs of literature and the fine arts, with little attention to the sciences, pure or applied. More broadly conceived, the American Philosophical Society itself is not without some regional bias or geographic concentration. Certain metropolitan areas seem to be disproportionately represented. Thus, for 1964, we found some 57 members living in Philadelphia or the immediate environs, as against but 61 for New York, and 78 for Cambridge and Boston. Again, 39 members resided in Princeton and 14 in Baltimore, as against only 19 in Berkeley, 18 in Chicago, and 17 in New Haven. It may be a fair conclusion, therefore, that the location of the American Philosophical Society in Philadelphia, with the natural effects of propinquity and better acquaintance, have generated a modest regional preference in the elections to membership, which in turn may have had its institutional accompaniment.

Another bias, or rather distinct emphasis, in the American Philosophical Society membership should be remarked. In 1964, the membership was balanced as follows: mathematics and the physical sciences, 137; geology and the biological sciences, 129; the social sciences, 126; the humanities, 94. The emphasis on the physical and biological sciences, the noticeably large representation for the social sciences, and the distinct under-representation of the humanities (and the fine arts) may in their turn have contributed to the building up of substantial delegations from colleges and universities with a like emphasis.

Notwithstanding such reservations, the membership of the American Philosophical Society has evidently been drawn from most of the great universities, and in numbers (with the exception possibly of the University of Pennsylvania) only modestly out of proportion. One notes the pre-eminence of the great private universities but the appearance also of six state universities, plus Pennsylvania and Cornell, among the nineteen leaders. Our twentieth-century importations of scholars from England and the continent--or the attractions of Berlin, Cambridge, Oxford, Paris, and Göttingen for American-born scholars--are also suggested in the figures. Altogether, almost one quarter of the total membership proved to have had some educational training at Harvard. Disregarding duplications, another quarter had studied at either Columbia, Princeton, or Yale. Still another (overlapping) quarter had enrolled at Pennsylvania, Johns Hopkins, M.I.T., Cornell, Brown, or N.Y.U.; and an equivalent number had achieved at least a part of their education in the Middle or Far West.

Educational backgrounds of the living members of the American
Philosophical Society in 1964.

College or University	Undergraduate Connections	Graduate or Professional	Net Total Individuals
HARVARD	60	100	119
COLUMBIA	17	45	50
PENNSYLVANIA	19	39	42
CHICAGO	14	36	39
PRINCETON	20	25	36
YALE	18	26	36
JOHNS HOPKINS	7	28	28
CALIFORNIA (Berkeley)	9	25	26
WISCONSIN	11	14	21
M.I.T.	10	13	17
CORNELL	7	10	14
MICHIGAN	8	9	13
ILLINOIS	6	10	12
MINNESOTA	8	10	12
BROWN	9	6	10
CAL. TECH.	4	8	10
N.Y.U.	5	4	8
STANFORD	7	4	8
MISSOURI	7	5	7
138 Other American Institutions	204	88	199
Foreign:			
BERLIN	3	15	18
CAMBRIDGE	3	15	18
OXFORD	1	18	18
PARIS	2	11	13
GÖTTINGEN	1	9	10
80 Other Foreign Institutions	30	109	92
Unknown			3
Net Total Individuals			486

Sources: American Philosophical Society Yearbook, 1964 (Philadelphia,
1965), and Who's Who in America.

K-7. HUMANISTIC SCHOLARSHIP--A.C.L.S. PRIZE AWARDS, 1958-62-- EDUCATION OF THE 50 SCHOLARS

Education of the 50 scholars awarded $10,000 each by the American Council of Learned Societies for the "distinguished accomplishment in humanistic scholarship" 1958-62.

College or University	Undergraduate Connections	Graduate or Professional	Net Total Individuals
HARVARD	7	13	16
COLUMBIA	1	5	5
CORNELL	2	4	5
CHICAGO	3	3	4
MICHIGAN	3	0	3
YALE	0	3	3
BRYN MAWR	0	2	2
HAMILTON	2	0	2
ILLINOIS	0	2	2
JOHNS HOPKINS	0	2	2
PRINCETON	0	2	2
28 Other American Colleges and Universities	19	13	18
26 Foreign Colleges and Universities	18	29	27
Net Total Individuals	45	47	50

The 50 A.C.L.S. Prize Awards of $10,000 each represented for the American academic world the recognition of singular distinction in humanistic scholarship. One notes in our table above the outstanding production of humanists by both Harvard College and the Harvard graduate or professional schools. Also the strong presence of British and continental universities: Our humanistic scholarship was still drawing inspiration from abroad.

Sources: Who's Who in America and The Directory of American Scholars.

K-8. HUMANISTIC SCHOLARSHIP--A.C.L.S. PRIZE AWARDS, 1958-62--
FACULTY CONNECTIONS OF THE 50 SCHOLARS

Faculty connections of the 50 scholars awarded $10,000 each by the American Council of Learned Societies for their "distinguished accomplishment in humanistic scholarship," 1958-62.

College or University	Faculty at Time of Award	Other Previous Faculty Memberships	Net Total Individuals
HARVARD	8	2	10
COLUMBIA	6	3	9
YALE	8	1	8
CHICAGO	3	4	7
PRINCETON	5	2	7
BRYN MAWR	3	2	5
JOHNS HOPKINS	3	1	4
CALIFORNIA	2	1	3
MICHIGAN	1	2	3
MINNESOTA	-	3	3
SMITH	1	2	3
TEXAS	1	2	3
VASSAR	-	3	3
CATHOLIC U.	1	1	2
CORNELL	-	2	2
ILLINOIS	-	2	2
IOWA	-	2	2
LOUISVILLE	-	2	2
N.Y.U.	2	-	2
PENNSYLVANIA	1	1	2
STANFORD	1	1	2
WISCONSIN	1	1	2

6 Other Colleges and Universities, Including 1 Foreign	6	16 Other American Colleges and Universities	16	21 Other American Colleges and Universities	21
		17 Foreign Colleges and Universities	19	18 Foreign Colleges and Universities	20
Total Connections at Time of Award	53	Total Previous Faculty Connects.	86	Net Total Faculty Connections	139

These two tables on the A.C.L.S. Awards in the Humanities suggest a rather significant magnetization of talent and distinction at certain leading universities. At the time of the awards, 27 of the 50 scholars were members of the faculties of Harvard, Yale, Columbia, or Princeton. The table on educational backgrounds showed a wider distribution in general, balanced by the tremendous individual contribution of Harvard. In a combined analysis we discover that Harvard had had some connection, at either the undergraduate or graduate or faculty level, with 20 of the 50 individuals laureated by the A.C.L.S. On the same basis Chicago, Columbia, and Yale could show 10 connections each, Oxford 9, Princeton 7; Berlin, Bryn Mawr, and Cornell, each 5; California, Michigan, and Minnesota, 4; Illinois, Prague (Charles U.), Smith, Vassar, and Wisconsin, each 3.

Sources: Who's Who in America and Directory of American Scholars.

197

On a number of occasions within the memory of those still teaching,
the scholars and administrators of our leading graduate universities have
attempted to assess the excellence of their competitive faculties, department by department--the pooled scores from these questionnaires or opinion
polls constituting a kind of over-all judgment or comparative rating for
all the faculties involved. On each occasion, needless to say, the results have been awaited with some anxiety. To a scholar the reputation of
his department among the many disciplines within his own university is of
substantial importance. But perhaps more important still is the reputation of his department in his own profession, nationally and abroad. For
beyond the matter of pride looms the effect of such ratings on the flow of
students and of budgetary support. Depending upon the rating given to his
department, it may become harder or easier to attract able colleagues or
financial assistance from the major foundations.

Our office has attempted to study and to relate the three most famous
of these studies, the Hughes survey of 1925, the Keniston ratings of 1957,
and the recently published "Assessment" of 1964 for the American Council
on Education.

Scholar and layman alike, of course, should be wary of giving too
much credence to the numerical scores in any of these surveys. The equiva-
lence between opinions and numbers is never exact. The quantitative addition of numerical quality ratings may ultimately greatly exaggerate or
greatly underestimate the differences between any two departments. In
sober reality, opinion polls, even in non-numerical terms, are no more
than approximate judgments; and they are sometimes in serious error.
Finally, the public reputation of a university or department may on occasion lag years behind its actual condition. A law school, for example,
may not gain public recognition as the most distinguished of its kind
until it has already been at or near the top for as much as ten or twenty
years--and it may retain the prestige of greatness when it is already a
decade past its prime. And even the knowledge of rival faculties in the
arts and sciences tends generally to be a little or considerably out-of-
date. Scholars themselves, particularly in the more specialized and rapid-
ly advancing fields, find it next to impossible to keep up with changes in
personnel at more than a handful of the most conspicuous institutions.
All of which is to say that the comparative ratings in the tables here
given should be understood as no more than very rough approximations of
quasi-informed opinions accumulated from incomplete samplings and by imperfect means in the months immediately preceding their study and publication.

Such reservations notwithstanding, the three surveys of 1925, 1957,
and 1964 emphasize on an over-all basis the extraordinary rise and spectacular distinction of the University of California at Berkeley, and ex-
plain why many of the Harvard faculty have in recent years come to regard
California as their chief rival. In a special summary review of "Patterns
of Quality in Universities" (pp. 106-07), Allan Cartter attempted to list
the highest rated universities in each of the five general divisions--
humanities, social sciences, biological sciences, physical sciences, and

COMPARATIVE RATINGS OF THE UNIVERSITY GRADUATE SCHOOLS, 1925, 1957, 1964

This table attempts to correlate the results of three independent investigations or self-evaluations by the leading universities of the country, spaced across forty years. The first of these now classic studies was reported by R. M. Hughes in A Study of the Graduate Schools of America (Miami University, 1925). The second or 1957 study was made as a part of a survey of the graduate school of the University of Pennsylvania and was reported by Hayward Keniston (together with recalculated figures for 1925) in Graduate Study and Research in the Arts and Sciences at the University of Pennsylvania (University of Pennsylvania Press, 1959), pp. 115-50. The third survey of graduate education was made for the American Council on Education by its Commission on Plans and Objectives for Higher Education, under the direction of Allan M. Cartter in the year 1964, and was published as An Assessment of Quality in Graduate Education (American Council on Education, Washington, D.C., 1966).

The emphasis of the first two surveys was on the strength of the departments, i.e., presumably on a combination of faculty distinction and quality of graduate program. The 1964 Assessment separated these two, and emphasized the ratings on the faculty distinction, which we have followed here.

Each of these surveys used its own scoring system and its own classification of departments within the major divisions of graduate instruction. To make their ratings more nearly comparable, we have undertaken to retabulate all three studies on the basis of the following scoring system: 15 points for the top department, 14 for the second, etc. In the same interest, the groupings of departments within the major divisions of study have been revised, wherever necessary, to make them conform. Particular discrepancies are noted in the individual tables. I am obliged to Dr. Allan M. Cartter of the American Council on Education for permission to see and to use the ACE tables prior to publication. For the rearrangement of his statistics and for any deviations from his published figures, I am entirely responsible.

Number of Departments in the Top Ten

1925		1957		1964	
CHICAGO	18	CALIFORNIA	24	CALIFORNIA	24
HARVARD	18	HARVARD	23	HARVARD	23
COLUMBIA	17	YALE	22	WISCONSIN	17
YALE	16	MICHIGAN	21	MICHIGAN	16
MICHIGAN	15	COLUMBIA	20	STANFORD	15
JOHNS HOPKINS	13	CHICAGO	19	YALE	15
PRINCETON	13	CORNELL	15	COLUMBIA	14
WISCONSIN	12	PRINCETON	14	PRINCETON	14
CORNELL	11	WISCONSIN	14	CHICAGO	13
ILLINOIS	11	ILLINOIS	9	CORNELL	9
CALIFORNIA	10	MINNESOTA	9	CAL. TECH.	8
PENNSYLVANIA	8	PENNSYLVANIA	9	ILLINOIS	7
CAL. TECH.	2	INDIANA	7	M.I.T.	7
IOWA	2	JOHNS HOPKINS	6	PENNSYLVANIA	7
M.I.T.	2	U.C.L.A.	6	JOHNS HOPKINS	6
NORTHWESTERN	2	STANFORD	4	MINNESOTA	6
Five Others	1	N.Y.U.	3	U.C.L.A.	6
		OHIO STATE	3	INDIANA	5
		WASHINGTON (Seattle)	3	ROCKEFELLER INST.	4
		IOWA	2	TEXAS	3
		NORTH CAROLINA	2	CALIFORNIA (Davis)	2
		NORTHWESTERN	2	IOWA	2
		TEXAS	2	NORTH CAROLINA	2
				OHIO STATE	2
				WASHINGTON (Seattle)	2
				Twenty Others	1

engineering--and stated: "California, Berkeley, appears in the leading group in all five divisions, a finding which supports the claim that it is the best balanced distinguished university in the country. Harvard and Stanford appear in four divisions; Columbia, Illinois, Yale, Princeton, Michigan, and Cal. Tech. in three; and M.I.T., Chicago, and Wisconsin in two." Yet it should be noted that Cartter's figures show Harvard leading California in each of the four major divisions of the arts and sciences, while trailing only in engineering.

These tables emphasize, in the second place, the remarkable expansion of the higher scholarship in this country, the growth in the number of substantial universities, and the very large growth in the number of excellent departments in the several major areas of graduate instruction. Ineluctably, the difficulty for any single university of ranking in the first ten departments in any given science or discipline has been steadily increasing--a fortiori the difficulty of fielding any great number of departments all of which rate in the top ten of their kind--as witness the marked decline in the number of top-ranked departments reported in 1964 for Michigan, Yale, Columbia, and Chicago.

A third point of interest attaches to the shifts in relative standing for certain universities across forty years. Observers acquainted with the history of twentieth-century scholarship in this country will not be surprised at Chicago's excellent showing in the 1925 survey, its somewhat more moderate success since. From the ACE:1964 study one may gather that no third university can today compare, either in the number of distinguished departments or in total scores, with Harvard and California. The same survey suggests that Columbia may have been going through a moderate depression, and that Yale's precarious hold on third place (table of Overall Scores) will soon be lost if it is unable to recoup its losses and increase once again the number of its outstanding departments.

Two technical omissions of some importance should be underlined. The earlier surveys did not include departments of engineering or such "state schools" as Penn State, Iowa State, or Michigan State; and the Keniston survey omitted also M.I.T. and California Institute of Technology. For purposes of fair comparison the engineering ratings of the ACE:1964 survey have therefore been cancelled out, to produce the scores given in our 1964 tables. How the universities would have ranked in numbers of departments in the top ten, and in over-all scores, had the engineering departments been included for 1964, is indicated by the following figures.

HUMANITIES*

1925		1957		1964		Average	
HARVARD	102	HARVARD	146	HARVARD	99	HARVARD	116
COLUMBIA	90	YALE	129	CALIFORNIA	93	COLUMBIA	95
CHICAGO	82	COLUMBIA	128	YALE	82	YALE	93
PRINCETON	68	CALIFORNIA	118	PRINCETON	78	CALIFORNIA	87
YALE	68	MICHIGAN	96	COLUMBIA	67	PRINCETON	74
JOHNS HOPKINS	61	PRINCETON	75	MICHIGAN	55	MICHIGAN	66
CORNELL	53	CHICAGO	61	WISCONSIN	47	CHICAGO	63
PENNSYLVANIA	53	PENNSYLVANIA	61	CHICAGO	46	CORNELL	51
CALIFORNIA	51	CORNELL	60	CORNELL	40	PENNSYLVANIA	50
WISCONSIN	50	WISCONSIN	51	PENNSYLVANIA	37	WISCONSIN	49
MICHIGAN	46	ILLINOIS	45	STANFORD	29	JOHNS HOPKINS	40
ILLINOIS	38	JOHNS HOPKINS	31	JOHNS HOPKINS	27	ILLINOIS	34
BRYN MAWR	25	N.Y.U.	30	U.C.L.A.	27	U.C.L.A.	16
MINNESOTA	12	INDIANA	28	ILLINOIS	19	INDIANA	15
NORTHWESTERN	10	WASHINGTON (Seattle)	23	TEXAS	19	STANFORD	15
STANFORD	9	U.C.L.A.	22	INDIANA	18	BRYN MAWR	14
OHIO STATE	7	MINNESOTA	18	NORTH CAROLINA	13	NORTH CAROLINA	12
NORTH CAROLINA	6	NORTH CAROLINA	18	BRYN MAWR	12	MINNESOTA	11

*In the area of the Humanities all three surveys included Classics, English, German, Philosophy--also the Romance Languages, which the 1964 survey separated into French and Spanish. Keniston also classified History under Humanities, so the ACE:1964 scores for History have been transferred from its Social Sciences classification into the present table. We found it impossible to correct for one difference: The 1957 study included departments of Fine Arts, Linguistics, Music, Oriental Studies, and Slavic Languages-- all of which the two other surveys omitted.

SOCIAL SCIENCES**

1925		1957		1964		Average	
CHICAGO	70	CHICAGO	85	CALIFORNIA	77	CHICAGO	74
HARVARD	65	CALIFORNIA	84	HARVARD	72	HARVARD	73
COLUMBIA	58	HARVARD	82	CHICAGO	66	CALIFORNIA	60
WISCONSIN	52	MICHIGAN	75	MICHIGAN	57	MICHIGAN	60
MICHIGAN	48	COLUMBIA	68	WISCONSIN	53	COLUMBIA	56
YALE	31	YALE	67	YALE	49	WISCONSIN	49
JOHNS HOPKINS	29	WISCONSIN	43	COLUMBIA	42	YALE	49
ILLINOIS	26	CORNELL	42	STANFORD	42	MINNESOTA	30
CORNELL	23	MINNESOTA	42	MINNESOTA	30	CORNELL	29
PENNSYLVANIA	23	STANFORD	27	U.C.L.A.	28	STANFORD	26
PRINCETON	21	U.C.L.A.	27	PRINCETON	27	PRINCETON	23
CALIFORNIA	19	PENNSYLVANIA	26	M.I.T.	22	PENNSYLVANIA	22
MINNESOTA	19	NORTHWESTERN	25	CORNELL	21	ILLINOIS	19
IOWA	17	WASHINGTON (Seattle)	25	NORTHWESTERN	20	U.C.L.A.	18
CLARK	15	INDIANA	22	PENNSYLVANIA	18	NORTHWESTERN	16
STANFORD	10	ILLINOIS	21	WASHINGTON (Seattle)	15	JOHNS HOPKINS	15
MISSOURI	9	PRINCETON	20	SYRACUSE	11	WASHINGTON (Seattle)	13
OHIO STATE	8	JOHNS HOPKINS	13	ILLINOIS	10	IOWA	11
		OHIO STATE	13				

**All three surveys of the Social Sciences included Economics, Political Science, and Sociology; and the two later surveys also rated departments of Anthropology. The ACE:1964 study originally classified History under the Social Sciences; but, for purposes of comparison, the scores obtained for this subject have been transferred to the Humanities. Reciprocally, the scores for Psychology which the ACE:1964 study placed under the Biological Sciences have been transferred into its Social Sciences tabulation to match the 1957 classi-fication; while Geography, which the Keniston survey placed under the Physical Sciences, has been transferred into its Social Sciences tabulation to accord with ACE:1964 and the more normal classification of this subject.

PHYSICAL SCIENCES*

1925		1957		1964		Average	
CHICAGO	71	HARVARD	70	HARVARD	69	HARVARD	68
HARVARD	65	CALIFORNIA	69	CALIFORNIA	68	CALIFORNIA	61
YALE	58	CHICAGO	57	CAL. TECH.	58	CHICAGO	55
PRINCETON	49	PRINCETON	52	PRINCETON	53	PRINCETON	51
CALIFORNIA	46	COLUMBIA	50	M.I.T.	43	YALE	46
WISCONSIN	41	YALE	45	STANFORD	41	COLUMBIA	42
COLUMBIA	40	MICHIGAN	40	CHICAGO	38	WISCONSIN	36
MICHIGAN	33	WISCONSIN	37	COLUMBIA	37	MICHIGAN	30
CORNELL	30	ILLINOIS	34	YALE	35	STANFORD	27
JOHNS HOPKINS	30	STANFORD	28	WISCONSIN	31	CAL. TECH.	27
CAL. TECH.	23	CORNELL	25	ILLINOIS	23	ILLINOIS	26
M.I.T.	22	MINNESOTA	16	MICHIGAN	17	CORNELL	23
ILLINOIS	21	OHIO STATE	14	CORNELL	15	M.I.T.	22
STANFORD	13	NORTHWESTERN	11	U.C.L.A.	13	JOHNS HOPKINS	15
MINNESOTA	12	INDIANA	10	N.Y.U.	8	MINNESOTA	11
NORTHWESTERN	9	JOHNS HOPKINS	10	PENN STATE	8	NORTHWESTERN	7
OHIO STATE	4	PENNSYLVANIA	10	TEXAS	5	U.C.L.A.	7
PENNSYLVANIA	4	N.Y.U.	8	JOHNS HOPKINS	4	OHIO STATE	6
		U.C.L.A.	8	MINNESOTA	4		

*In the area of the Physical Sciences all three surveys listed the departments of Astronomy, Chemistry, Geology, Mathematics, and Physics. Keniston also included Geography which has, however, in our tables been transferred to the Social Sciences.

BIOLOGICAL SCIENCES**

1925		1957		1964		Average	
CHICAGO	29	HARVARD	30	CALIFORNIA	89	HARVARD	47
COLUMBIA	29	CALIFORNIA	28	HARVARD	83	CALIFORNIA	43
HARVARD	27	WISCONSIN	22	WISCONSIN	54	WISCONSIN	32
JOHNS HOPKINS	20	INDIANA	20	ROCKEFELLER INST.	53	MICHIGAN	25
CORNELL	19	YALE	20	STANFORD	43	JOHNS HOPKINS	23
WISCONSIN	19	MICHIGAN	17	MICHIGAN	40	ILLINOIS	22
MICHIGAN	18	COLUMBIA	14	ILLINOIS	39	CORNELL	20
ILLINOIS	17	CORNELL	14	JOHNS HOPKINS	39	YALE	20
YALE	14	PENNSYLVANIA	12	CAL. TECH.	37	STANFORD	19
CALIFORNIA	12	U.C.L.A.	12	MINNESOTA	30	COLUMBIA	19
MINNESOTA	10	ILLINOIS	11	CORNELL	26	ROCKEFELLER INST.	18
PRINCETON	10	JOHNS HOPKINS	10	YALE	25	MINNESOTA	16
STANFORD	8	MINNESOTA	8	PENNSYLVANIA	21	CHICAGO	15
BRYN MAWR	3	PRINCETON	7	CALIFORNIA (Davis)	20	INDIANA	13
OHIO STATE	3	CHICAGO	6	INDIANA	20	CAL. TECH.	12
PENNSYLVANIA	3	DUKE	5	WASHINGTON (Seattle)	19	PENNSYLVANIA	12
MISSOURI	1	STANFORD	4	U.C.L.A.	17	U.C.L.A.	10
		OHIO STATE	3	COLUMBIA	13	PRINCETON	7

**In the area of the Biological Sciences all three surveys rated departments of Botany and Zoology. The ACE:1964 study also included ratings for Bacteriology/Microbiology, Biochemistry, Entomology, Pharmacology, and Physiology. As stated above, the ACE:1964 study likewise classified Psychology under the Biological Sciences, but its scores for this subject have been transferred in our tables to the Social Sciences.

OVER-ALL SCORES*

1925		1957		1964		Average	
HARVARD	259	HARVARD	328	CALIFORNIA	327	HARVARD	303
CHICAGO	252	CALIFORNIA	299	HARVARD	323	CALIFORNIA	251
COLUMBIA	217	YALE	261	YALE	191	COLUMBIA	212
YALE	171	COLUMBIA	260	WISCONSIN	185	YALE	208
WISCONSIN	162	MICHIGAN	228	MICHIGAN	169	CHICAGO	207
PRINCETON	148	CHICAGO	209	PRINCETON	163	MICHIGAN	181
MICHIGAN	145	PRINCETON	154	CHICAGO	160	WISCONSIN	167
JOHNS HOPKINS	140	WISCONSIN	153	COLUMBIA	159	PRINCETON	155
CALIFORNIA	128	CORNELL	141	STANFORD	155	CORNELL	123
CORNELL	125	ILLINOIS	111	CORNELL	102	ILLINOIS	101
ILLINOIS	102	PENNSYLVANIA	109	CAL. TECH.	95	JOHNS HOPKINS	92
PENNSYLVANIA	83	MINNESOTA	84	ILLINOIS	91	PENNSYLVANIA	90
MINNESOTA	53	INDIANA	80	U.C.L.A.	85	STANFORD	87
STANFORD	40	U.C.L.A.	69	PENNSYLVANIA	77	MINNESOTA	68
BRYN MAWR	30	STANFORD	66	M.I.T.	75	U.C.L.A.	51
CAL. TECH.	23	JOHNS HOPKINS	64	JOHNS HOPKINS	72	INDIANA	41
IOWA	22	WASHINGTON (Seattle)	52	MINNESOTA	67	CAL. TECH.	39
M.I.T.	22	NORTHWESTERN	47	ROCKEFELLER INST.	53	M.I.T.	32
OHIO STATE	22	N.Y.U.	38	INDIANA	44	NORTHWESTERN	31
NORTHWESTERN	21	OHIO STATE	37	TEXAS	35	WASHINGTON (Seattle)	29
CLARK	15	NORTH CAROLINA	26	WASHINGTON (Seattle)	34	OHIO STATE	25
NORTH CAROLINA	13	IOWA	20	NORTHWESTERN	25	NORTH CAROLINA	20
MISSOURI	10	TEXAS	14	CALIFORNIA (Davis)	20	IOWA	19
		DUKE	10	NORTH CAROLINA	20	ROCKEFELLER INST.	18
		BRYN MAWR	4	IOWA	16	N.Y.U.	17
				OHIO STATE	16	TEXAS	16
				BROWN	14	BRYN MAWR	15
				BRYN MAWR	12	CALIFORNIA (Davis)	7
				N.Y.U.	12	DUKE	7
				WESTERN RESERVE	12	CLARK	5
				KANSAS	11	BROWN	5
				SYRACUSE	11	WESTERN RESERVE	4
				UTAH	11	KANSAS	4
				DUKE	10	SYRACUSE	4
				YESHIVA	9	UTAH	4
				EMORY	8	MISSOURI	3
				PENN STATE	8	YESHIVA	3
				PITTSBURGH	8	EMORY	3
				PURDUE	8	PENN STATE	3
				BRANDEIS	7	PITTSBURGH	3
				IOWA STATE	7	PURDUE	3
				ROCHESTER	7	BRANDEIS	2
				WASHINGTON (St. L.)	7	IOWA STATE	2
				CINCINNATI	6	ROCHESTER	2
				KANSAS STATE	6	WASHINGTON (St. L.)	2
				LOUISIANA STATE	6	CINCINNATI	2
				ARIZONA	4	KANSAS STATE	2
				CARNEGIE TECH.	3	LOUISIANA STATE	2
				MICHIGAN STATE	2	ARIZONA	1
						CARNEGIE TECH.	1
						MICHIGAN STATE	1

*The Hughes and Keniston surveys did not include departments of Engineering, hence Engineering has been dropped from the ACE:1964 figures. The two earlier surveys also left out of account such "state schools" as Penn State, Iowa State, or Michigan State. The Keniston survey also excluded M.I.T. and California Institute of Technology, two institutions of limited range but of marked excellence in certain categories of graduate study--an omission which prejudices their over-all average score in the last column.

Number of Departments in Top Ten		Over-all Scores	
CALIFORNIA	28	CALIFORNIA	378
HARVARD	25	HARVARD	339
MICHIGAN	20	WISCONSIN	210
STANFORD	19	MICHIGAN	203
WISCONSIN	18	STANFORD	199
COLUMBIA	16	YALE	191
PRINCETON	15	PRINCETON	177
YALE	15	COLUMBIA	174
CHICAGO	13	CHICAGO	160
CAL. TECH.	12	CAL. TECH.	139
ILLINOIS	11	M.I.T.	132
M.I.T.	11	ILLINOIS	131
CORNELL	10	CORNELL	116
MINNESOTA	8	MINNESOTA	92
PENNSYLVANIA	7	U.C.L.A.	85
JOHNS HOPKINS	6	PENNSYLVANIA	80
U.C.L.A.	6	JOHNS HOPKINS	76
		ROCKEFELLER INSTITUTE	53
		INDIANA	44
		TEXAS	43
		NORTHWESTERN	41

In his review of the "Patterns of Quality in Universities," Allan Cartter noted a number of interesting concentrations. "For example, of the eight departments at Chicago receiving 'Distinguished' ratings, six are in the social sciences. M.I.T. has seven of its nine 'Distinguished' ratings in engineering and the physical sciences; Cal. Tech. has six of its eight in those areas. Eight of Stanford's ten 'Distinguished' departments are in the sciences and engineering, while seven of Yale's ten are in humanities and social sciences."

One final comment may be in order. Readers of the ACE An Assessment of Quality in Graduate Education will find in it a set of parallel tables scoring the leading departments "by rated effectiveness of graduate program." These tables were based on a section of the ACE questionnaire asking how each responding scholar would rate the universities in his field in attractiveness for study for the Ph.D. Respondents were asked to take into account the accessibility of faculty as well as their scholarly competence, the character of the curriculum, the educational and research facilities, the quality of graduate students, and other factors contributing to the effectiveness of the doctoral program. On this basis the private universities frequently seem to have improved their ranking while the public universities and especially the city universities suffered a decline. Thus in English, by rated quality of graduate faculty, Columbia and Chicago ranked fifth and sixth but by rated effectiveness of graduate program they dropped to seventh and tenth, while Stanford rose from seventh to fifth, Cornell from eighth to sixth, and Johns Hopkins from eleventh to eighth. By the same criterion, California (Berkeley) dropped in classics from second to third, in French from fourth to fifth, in German from first to third, in anthropology from third to fourth, in history from

second to third, and in sociology from first to second. In Allan
Cartter's interpretation "departments in the larger and somewhat more
impersonal universities generally fared less well" on this question of
effectiveness of program. One suspects that stiffer attitudes toward
marginal students and the M.A. degree, with concentration on the doctorate in some of the private universities, as against the unavoidable
admixture of large numbers of courses and students for the M.A. in certain of the city and state universities, also has a good deal to do with
it. At all events a cumulative rating by effectiveness of graduate program would show the following results for the Humanities:

HARVARD	99	STANFORD	38
CALIFORNIA	88	PENNSYLVANIA	36
YALE	88	JOHNS HOPKINS	32
PRINCETON	83	NORTH CAROLINA	20
MICHIGAN	58	INDIANA	19
COLUMBIA	52	U.C.L.A.	17
CORNELL	44	TEXAS	16
WISCONSIN	42	BRYN MAWR	12
CHICAGO	40	ILLINOIS	12

THE PROMISE OF LEADERSHIP IN
EDUCATION AND SCHOLARSHIP

Thus far our tables have concentrated on established leadership, on men elected to higher office, awarded distinguished medals, or rated preeminent in their professions and vocations by their contemporaries and by those who came after. Of such groups of outstanding individuals we have asked where they went to college or to graduate or professional school. The effort has been to deal as far as possible with the leaders of our society in the immediate or recent past. And the statistical results speak in many accents (yet often give the same message).

Unfortunately the leaders of today or of yesterday are almost necessarily men in their fifties and sixties or even older, hence graduates already thirty to fifty years out of college. So one wonders whether the statistical message can after all be related with any accuracy to present circumstance. Are the major colleges and universities of 1966 still producing as they did in 1926 and 1936? Is there any reliable way of judging promise of leadership?

Of course we do not know who will be the leaders of tomorrow. Strictly speaking, the most we can hope to do is to imagine from what groups the majority of such leaders may emerge. But are there any ways of identifying such groups? It occurred to our office that if we could catch the intending scholar not just at the absolute beginning of his career but somewhere a little farther along--say, at the achievement of his Ph.D., or the winning of prizes and fellowships, or the election to scientific societies--we might perhaps be able to make, not a reliable prediction, but an educated guess as to the sources of tomorrow's leadership in education and scholarship. Accordingly, we have put together a small series of tables aimed at penetrating the mists that to a degree still obscure the comparative performances of our colleges and universities since World War II.

One rather interesting way of measuring the continuing output of
talent from our colleges, much of it destined to go into teaching either
at the college or preparatory school level, was to study the award of
Rhodes Scholarships in the 60 years since their establishment. Investigation promptly showed that for many years Princeton was the preeminent
producer of Rhodes Scholars (with the Harvard law or graduate schools a
not unlikely point of return). By 1954 no fewer than 84 Rhodes Scholars
had taken their B.A.'s at Princeton, to 77 at Harvard and 76 at Yale.
Given Princeton's smaller enrollments, this represented a noteworthy
achievement. In the last 10 years, however, Harvard has surged ahead,
while Yale still finds itself in third place. Year in and year out Princeton has almost invariably produced a respectable delegation of Rhodes
Scholars, missing out entirely only in 3 years. Yale also missed out
only 3 times, but its representation showed wider variations. Harvard
failed to place a man on 5 occasions.

RHODES SCHOLARS, 1904-64

Yearly election of Rhodes Scholars from the three leading colleges and from all others. Each Rhodes Scholar has been credited to the institution of his undergraduate affiliation.

Year	Harvard	Princeton	Yale	Other U.S. Colleges	Total
1904	1	1	0	41	43
1905	1	2	1	34	38
1907	2	1	2	40	45
1908	0	1	2	42	45
1910	1	1	1	41	44
1911	1	1	3	41	46
1913	2	1	1	39	43
1914	1	5	1	40	47
1916	1	0	1	30	32
1917	0	1	1	26	28
1918	0	1	1	29	31
1919	2	1	1	32	36
1920	1	2	2	26	31
1921	1	0	0	32	33
1922	3	2	2	25	32
1923	1	5	2	24	32
1924	3	2	1	28	34
1925	2	3	1	25	31
1926	2	3	1	27	33
1927	1	4	1	27	33
1928	0	2	3	28	33
1929	2	1	4	26	33
1931	1	2	1	29	33
1932	3	1	0	28	32
1933	2	4	1	26	33
1934	3	3	4	22	32
1935	1	2	4	25	32
1936	1	2	2	27	32
1937	2	4	1	25	32
1938	4	1	1	26	32
1939	0	2	2	27	31
1947	3	5	1	38	47
1948	2	6	4	36	48
1949	4	0	2	25	31
1950	2	3	4	23	32
1951	2	3	4	23	32
1952	3	3	4	22	32
1953	3	2	5	22	32
1954	4	2	4	22	32
1955	4	3	2	23	32
1956	4	3	1	24	32
1957	3	4	3	21	32
1958	4	3	2	23	32
1959	5	3	1	23	32
1960	7	3	5	17	32
1961	4	1	4	23	32
1962	6	3	4	19	32
1963	4	2	2	24	32
1964	6	3	2	21	32
Total	115	113	102	1,367	1,698

K-11. RHODES SCHOLARS FROM HARVARD, PRINCETON, AND
YALE BY STATES OF APPOINTMENT, 1904-64

The breakdown of Rhodes Scholars by states of appointment and by recent years gives clues not only to Harvard's upsurge but to the concentration or comparative distribution of the selected students by state of
appointment since the Rhodes scholarships were begun. Thus it would appear that Harvard has recently fielded strong delegations from Massachusetts, Maine, New York, Utah, and Oregon (the last two states having
produced virtually no Rhodes Scholars in the earlier years). The over-
all count shows that Connecticut has contributed the largest number of
Scholars (most of them through Yale), while Princeton and Harvard have
each benefited from, or given strength to, their own states.

With a smaller grand total Yale has seemingly had the widest distribution, having been unrepresented in only eleven states against fourteen
for Harvard and fifteen for Princeton.

Only Nevada and West Virginia have never produced a Rhodes Scholar
for anyone, but Vermont has produced just one. Six states in the north
central and southern regions have produced only two each, while Maine,
Utah, Oregon, and New Hampshire have only recently achieved real representation. Whether these contrasting performances reflect the origins of the
student bodies of Harvard, Princeton, and Yale, or the genuine scarcity of
talent in certain areas, or recent efforts of the adjudicating committees
to encourage the underdeveloped states, is not altogether clear. Whatever
the explanation, the benefits have accrued to the seniors of Harvard.

Between them in the last 10 years Harvard, Princeton, and Yale have
produced 102 out of 320, or almost 32 per cent of the total for the country as a whole (in contrast to 16.6 per cent for the first 50 years).

A study made in 1960 (quoted in The New York Times, April 6, 1961)
showed that up to that time the next most productive colleges had been
U.S. Military Academy, Dartmouth, Virginia, Brown, Wisconsin, Reed,
Williams, Michigan, and Washington--with scores ranging from forty-five
down to twenty.

RHODES SCHOLARS FROM HARVARD, PRINCETON, AND YALE
BY STATES OF APPOINTMENT, 1904-64

State	Recent Appointments 1955-64				Cumulative Appointments 1904-64			
	Harvard	Princeton	Yale	Total Scholars from H.P.Y.	Harvard	Princeton	Yale	Total Scholars from H.P.Y.
Connecticut	0	2	1	3	0	3	29	32
New Jersey	0	6	2	8	0	28	3	31
Massachusetts	6	1	1	8	21	3	2	26
New York	3	1	3	7	6	7	5	18
Florida	2	0	1	3	4	5	2	11
Maryland	1	0	0	1	4	5	2	11
Texas	2	1	0	3	3	4	4	11
Colorado	0	0	1	1	1	2	7	10
Illinois	1	1	1	3	6	2	2	10
Missouri	0	1	1	2	3	3	3	9
Delaware	0	0	0	0	1	6	1	8
Michigan	2	1	1	4	5	2	1	8
Pennsylvania	0	4	1	5	1	6	1	8
Indiana	0	0	1	1	4	1	2	7
Ohio	0	1	2	3	0	5	2	7
Virginia	1	0	1	2	1	2	4	7
Wisconsin	1	2	0	3	2	4	1	7
California	2	0	3	5	2	1	3	6
Louisiana	0	1	1	2	0	5	1	6
Oklahoma	1	0	2	3	3	0	3	6
Rhode Island	2	1	0	3	4	1	1	6
South Carolina	0	0	1	1	0	1	5	6
Arkansas	1	0	0	1	3	1	1	5
Georgia	0	1	0	1	2	2	1	5
Kansas	2	0	0	2	3	0	2	5
Utah	3	0	0	3	4	1	0	5
Iowa	1	0	0	1	3	0	1	4
Maine	3	0	0	3	4	0	0	4
New Hampshire	2	0	1	3	3	0	1	4
Oregon	3	0	0	3	3	0	1	4
Washington	2	0	0	2	2	1	1	4
Arizona	0	0	0	0	2	0	1	3
Idaho	2	0	0	2	3	0	0	3
Minnesota	1	0	0	1	2	1	0	3
Mississippi	0	0	0	0	0	2	1	3
Montana	1	0	0	1	3	0	0	3
Nebraska	0	1	1	2	0	1	2	3
North Carolina	0	0	1	1	1	1	1	3
Alabama	0	1	0	1	0	2	0	2
Kentucky	0	1	0	1	0	1	1	2
New Mexico	0	0	0	0	2	0	0	2
North Dakota	1	0	0	1	1	1	0	2
South Dakota	1	0	0	1	2	0	0	2
Tennessee	0	0	0	0	0	0	2	2
Wyoming	0	1	0	1	0	1	1	2
Vermont	0	0	0	0	0	0	1	1
Nevada	0	0	0	0	0	0	0	0
West Virginia	0	0	0	0	0	0	0	0
(At Large)	0	0	0	0	2	1	1	4
Totals	47	28	27	102	116	112	103	331

In view of the prominence given in recent years to studies of the undergraduate origins of natural scientists, it is of interest that . . . 485 out of 856 fellows received their bachelor's degrees at universities which are now members of the Association of American Universities, while only 146 were graduates of independent liberal arts colleges. Nevertheless, three such colleges are among the 21 institutions listed in the first table, from which 10 or more fellows received their A.B.'s or B.S.'s. A total of 188 colleges and universities in the United States and Canada, and institutions in 12 foreign countries have conferred undergraduate degrees upon the 856 fellows.

The list of universities in which fellows received the doctoral degree, or last pursued graduate study if they had not yet received that degree, is of course much shorter than that of their undergraduate institutions. Forty-two universities in the United States and Canada, and 12 in foreign countries are represented. Three universities account for 48 percent of the total. Institutions attended by 10 or more fellows are shown in the second table.

A considerable proportion, over two fifths, of the fellows spent all or some part of their terms in foreign parts of the world. Especially in the years before World War II, large numbers of fellows studied or carried on research in Europe, even though many of them did not intend to be what is now known as "Area specialists." Since 1948, Area Research Training Fellows have been required to go abroad, excepting only those whose areas of interest are closed to American students and scholars.

Quoted by permission from Joseph B. Casagrande and Elbridge Sibley, "Fellows of the Social Science Research Council, 1925-1951: Some Statistics," in _Items_, Vol. 6, No. 2, June, 1952, p. 16.

Our own comparison of these materials with previous tables and our other statistics of scholarship suggests a strong interest in the social sciences in many of the state universities and a particular emphasis in certain city colleges, e.g., Chicago, C.C.N.Y., and Columbia. Yale as a college had done rather less well than we had expected but the Yale graduate departments in the social sciences perhaps better. Columbia's record of having given graduate instruction to 17.8 per cent of all the Social Science Research Council Fellows through twenty-six years rates as spectacular.

SOCIAL SCIENCE RESEARCH COUNCIL FELLOWSHIPS, 1925-51

Educational backgrounds of 856 scholars awarded fellowships in the social sciences in the following categories: research fellowships for post-doctoral fellows, 1925-34, 198; field fellowships, 1935-46, 157; research training fellowships, 1935-51, 264; agricultural fellowships, 1928-33, 106; southern fellowships, 1929-33, 59; graduate study fellowships, 1935-37, 22; demobilization awards, 1944-46, 151; economic history fellowships, 1947-49, 10; area research training fellowships, 1948-51, 100; faculty research fellowships, 1950-51, 12.

Colleges from Which 10 or More Fellows Received Their Bachelor's Degrees			Universities in Which 10 or More Fellows Received the Ph.D. Degree, or Pursued Advanced Graduate Study		
College	Number of Fellows	Per Cent of Total	University	Number of Fellows	Per Cent of Total
HARVARD	53	6.2	COLUMBIA	152	17.8
CHICAGO	44	5.1	HARVARD	141	16.5
C.C.N.Y.	40	4.7	CHICAGO	114	13.3
CALIFORNIA	38	4.4	YALE	52	6.1
COLUMBIA	31	3.6	CALIFORNIA	48	5.6
MICHIGAN	31	3.6	WISCONSIN	35	4.1
WISCONSIN	31	3.6	CORNELL	30	3.5
YALE	24	2.8	MICHIGAN	30	3.5
PRINCETON	22	2.6	PENNSYLVANIA	30	3.5
MINNESOTA	21	2.5	MINNESOTA	25	2.9
CORNELL	19	2.2	PRINCETON	25	2.9
STANFORD	15	1.8	STANFORD	22	2.6
PENNSYLVANIA	14	1.6	NORTHWESTERN	21	2.5
WASHINGTON	14	1.6	JOHNS HOPKINS	15	1.8
ILLINOIS	13	1.5	OHIO STATE	12	1.4
NORTHWESTERN	13	1.5	M.I.T.	11	1.3
OBERLIN	13	1.5			
OHIO STATE	12	1.4			
TORONTO	12	1.4			
AMHERST	11	1.3			
REED	10	1.2			
All Other Colleges	375	43.8	All Other Universities	93	10.9
Total Number of Fellows	856	100.0	Total Number of Fellows	856	100.0

Source: Social Science Research Council *Items*, Vol. 6, No. 2, June, 1952, pp. 16-17, reproduced by permission.

By contrast to authentic honor rolls for achievement, such as are
represented by the fifty Scholars who were awarded prizes by the A.C.L.S.,
a fellowship list presents at the best the promise of achievement by the
winners of the fellowship and a demonstrated production of promising
talent by the college or university where the candidate had been educated.
With this limited expectation, our office undertook a study of fellowship
and doctoral awards in certain of the major divisions of learning. A
sampling for the area of the social sciences has already been presented.
Ideally one of the best measures of the distribution of promise and talent
in the wide fields of humanistic scholarship over the years ought to be a
cumulative study of Guggenheim Fellowship awards. Unfortunately, manpower
was lacking to do more than attempt a sampling for three different years:
one before World War II, and the others within the decade after it ended.

A study of these samplings suggested that there may have been considerable swings in the availability of talent or the energy of application
from year to year. Hence no attempt should be made to translate these
statistics into fixed rankings. Cornell, for example, ranked ahead of
Columbia and second only to Harvard in the number of individuals receiving Guggenheim Fellowships for 1939, whereas in 1949 its delegation was
cut in half, and in 1954, despite recovery, Cornell placed only half as
many as Wisconsin.

Another point of some interest was the evident tendency of scholars
trained elsewhere to gravitate to the faculty of the University of
California at Berkeley--with Columbia doing rather less well than might
have been expected, and Harvard and Yale somewhere in between.

GUGGENHEIM FELLOWSHIPS: SAMPLE YEARS

College and university connections of all U.S. appointments to Guggenheim Fellowships for the years 1939, 1949, and 1954.

College or University	Undergraduate Connections			Graduate or Professional			Net Total Individuals			Faculty Affiliations		
	1939	1949	1954	1939	1949	1954	1939	1949	1954	1939	1949	1954
HARVARD	3	11	13	10	24	32	12	29	36	1	9	14
COLUMBIA	3	5	14	4	14	17	5	18	25	1	1	11
CALIFORNIA	2	9	13	4	16	19	4	18	24	2	13	20
CHICAGO	1	4	5	3	7	11	4	9	12	2	1	8
YALE	0	6	5	3	11	10	3	11	11	0	7	8
WISCONSIN	1	1	2	4	2	12	4	3	14	4	1	4
CORNELL	3	2	1	4	2	6	6	3	7	2	2	6
PRINCETON	0	1	3	1	5	7	1	5	10	0	5	3
Totals for All Other American Colleges and Universities	27	72	107	12	39	81	29	78	122	22	52	109
Foreign Colleges and Universities	5	18	39	9	23	56	11	29	63	0	1	0
Individuals with Known College or University Connection	45	116	190	39	97	191	45	117	205	37	89	173
No Institutional Connection							7	3	3			
Net Total Individuals							52	120	208			

Source: Based on the Reports of the Secretary of the John Simon Guggenheim Memorial Foundation for the years 1939, 1949, and 1953-54.

The American Council of Learned Societies has included the American Economic Association, the Association of American Law Schools, the American Anthropological Association, the American Political Science Association, the Association of American Geographers, and the American Sociological Association, in addition to the American Historical Association, the Modern Language Association, the American Philosophical Association, the Medieval Academy, and a large number of others which clearly belong in the field of humanistic scholarship. The fellowships and grants-in-aid of the A.C.L.S. may therefore be regarded as one measure of the talent coming forward in the humanistic disciplines and in those social science disciplines with humanistic elements or connections.

On examination, the statistics supplied by Professor Robert H. Knapp in his The Origins of American Humanistic Scholars confirm and emphasize the strength of the humanities in the private universities in the East. Alike in attracting talent into the humanities and in giving it professional training, Harvard has clearly excelled, with Columbia, Princeton, and Yale following. From these colleges have come in impressive numbers the young men who would go on to the Ph.D. and later receive an A.C.L.S. fellowship or grant-in-aid: The bachelors of Harvard, Columbia, Princeton, and Yale accounted for 22 per cent of the winners who had gone to college in this country.

At the graduate level the preeminence of these 4 universities has evidently been even more marked, accounting for 55 per cent of all the American-educated Ph.D.'s who would win such honors. The impression of quality as well as quantity was confirmed by the ratios of productivity. That is, when we compared the number of grantees to the total number of students sent forward by each university in the humanities, we found that Harvard in the years 1936-56 produced 378 undergraduates who would later go on to doctorates in one or the other of the humanistic disciplines. Harvard's 32 A.C.L.S. winners therefore represented 8.5 per cent of all the candidates from Cambridge who could possibly have won that honor. On the same basis Princeton and Columbia graduates made 8.2 per cent showings. Yale sent forward 247 B.A.'s out of whom only 11 or 4.5 per cent earned A.C.L.S. grants. The comparable percentage for California was 3.6 per cent.

Turning to the doctorates, we found that the 60 Harvard awards represented 5.1 per cent of all possible Ph.D. winners from Harvard for the years 1936-56. The percentages for Yale and Princeton for the same period were 4.8 per cent, for Columbia 2.8 per cent, for Chicago 2.4 per cent, and for California 1.8 per cent.

Such ratios are illuminating but must be used with considerable caution. It has been noted, for example, that the students or graduates of certain institutions were slower to awake to the opportunities of the A.C.L.S. awards and decidedly slower in "getting on the gravy train." Notwithstanding, the raw statistics in these tables suggest irresistibly where humanistic scholarship in this country has been nourished, strengthened, and trained.

216

A.C.L.S. FELLOWSHIPS AND GRANTS-IN-AID, 1958-62

Baccalaureate and doctoral origins of individuals awarded A.C.L.S. fellowships or grants-in-aid for the five years 1958 through 1962.

Baccalaureate Origins		Doctoral Origins	
HARVARD	32	HARVARD	60
COLUMBIA	14	YALE	37
PRINCETON	14		
		COLUMBIA	36
YALE	11	PRINCETON	18
OBERLIN	9		
		CHICAGO	16
CALIFORNIA (Berkeley)	8		
N.Y.U.	8	CALIFORNIA (Berkeley)	10
		WISCONSIN	10
C.C.N.Y.	7		
		MICHIGAN	9
CHICAGO	6		
CORNELL	6	PENNSYLVANIA	7
MICHIGAN	6		
WESLEYAN	6	CORNELL	5
WISCONSIN	6	N.Y.U.	5
		RADCLIFFE	5
DARTMOUTH	5		
SYRACUSE	5	ILLINOIS	4
		JOHNS HOPKINS	4
BROWN	4		
DAVIDSON	4	NORTH CAROLINA	3
ILLINOIS	4	OHIO STATE	3
U.C.L.A.	4	U.C.L.A.	3
WESTERN RESERVE	4	VIRGINIA	3
		WASHINGTON U.	3
ARIZONA	3		
BAKER	3	BOSTON U.	2
NEW MEXICO	3	BRYN MAWR	2
NORTHWESTERN	3	INDIANA	2
OHIO STATE	3	NEW MEXICO	2
RUTGERS	3	ROCHESTER	2
SWARTHMORE	3	STANFORD	2
WABASH	3	WESTERN RESERVE	2
WILLIAMS	3		
		18 Other Institutions	18
Other Institutions	122		
		No Formal Doctorates	18
Foreign Institutions	51		
		Foreign Institutions	39
No Degrees or Unknown	34		
		Doctorate Before 1936 (unidentified)	67
Total	397	Total	397

Source: Statistics taken from Tables 37 and 48 in Robert H. Knapp, The Origins of American Humanistic Scholars, Prentice-Hall Inc., 1964, by permission.

Once it was thought (or hoped) that the doctorate and distinction were pretty close to synonymous. That theme of academic wishfulness has now faded on the horizons. Too many of our Ph.D.'s have been mediocre talents turning out mediocre work on insignificant subjects. Yet perhaps it has become truer than ever that a man who wishes to do advanced scholarship and teaching in his field must have the training of the Ph.D. The doctorate has therefore become more miscellaneous yet at the same time more necessary.

Yale first offered the Ph.D. in 1861, and for nine years there were no universities to rival it. In 1870 Pennsylvania offered its first Ph.D.'s, to be followed in 1872 by Cornell, in 1873 by Harvard, and in 1876 by the founding of Johns Hopkins (first Ph.D. 1878). It has been estimated that in the centennial year of 1876 there were in the United States 400 graduate students; forty-four Ph.D.'s were actually awarded, and Yale had given one third of all the Ph.D.'s granted up to that moment.

The rise of Hopkins, then Harvard and Chicago, in the world of graduate education is an oft-told tale. By 1935, on the basis of total accumulated production of doctors, the universities ranked in the following order: Chicago first, then Columbia, Harvard, Cornell, and Yale. By the late 1930's Columbia had become the greatest producer of them all, in part because of its development of professional studies for the metropolitan community, but in large part because of the great numbers of Ph.D.'s turned out in education by Teachers College. Meanwhile the great Johns Hopkins, unable to muster any such numbers, had fallen far behind.

In the 20-year period between the depths of the depression and the mid-1950's there evidently took place a second revolution in this educational world: The state universities of Wisconsin, California, Illinois, Ohio State, Michigan, and Minnesota came surging forward (see the last five columns of our table), while Chicago and Harvard changed places, and Stanford and M.I.T. joined the list of substantial producers.

Those who are interested in pursuing this subject since 1956 should consult Doctorate Production in United States Universities, 1920-1962, With Baccalaureate Origins of Doctorates in Sciences, Arts, and Professions (Publication 1142, National Academy of Sciences-National Research Council, 1963). Here will be seen the tremendous dispersion of baccalaureate origins, and the growing diffusion of doctorate production. According to the 1960 and 1961 figures there given (pages 19 and 31), Columbia still ranked first as a producer of Ph.D.'s, but Illinois had shot up to second, and Wisconsin, Harvard, California, N.Y.U., Michigan, Ohio State, Cornell, Minnesota, Purdue, and Yale followed after. The same two years saw C.C.N.Y. rising to the top as the largest baccalaureate source for future Ph.D.'s, followed by California, Illinois, Harvard, Michigan, Wisconsin, N.Y.U., Minnesota, Brooklyn College, U.C.L.A., Cornell, Columbia, Chicago, M.I.T., and Yale.

The crude mathematical implications, or scale of expectation, may be suggested by the fact that Yale, ranking twelfth among the graduate

PRODUCTION OF PH.D.'S, 1861-1956

University	Date of First Ph.D.	Total Ph.D.'s By 1956
COLUMBIA	1875	9,711
CHICAGO	1893	7,291
HARVARD	1873	6,597
WISCONSIN	1892	5,971
CALIFORNIA	1885	5,549
CORNELL	1872	5,453
YALE	1861	4,853
ILLINOIS	1900	4,356
N.Y.U.	1887	4,156
MICHIGAN	1876	4,103
OHIO STATE	1879	3,830
MINNESOTA	1888	3,392
IOWA	1900	3,030
STANFORD	1894	2,358
M.I.T.	1907	2,228

University	1936-42	1943-49	1950-56	Total Ph.D.'s 1936-56
COLUMBIA	1,690	1,609	3,896	7,195
WISCONSIN	1,028	945	2,436	4,409
HARVARD	967	928	2,264	4,159
CHICAGO	1,122	1,072	1,895	4,089
CALIFORNIA	784	756	2,078	3,618
ILLINOIS	824	718	1,943	3,485
CORNELL	906	844	1,593	3,343
OHIO STATE	722	734	1,783	3,239
N.Y.U.	808	673	1,744	3,225
MICHIGAN	776	569	1,783	3,128
MINNESOTA	693	654	1,492	2,839
YALE	838	619	1,360	2,817
IOWA	675	474	1,141	2,290
STANFORD	372	508	1,236	2,116
M.I.T.	415	544	1,133	2,092

Sources: Walter Crosby Eells, "Earned Doctorates in American Institutions of Higher Education," Higher Education, Vol. XII, No. 7, pp. 109-13, and National Academy of Sciences--National Research Council, Washington, D.C., Doctorate Production in United States Universities, 1936-1956, Tables 4 and 6. Quoted by permission.

schools, was apparently producing about 2.2 per cent of the Ph.D.'s;
while in fifteenth place as a baccalaureate producer of future Ph.D.'s,
it had apparently generated only 1.02 per cent of all such future
scholars. Harvard, in fourth place now in each category, produced 3.4
per cent of all the Ph.D.'s, and had been the baccalaureate source for
1.38 per cent. Consideration of these ratios will suggest the odds faced
by our major universities in the competition for positions of leadership
in the scholarly world.

K-16. LEADING DOCTORATE PRODUCERS IN THE HUMANITIES, 1920-61

The quantitative production of Ph.D.'s may be a function only in-
directly connected with the nurture of excellence. When, for example, an
institution has few or no competitors, it may be because it is the only
reputable university willing to offer the Ph.D. in a new or somewhat doubtful learning. If the field has many competitors, however, and still a
single university or pair of universities clearly outproduces all the
rest, then one may have confidence in the competence of that particular
faculty or faculties, and may with some reason assume a considerable excellence, if not in the present at least in the generation just passed.
A second probability, related to the foregoing, is that the popularity or
reputation of a university in a given field tends to be slow to build but
self-perpetuating. When a graduate school succeeds in turning out more
M.A.'s and Ph.D.'s, it will before long have placed more instructors and
professors on the faculties of rival and feeder institutions. In turn
these instructors and professors will tend to send their own best undergraduates back to take their doctorates at the place where they were themselves trained. Evidently there is a self-feeding principle involved.
It has been noticeable at Yale in English literature, and very marked in
history at Harvard and Columbia.

Returning to the problem of numbers one may observe that genuine excellence in the humanities does not necessarily generate large numbers of
Ph.D.'s. Thus Princeton has for several generations been one of the smaller but very high quality universities for the study of the humanities, yet
in production of Ph.D.'s it ranks in the first 10 only for foreign languages and literature. Cornell has generated some most distinguished historians but falls out of the top 10 in that category. The only university,
incidentally, to qualify in the top 10 (in our table) in all 5 divisions
of the humanities was Harvard. Yale and Columbia both failed to register
under Arts and Professional (they had produced 122 and 100 Ph.D.'s respectively).

Over-all, Columbia and Harvard turn out to have been the outstanding
producers. With only two thirds as many Ph.D.'s to its credit, Yale held
third place by a modest margin over Chicago and Wisconsin. After these
five leaders our statistics recorded another great drop to the tight cluster of Michigan, Pennsylvania, Iowa, and Berkeley--then, finally, Cornell.

LEADING DOCTORATE PRODUCERS IN THE HUMANITIES, 1920-61

History		English Lit.		Foreign Langs. and Lit.		Arts and Professional		Philosophy		Totals	
Institution	No.	Institution	No.	Institution	No.	Institution	No.	Institution	No.	Institution	No.
HARVARD	725	YALE	558	COLUMBIA	669	HARVARD	482	COLUMBIA	312	COLUMBIA	2,304
COLUMBIA	694	COLUMBIA	529	CHICAGO	384	STATE U. OF IOWA	408	HARVARD	287	HARVARD	2,276
CALIFORNIA, Berkeley	417	HARVARD	425	YALE	373	NORTHWESTERN	325	FORDHAM	192	YALE	1,489
WISCONSIN	405	WISCONSIN	338	HARVARD	357	WISCONSIN	249	CATHOLIC U.	187	CHICAGO	1,350
CHICAGO	391	CHICAGO	331	WISCONSIN	318	MICHIGAN	227	YALE	166	WISCONSIN	1,347
YALE	270	PENNSYLVANIA	327	JOHNS HOPKINS	244	U. SOUTHERN CALIFORNIA	199	CHICAGO	119	MICHIGAN	971
PENNSYLVANIA	269	MICHIGAN	266	CALIFORNIA, Berkeley	242	ROCHESTER	195	BOSTON U.	107	PENNSYLVANIA	962
MICHIGAN	210	STATE U. OF IOWA	244	PRINCETON	241	OHIO STATE	184	CORNELL	78	STATE U. OF IOWA	959
TEXAS	207	CORNELL	240	ILLINOIS	240	CORNELL	154	CALIFORNIA, Berkeley	74	CALIFORNIA, Berkeley	951
ILLINOIS	205	ILLINOIS	222	PENNSYLVANIA	220	N.Y.U.	146	MICHIGAN	73	CORNELL	867

Source: Doctorate Production in United States Universities, 1920-1962, With Baccalaureate Origins of Doctorates in Sciences, Arts and Professions, National Academy of Sciences-National Research Council, publication 1142, 1963, Appendix 3.

This final table or measurement of promise, as adapted from the well-known study by Robert H. Knapp and Joseph J. Greenbaum, represents an attempt to assess the production of successful graduate scholars in the three major areas of learning for the years immediately after World War II. The figures suggest as well a qualitative evaluation of the contributions of our leading colleges great and small. The authors did not attempt to count in those college graduates who, in this period, won teaching awards or were earning their way in part by teaching assistantships: an omission which may have tended to reduce the apparent contributions of certain state universities. It should be noted also that no effort was made to measure graduate work in medicine, law, divinity, etc.

The index of productivity (or awards per thousand college graduates-- second numerical column) speaks eloquently for the outstanding contribu-tions made by some of the best of our small private colleges. It is notable that these small colleges (and California Institute of Technology) walked off with eight of the top twelve places in the "male index" column. On total awards Harvard, California, and Yale headed the list, with Chicago, Wisconsin, Illinois, Purdue, and Princeton following, ahead of Cornell, Columbia, Michigan, and N.Y.U. Without exception the state uni-versities ranked low in productivity per thousand college graduates, yet produced such graduates in considerable numbers. The reader will note that for all their productivity the thirteen small colleges together just barely managed to produce as many promising young scholars as did Harvard alone.

It should also be noted that both the productivity column and the "male index" column are open to some question because of a possible hidden bias in favor of government-supported science. It is notable that Swarth-more, Reed, and California Institute of Technology among the smaller insti-tutions, with Chicago among the larger, owed no small part of their high ranking to their degrees, awards, and grants in the sciences and from the federal government. A comparison of our table with the A.C.L.S. fellow-ships and grants-in-aid for the humanities will indicate that these insti-tutions did not do so well in the humanistic fields.

COLLEGE ORIGINS OF THE YOUNGER AMERICAN SCHOLAR, 1946-51

Analysis of the undergraduate educational backgrounds of those younger scholars who in the years 1946-51 took graduate work at twenty-five leading universities in the arts and sciences and either (1) won a Ph.D. degree or (2) won a university fellowship or scholarship, or (3) received a fellowship from one of nine private foundations (including A.C.L.S., S.S.R.C., National Research Council, Rhodes Scholarship Trust, Woodrow Wilson Fellowship Foundation, or finally (4) were awarded a government fellowship from the U.S. Public Health Service, Atomic Energy Commission, or the U.S. State Department under the Fulbright Program. Only American educated students were considered and only those fellowship winners whose awards exceeded $400.

University College	Total Male Awards	Awards per 1,000 College Grads.	Productivity by Fields				Source of Awards			Highest Male Index
			Sciences	Social Sciences	Humanities	Ph.D.	Univ. Fellowship	Govt. Grants	Private Foundations	
HARVARD	288	27.3	10.1	9.2	8.0	5.2	14.7	4.7	2.7	10
CALIFORNIA	238	8.3	4.7	2.2	1.5	1.9	5.0	1.2	0.3	--
YALE	211	27.2	9.2	9.5	8.4	5.2	13.5	4.5	4.0	11
CHICAGO	186	48.4	27.7	14.6	6.3	18.5	15.7	12.3	2.1	3
WISCONSIN	186	12.3	7.8	3.2	1.3	4.4	6.0	1.5	0.5	36
ILLINOIS	177	9.6	7.8	1.7	1.7	3.6	4.5	1.3	0.3	--
PURDUE	154	12.8	12.5	0.3	0.0	2.9	8.9	1.0	0.0	34
PRINCETON	148	32.4	10.9	10.3	11.2	5.2	15.8	3.3	8.1	8
CORNELL	142	19.5	12.0	4.0	3.6	6.6	9.2	2.5	1.2	20
COLUMBIA	129	17.7	6.9	4.5	6.3	2.7	10.4	3.6	1.0	23
MICHIGAN	128	9.1	6.5	1.6	1.1	1.7	4.8	1.8	0.9	--
N.Y.U.	100	5.2	2.5	1.5	1.1	1.2	2.9	0.9	0.2	--
Most Productive Small Colleges										
SWARTHMORE	45	61.2	34.6	19.9	6.6	9.3	26.6	17.3	6.7	1
REED	24	53.1	26.5	17.7	8.8	2.2	17.7	15.5	17.7	2
OBERLIN	49	39.8	15.4	12.2	12.2	8.1	20.3	8.1	3.3	4
HAVERFORD	25	39.5	4.7	11.1	23.7	3.1	23.7	4.7	7.9	5
CAL. TECH.	36	38.2	38.2	--	--	11.7	19.5	17.0	--	6
CARLETON	22	35.4	12.8	12.8	9.7	3.2	16.1	8.0	8.0	7
ANTIOCH	16	31.5	13.8	11.8	5.9	3.9	15.8	7.9	3.9	9
GRINNELL	13	23.7	7.3	7.3	9.1	0.0	20.0	3.6	0.0	13
WESLEYAN	22	22.5	8.8	8.8	3.9	2.9	10.8	2.0	5.9	14
KENYON	10	22.4	0.0	2.2	20.2	0.0	6.7	11.2	4.5	15
U. OF SOUTH	9	20.2	2.2	13.4	4.5	2.2	11.2	6.7	0.0	18
KNOX	11	19.6	7.1	3.6	8.9	1.8	14.2	1.8	1.8	19
BELOIT	11	17.9	7.4	9.8	4.9	3.3	17.9	0.9	0.0	22

Sources: Adapted by permission from Robert H. Knapp and Joseph J. Greenbaum, The Younger American Scholar: His Collegiate Origins (University of Chicago Press and Wesleyan University Press, 1953).

CHAPTER L FOR THE TWENTIETH CENTURY:
TWO OVER-ALL INDEXES
OF ACHIEVEMENT

After analyzing an extensive and most varied assortment
of honor lists for many of the important vocations and professions in the twentieth century--but failing to achieve any
measurements at all for leadership in a regrettable range of
significant occupations--our office cast about for some com-
prehensive over-all assessments of contemporary leadership in
American life. Ultimately it was decided to study two quite
different rolls of honor, one extremely selective, the other
very general. The first was composed of the winners of the
President's Freedom Medal in the years 1963 and 1964.

The original list of 31 distinguished individuals for the first Freedom Medal was made up for President John F. Kennedy, then enlarged to 33 by the inclusion of Pope John XXIII and President Kennedy himself after their deaths. The next list of 30 was made up for President L. B. Johnson (as can perhaps be detected from certain of the choices).

Of the 63 individuals, thus honored in 1963 and 1964, 18 could be classified only in a marginal way. Pope John XXIII had been educated entirely in Europe. No academic information whatever could be obtained for 4: Genevieve Caulfield, Karl Holton, J. Clifford MacDonald, and Annie D. Wauneka. Ten others appeared to have received no formal higher education: the labor leaders John L. Lewis and George Meany, the European economic planner Jean Monnet, the singer Marian Anderson, the actress Lynn Fontanne, the musicians Pablo Casals and Rudolph Serkin, the photographer Edward Steichen, the landscape painter Andrew Wyeth, and the animated cartoonist Walt Disney. Three--Robert J. H. Kiphuth, Mies van der Rohe, and Aaron Copland--without ever attending college had achieved faculty connections respectively at Yale, Illinois Institute of Technology, and Harvard.

Of the remaining 45 individuals honored with the Freedom Medal, 25 had had one or more connections with Harvard, Yale, or Princeton. The outstanding representation of 18 men and women from Harvard was made up of 9 Harvard undergraduates with 2 from Radcliffe, supplemented at the graduate level by 3 Yale men and 1 each from Princeton, C.C.N.Y., and Amherst, with Aaron Copland (no previous affiliation) as a faculty member. Nine of these were from the Johnson honor list and 9 from the Kennedy list. By contrast 6 of Yale's representatives and all 3 of Princeton's graduates appeared on the Kennedy list; the Johnson list named but 3 Yale men and no Princetonians at all.

Kennedy List	Johnson List
Marian Anderson	Dean Acheson
Ralph J. Bunche	Detlev W. Bronk
Ellsworth Bunker	Aaron Copland
Pablo Casals	Willem de Kooning
Genevieve Caulfield	Walt Disney
James B. Conant	J. Frank Dobie
John F. Enders	Lena F. Edwards
Felix Frankfurter	T. S. Eliot
Karl Holton	John W. Gardner
Pope John XIII	The Rev. T. M. Hesburgh
John F. Kennedy	Clarence L. Johnson
Robert J. H. Kiphuth	Frederick R. Kappel
Edwin H. Land	Helen A. Keller
Herbert H. Lehman	John L. Lewis
Robert A. Lovett	Walter Lippmann
John J. McCloy	Alfred Lunt and
J. Clifford MacDonald	Lynn Fontanne
George Meany	Ralph Emerson McGill
Alexander Meiklejohn	Samuel Eliot Morison

THE FREEDOM MEDAL, 1963, 1964

The educational backgrounds and faculty affiliations of the thirty-three winners of the Freedom Medal in 1963 and the thirty winners in 1964.

College or University	Undergraduate Connections	Graduate or Professional	Faculty Affiliations	Net Total Individuals
HARVARD	11	12	7	18
YALE	5	1	3	9
CALIFORNIA	2	1	3	4
C.C.N.Y.	3	-	-	3
CORNELL	1	1	1	3
PENNSYLVANIA	1	1	3	3
PRINCETON	2	2	-	3
STANFORD	2	1	1	3
AMHERST	1	-	1	2
BROWN	2	1	1	2
COLUMBIA	1	1	-	2
HOWARD	-	1	2	2
JOHNS HOPKINS	-	1	2	2
MICHIGAN	1	2	1	2
NEW SCHOOL FOR SOCIAL RESEARCH	1	-	1	2
Total for 37 Other American Colleges and Universities	16	8	14	37
Total for Foreign Colleges and Universities	2	6	2	9
No Acad. Connections				10
Unknown				4
Net Total	45	28	22	63

L. Mies van der Rohe
Jean Monnet
Luis Munoz-Marin
Clarence B. Randall
Rudolph Serkin
Edward Steichen
George W. Taylor
Alan T. Waterman
Mark S. Watson
Annie D. Wauneka
E. B. White
Thornton Wilder
Edmund Wilson
Andrew N. Wyeth

Lewis Mumford
Edward R. Murrow
Reinhold Niebuhr
Leontyne Price
A. Philip Randolph
Carl Sandburg
John Steinbeck
Helen B. Taussig
Carl Vinson
Thomas J. Watson, Jr.
Paul Dudley White

L-2. COLLEGE GRADUATES IN WHO'S WHO IN AMERICA, 1928, 1938, 1950, 1962

Where a Freedom Medalist may represent distinction at the highest level
(or even selectivity carried to the point of symbolism and arbitrary choice),
perhaps the widest and most impartial samplings of achievement in twentieth-
century America have been the lists published every two years by Marquis-
Who's Who, Inc. under the now established rubric of Who's Who in America.

The Who's Who lists themselves are not wholly satisfactory. It would
appear that the standards for selection have changed somewhat over the
years. Where once there may have been a bias in favor of writers and aca-
demicians, or of those who had published a book, in recent times the representation of men in business and industry, and in government and the arts,
has been greatly enlarged. Again the counting of educational connections,
or the assignment of given individuals to one college or another, has left
something to be desired, so that the figures here given must be taken as
approximations rather than exact tallies.* Nevertheless, this sampling

_____

*Ideally the figures stated under "Number of Graduates Listed" should
indicate the number of men who graduated from the college of each institution and were then listed in Who's Who in America of the years specified.
In point of fact the counts were based--both by Who's Who in America for
1962 and by Kunkel and Prentice for 1928, 1938, and 1950--on the first or
baccalaureate degree. They would include such degrees as LL.B. and B.D.
if no B.A., B.S., or Ph.B. were mentioned in the Who's Who sketch. They
would include also those who attended a given institution, did not get a
degree, but did not subsequently take a degree at some other higher educational institution (e.g., for their 1950 count Kunkel and Prentice found
that approximately 3 per cent of the Yale names represented such professional school degrees or nongraduating attendance). It should be noted
again that the counts in each case have been subject to human miscalcula-
tion (e.g., the 1962 figure for Yale supplied by Who's Who in America was
1,999, but on checking some duplications and stenographic errors were discovered which reduced the count to 1,884). Unfortunately the sheer magnitude of the task made it impossible for us to verify the publisher's tabulations by a recount for all the universities in our own office. In the
circumstances I should like here to record my great indebtedness to Nealy,
Kunkel, and Prentice both for their generosity in making available to me
their statistical information and for their sympathetic advice and help.

COLLEGE GRADUATES IN <u>WHO'S WHO IN AMERICA</u>, 1928, 1938, 1950, 1962

Holders of bachelors' degrees listed in <u>Who's Who in America</u> for 1928-29, 1938-39, 1950-51, and 1962-63.

Rank in 1928	Rank in 1938	Rank in 1950	Rank in 1962	Number of Graduates Listed				Institutions
				1928	1938	1950	1962	
1	1	1	1	1,374	1,409	1,566	2,237	HARVARD
2	2	2	2	937	1,006	1,299	1,884	YALE
3	3	4	3	480	515	746	1,379	PRINCETON
4	5	3	4	470	454	754	1,173	MICHIGAN
5	4	5	5	402	461	653	1,048	COLUMBIA
15	8	11	6	185	289	485	1,006	CALIFORNIA
6	6	7	7	401	413	630	881	CORNELL
10	9	12	8	261	288	413	860	PENNSYLVANIA
?	16	13	9	?	186	402	859	ILLINOIS
8	7	8	10	287	342	585	857	WISCONSIN
20	10	10	11	170	279	517	837	CHICAGO
?	42	31	12	?	79	209	736	NEW YORK UNIVERSITY
14	19	9	?	186	189	566	507	U.S. NAVAL ACADEMY
12	15	6	?	235	221	631	463	U.S. MILITARY ACADEMY

Sources: This table has been in part constructed from information supplied by Arthur E. Nealy, Educational Director of Marquis-Who's Who, Inc., and in part adapted from tables published in <u>School and Society</u>, November 1, 1930 and October 20, 1951, by B. W. Kunkel, of Lafayette College, and D. B. Prentice, of Rose Polytechnic Institute and the Scientific Research Society of America.

table for the years 1928, 1938, 1950, and 1962 represents the best <u>general</u> <u>estimates</u> we have yet been able to reach of the relative representation of the graduates of our major colleges in the important offices and significant activities of twentieth-century American life.

With due allowance for approximations, this table of <u>Who's Who</u> listings will repay considerable study and reflection. First of all, the table demonstrates beyond question the leadership of Harvard in numbers of eminent graduates. In undisputed second place has been Yale. Princeton has educated the third largest number of men in <u>Who's Who</u> in all the editions under study, except for 1950 when Michigan surpassed the Princeton delegation by 8 names (it may be pertinent to observe that the available reservoir of Michigan alumni was many times that of Princeton). Columbia has ranked fifth as a producer in all the editions except that for 1938, when it surpassed Michigan by 7 names. Through a span of 34 years these 5-- Harvard, Yale, Princeton, Michigan, and Columbia--have led the procession. In the same interval the University of California at Berkeley has come forward to the unchallenged leadership of the second five. At one time Chicago promised as well, but seems not to have fully realized on that promise. In the same interval Illinois and N.Y.U. have come from nowhere to positions of substantial achievement, while Pennsylvania has improved its position slightly, Cornell and Wisconsin have suffered slight declines, and the representation of the Naval and Military Academies, after the wartime boom, has been drastically reduced.

Calculations have shown that the numbers of graduates from our leading institutions have increased from year to year but not quite in the proportion of the total increase in the <u>Who's Who in America</u> listings. Thus, in an unpublished article of 1950 which they have most kindly allowed me to use, Professors Kunkel and Prentice observed that "whereas in 1938, Harvard, Yale, Princeton, Columbia, and Cornell furnished together 30.5% of all the college graduates in <u>Who's Who</u>, in 1950 they furnished only 23.4%." Evidently, the percentage decline had been shared by each of these universities. "In 1928 5.70% of all the college graduates in <u>Who's</u> <u>Who</u> were Yale graduates, in 1938 the percentage had dropped slightly to 5.34% and in 1950 to 4.45%. Harvard's representation relative to the whole collegiate branch of the family declined from 8.25% to 7.49% and finally, in 1950, to 5.36%." By 1962, we may add, the percentages for Harvard and Yale had declined still further to approximately 4.79 per cent and 4.03 per cent.

Too hasty conclusions should not be drawn from these percentages, however, for the explanation has lain not in a decreasing effectiveness on the part of our major universities but in the increasing spread of college education. In effect the state universities have enlarged their own roles less at the expense of the Ivy League than by the diminution of the sector of self-made men. A second glance at the figures in our table will show, for example, that the so-called Big Three registered larger increases between 1928 and 1962 than any other universities. Subtracting the listings of 1928 from those for 1962 we find the following figures and ranking for absolute net growth:

1.	Yale	947	8.	Chicago	667
2.	Princeton	899	9.	Columbia	646
3.	Harvard	863	10.	Pennsylvania	599
4.	California	821	11.	Wisconsin	570
5?	Illinois	(c.800)	12.	Cornell	440
6.	Michigan	703	13.	U.S. Naval Acad.	322
7.	N.Y.U.	(c.700)	14.	U.S. Military Acad.	228

Evidently, Harvard, Yale, and Princeton have not lost their appeal for young men of ability (or their own ability to make something of the human material admitted to their colleges). Whether in the decades to come the University of California will be able to penetrate the top echelon in this regard, and whether Columbia will be able to withstand the challenge of institutions like N.Y.U. and Illinois, will be interesting to see.

L-3. H-Y-P RATIOS OF ELECTION TO WHO'S WHO IN AMERICA,
1928, 1938, 1950, 1962

This table perhaps speaks for itself, but it may be worth remarking how close together our most celebrated colleges have grown in their ratios of outstanding production in this century.

Some years ago Arthur E. Traxler, Executive Director of the Educational Records Bureau, New York, prepared a paper for the annual meeting of the American Association for the Advancement of Science meeting in Indianapolis, December 29, 1957, in which he made an appraisal of American colleges on the basis of male graduates listed in Who's Who in America. His estimates showed that the 25 colleges and universities with the largest number of men graduates, of the classes 1920-49, who were listed in Who's Who in America for 1956-57, were headed by Harvard with 881, Yale 751, Princeton 556, Michigan 426, followed by Illinois, California, Wisconsin, Columbia, Chicago, Cornell, Pennsylvania, Minnesota, Dartmouth, and Stanford. Next, in 15th and 16th places, came the Military and Naval Academies followed by M.I.T., N.Y.U., Ohio State, Northwestern, Texas, Missouri, Iowa, Washington, and Nebraska.

To convert these quantitative figures into a qualitative estimate or ratio of production, Traxler divided the total number of men graduates from each institution during the 30-year period by the number of its graduates listed in Who's Who in America. By this method he was able to obtain an index number or ratio for each college or university, and a median index number for categories or groups of colleges or for the entire list of institutions represented in Who's Who. Thus he found that the median index number for the group of 302 colleges responding to his questionnaire was 186, i.e., 1 out of every 186 graduates of all those colleges appeared in Who's Who in America. This compared with an estimated 1 in 1,000 for the male population as a whole--which was to say that the college graduate had more than a 5 to 1 advantage or chance of achieving distinction.

Looking more closely, Traxler found that Yale, Princeton, and Harvard had index numbers ranging from 22 to 26, indicating that about 1 in every 25 graduates of these institutions appeared in Who's Who in America. No other institution could claim an index number below the 30's. Tied for fourth were Williams and Oberlin, however, with index numbers of 36, followed by Amherst 38, DePauw 40, Swarthmore 41, U.S. Military Academy and Park College, Missouri, each 44, Wesleyan 45, Dartmouth 48, Carleton and Reed each 49, Wabash 51, and Hamilton 52. Altogether 67 colleges and universities proved to have index numbers under 100.

When Traxler came to group his colleges and universities into categories, he found that next to Y-P-H with their index of 25, came 5 small highly selective Eastern colleges (Williams, Amherst, Swarthmore, Wesleyan, and Hamilton) with a median index of 41; then the 7 Ivy League colleges (adding Dartmouth, Brown, Cornell, and Pennsylvania to Y-P-H) with a median index of 48; next a select group of 13 non-Eastern independent colleges with index numbers ranging from 36 to 63 and a median of 53. When the groups were enlarged the range or variations increased and the median

H-Y-P RATIOS OF ELECTION TO WHO'S WHO IN AMERICA
1928, 1938, 1950, 1962

Percentages of living alumni of the undergraduate colleges of Harvard, Yale, and Princeton listed in the four issues of Who's Who in America at or about the times when the biographical listings were closed. Sources for Who's Who as in Table L-2. Living alumni figures drawn from the respective alumni registers and from correspondence with alumni officers.

College	1928	1938	1950	1962
HARVARD COLLEGE AND LAWRENCE SCIENTIFIC SCHOOL	4.8%	4.1%	3.9%	4.5%
YALE COLLEGE, SHEFFIELD SCIENTIFIC SCHOOL, AND ENGINEERING SCHOOL	3.8%	3.7%	3.8%	4.3%
PRINCETON COLLEGE	3.4%	2.9%	3.2%	4.5%

Note: These H-Y-P percentages are approximations based on the original count of bachelors' degrees by Kunkel and Prentice and by the office of Arthur E. Nealy of Who's Who in America. For purposes of calculation the assumption was made that all bachelors' degrees were obtained in the under- graduate college: an assumption which tends very faintly to inflate each ratio of election. A second factor of uncertainty derives from the fact that the Harvard, Princeton, and Yale alumni directories have been issued at different times and do not perfectly correspond. Thus the number of living alumni had to be estimated for all three institutions in calculating the 1928 and 1938 ratios, while the ratios for 1950 were based on living alumni figures for 1948.

Additional note: It may also be of some interest to state that in prepara- tion for their unpublished essay on "Yale and Who's Who," Kunkel and Pren- tice analyzed the vocational distribution of the Yale College men listed in the 1950-51 edition of Who's Who in America. They found that 38.8% of the Yale graduates recorded in that year were business executives, bankers, financiers, and manufacturers as against 20.4% for the national average; also that 15.5% of all Yale W. W. in A. graduates were in the law as as against the national figure of 6%. In writing, editing, and journalism, the percentages were about even, as was true also in medicine. In educa- tion, the Yale list showed 18.5% against 25.4% for all the names in Who's Who, and in government 3.5% versus 6% for the nation as a whole. If com- parable figures were available for Harvard College, no doubt they would reflect Harvard's strength in letters and scholarship, as well as in business, medicine, and the law.

One further defect of our statistics needs to be noted. Our tables summarize the findings of researchers who were primarily interested in bachelor degrees and undergraduate origins. So they tell us virtually nothing about the graduate or professional connections of the men and women in Who's Who.

index number rose markedly. At the head of the state universities were Virginia 78, Michigan 82, North Carolina 87, and Wisconsin 89, but the 33 state universities as a group had a median index figure of 145. In the same way some 90 Midwestern and Western colleges had a median index number of 154, some 46 Eastern independent colleges had a median index number of 175, some 15 state technological and agricultural colleges had a median of 231, some 20 state teachers colleges soared to a median of 450, and a dozen other state colleges registered 575. From all these figures Traxler drew some interesting conclusions, in particular the implication that "while a small number of highly selective and prestigeful eastern institutions have some advantage on the basis of this criterion, the results indicate that many other colleges throughout the United States are "good" in the sense that a noteworthy proportion of their graduates become leaders in later life. It is suggested that able high school graduates and the parents of these graduates may well be advised to consider applying to these colleges. . . ."

The other side of this yield may be more fully appreciated by comparing the enrollment figures and the total living alumni figures of some of the major state universities as given in Tables N-2, N-3, and N-4 with their production of names for Who's Who as given in the preceding table L-2. Using Traxler's figures, if the median index number for Y-P-H was about 25, and for the best liberal arts colleges about 53, and for the state universities 145, and for the 302 contributing colleges 186, then one could say that the chances of an undergraduate for eventual listing in Who's Who differed greatly between these institutions. A Princetonian, for example, would have about twice the chance of a man in a good liberal arts college, about 6 times the chance of a man in an average state university, and more than 7 times the chance of college undergraduates in general.

It may be observed that too much may be made of ratios, especially where a college is able to produce only a few men to become leaders in our society. Perhaps the best final measurement is therefore the combination of a high ratio of production with a reasonably large volume at the same time. In other terms, this describes a college of substantial size attended by an undergraduate body of a very high average level of ability: a combination achieved in some degree by a fair number of our colleges but hardly with an equal measure of success.

No study has been made of the total alumni bodies, living and dead, as against the total registration in all the volumes of Who Was Who and Who's Who in America, but it would perhaps be a fair guess that at least 10 per cent of the undergraduate classes at Harvard, Yale, or Princeton have on the average eventually found themselves listed in Who's Who in America.

CHAPTER M SUMMARY AND CONCLUSIONS

What has been the education of American leadership?

The first findings of our statistical investigations seem clear and unarguable. In times past many have not gone to college at all. But increasingly Americans of all kinds have gone to college. The more able and ambitious had been in the van of the movement. And those destined for high office and national distinction have now led the parade beyond college into graduate and professional training.

But where have outstanding Americans gone to college? And "in what proportions or relative volume has each of our colleges, and each of our major universities, contributed to the production of American leadership?" To these more delicate and searching questions our 100-odd statistical inquiries, for all their inadequacies and imperfections, supply some arresting answers.

To begin with, it would seem that most of our colleges, and all but a small handful of our universities, have been somewhat uneven in their appeal and in their performance. As the generations have passed, they have known ups and downs. As the professions and public callings developed, their graduate constituencies also responded unequally, compiling a stronger record, perhaps, in medicine than in divinity, or in law than in literature, or in business than in science or the fine arts. Thus, from the Dictionary of American Biography and from certain of our inquiries into "The Making of Statesmen," it is possible to deduce that in the first fifty years of our national existence the men from Princeton achieved extraordinary eminence in public affairs. The same tables document the very early decline of William and Mary, the strong but law-oriented performance of the men from Virginia, the spectacular but spasmodic achievements of the graduates from West Point, as perhaps also the more recent role of the University of Alabama in Southern state politics. In medicine one encounters the unmistakable distinction of the University of Pennsylvania, which through its college and its M.D. graduates helped make Philadelphia into a leading center for this science. Again our statistics suggest that M.I.T., through its training and its alumni, quickly achieved an unusual distinction in architecture, and in due course made substantial contributions to leadership in big business as well as in engineering--yet in many another field contributed hardly at all. From Table K-9 one learns that the University of Chicago faculties required only thirty years to rise to the top in graduate scholarship (a position they then were unable to hold), while other returns (E-2 and J-7) suggest that Columbia has been stronger in the Protestant ministry and in twentieth-century literature than has popularly been supposed.

In our general table, CAREER EMPHASIS AND SUCCESS IN THE COLLEGE CONSTITUENCIES (p. xxiv), an attempt has been made to estimate the comparative achievements of each of our major colleges in the more important professions and callings. These estimates are certainly open to modification. Had we been able to command more usable indexes of distinction in the sciences, for example, it seems almost certain that the rankings for California, Chicago, Johns Hopkins, and M.I.T. would have had to be improved, particularly for the recent decades, while the ratings for Yale and Cornell would need to be revised downward. Again, under the heading of Protestant divinity it may seem improbable that the graduates of Harvard actually played a larger role than those from Princeton. And no doubt there are other rank orderings which are open to improvement. The reader who cares to verify or to correct the priorities here assigned may refer back to our occupational tables, then undertake his own studies in other honor lists, or in the cumulative listings of the American Who's Who.

This same general table, meanwhile, suggests a second major conclusion. Whatever the variations of interest, or vicissitudes of fortune, or uncertainties of intermediate ranking, the evidence is incontrovertible that three colleges have been exceptionally distinguished. In one calling after another the same three have headed the parade and have been producing more outstanding leaders than any others, beginning with the statesmen of the American Revolution, carrying on through the nineteenth century, and continuing right down to our own day. For Princeton, given its distinctly limited enrollments and alumni constituencies, the almost consistent third-place ranking over a span of two hundred years represents an extraordinary achievement. While the rivalry of Harvard and Yale for preeminence in the world of colleges has become legendary, and has sometimes been interpreted in somewhat invidious terms, the solid performance of their graduates is here unarguably confirmed. The men of Harvard have indeed excelled in literature and the arts, in science and medicine and scholarship; while the sons of Yale have demonstrably lived up to their reputation for practical affairs and public service, as witness their records in government and the law, in business and philanthropy, in education and the Christian ministry.

240

How strong have been the H-Y-P contributions--and how decisive have been the differences between these and other collegiate rivers of supply? The reader is now referred to our three Summary Tables (M-1, M-2, and M-3) for the Colleges, for the Graduate and Professional Schools, and for the Universities. Here will be found tabulated the number of times the alumni constituencies of each of our leading institutions rated first or second or third, etc., in the supply of leaders (all the vocations and professions in all the appropriate statistical tables here included). To elucidate the method: On recapitulation we found that there had been 85 usable tabulations for the graduates of our colleges (M-1   SUMMARY TABLE FOR THE COLLEGES). In 84 out of 85 of these tables the alumni of Harvard had mustered such a cluster of participants that they could not be lumped with the "also-rans"; instead Harvard had to be listed as a major contributor. Moreover, out of these 84 listings or "mentions," 83 were toward the top of the table, only one competitive ranking being lower than 15th. On the same basis, the men who had studied in Yale College or Sheffield Scientific School were found in 82 out of 85 leadership groups and in only two of these ranked lower than 10th. By contrast, the Princeton and Columbia college constituencies showed 70 or 71 leadership mentions but only 68 or 58 in the top ten. On the same cumulative scale Michigan rated a clear 5th, with 49 out of 62 delegations in the top ten--to be followed by Pennsylvania and California; Chicago and Cornell; Wisconsin, M.I.T., and Dartmouth. In 14th place one finds the alumni of Stanford with 25 mentions out of 86 but only 15 of these in the top ten--and roughly at the same level may be placed Illinois and N.Y.U., whose alumni had earned 17 out of 29 top ratings or 12 out of 35.

Such comparisons suggest, by way of quantitative assessment, that the men who had chosen to go to Stanford for their college experience had mustered an appreciable group of representatives in about 30 per cent as many leadership groups as the alumni of Harvard or Yale, and had rated in the top ten less than 20 per cent as often. But perhaps an even more persuasive way to read this first table is to note that, out of 85 possible ratings, the men of Harvard College ranked 40 times in undisputed first place, 5 times tied for first, 20 times clearly second, 2 times tied for second, and 5 more times either third or tied for third (a total of 72). By the same mode of counting, the alumni of Yale had apparently earned 25 first places and 5 ties, 20 second places and 5 ties, 4 third places and 3 ties (a total at these ranks of 62). In like fashion we can observe that Princeton graduates had appeared 41 times in first, second, or third place, and Columbia men had earned the same high ranking 15 times. But no other college constituency could claim more than 9 such leadership ratings out of the possible 85.

Ratings of alumni constituencies in 85 leadership listings (all periods and categories).

College or University	Number of Listings at Each Rank								
	1	2	3	4	5	6	7	8	9
HARVARD	40-TTTTT*	20-TT	3-TT	3-T	2-TT			1-TT	
YALE	25-TTTTT	20-TTTTT	4-TTT	8-TTT	T	1	TT	1-T	1
PRINCETON	2-T	6-TTTT	23-TTTTT	5-TTTTT	5-T	2-T	TTTT	1-T	2
COLUMBIA	2	2-TTT	5-TTT	5-TTT	9-TTTTT	3-T	2	2-TTTTT	4-T
MICHIGAN	1	3-T	1-TTT	5-TTTT	4-TTT	5-TTTT	4-T	TTTT	1-TT
PENNA.	1-T	TT	3	3-TT	2-TTT	1	1-TTT	5-TTTT	2-TTTT
CALIFORNIA	1	4	3-T	4-TTT	2-TT	3-T	2-TTTT	3-T	1-T
CHICAGO	T	1-TTT	2	1-TT	2	5-T	1-TTT	1-TT	1-TT
CORNELL			3-TT	4-TT	3-T	4	3-TT	TT	1-T
WISCONSIN			1	2-TT	1-TT	T	2-TTTTT	6-TT	TT
M.I.T.	1-T	1-T	2-TT	2-TT	TTT	1-T	2-TTT	1-T	2
DARTMOUTH			T	2-T	3-TTTTT	1-T	TT	TTT	1-TT
MINNESOTA		1	T	TT	2-TT			1-T	2-TT
ILLINOIS	1			1	3	4-TT	TT	1	1-T
N.Y.U.		T	1		T	T	1-T	TT	1-TTT
STANFORD			T	TTT	T	2	1	1-T	TT
WILLIAMS				1-TT	TTT	T	1-T	T	

*The numeral indicates an undisputed rank, the "T" a tie at that rank. Thus 40-TTTTT means 40 undisputed first places and five ties for first.

10	11	12	13	14	15	16 or More	In Top 10	In Top 15	Total Mentions	Approx. Rank	
						1	83	83	84	1	HARVARD
	1		1				80	82	82	2	YALE
	T	1					68	70	70	3	PRINCETON
1-T	1-T	T	1	1-T	1	6	58	65	71	4	COLUMBIA
1-TT	2-TTTT	T	2	1-T	T		49	62	62	5	MICHIGAN
3-TTT	1-T	3	T		T	6	43	50	56	6T	PENNA.
2-TT	1-TTTT		1		1	1	40	47	48	6T	CALIFORNIA
3-T	1	T	2	1-T		6	32	38	44	8T	CHICAGO
TT	2-TTT	3	1-TT	T	1	2	30	43	45	8T	CORNELL
2-T	2-TTT	1	T	T		2	30	38	40	10T	WISCONSIN
T	1				T	2	26	28	30	10T	M.I.T.
T	1	1	T	T	T	3	24	29	32	10T	DARTMOUTH
3-TTT	1-TT	1-T	1-T	1	T	3	20	29	32	13	MINNESOTA
T	TTT		1	1	1-T	5	17	24	29	14T	ILLINOIS
	2-TT	4	T	TT	2	10	12	25	35	14T	N.Y.U.
2-T	T	1	TT		1-T	4	15	20	25	14T	STANFORD
1-TT	1-TT				T	2	13	17	19	17	WILLIAMS

It should be observed that these are cumulative tables, lumping together two centuries of American leadership and in the process weighting the professions quite unequally. What confidence may be given to a score card which assigns a much fuller opportunity to lawyers and educators than to ministers, artists, or engineers? Is it proper, for example, to add only one table for the Signers to thirteen for Big Business? Are all the callings, and all the honor lists great and small, to be given an equal weight? The compilers of this statistical summary have asked themselves precisely such questions repeatedly--and have found no altogether satisfying answers. Yet it may be noted that our society has not given equal weight to the learned professions or rewarded the other callings with an altogether even hand. In any case certain limited correctives can readily be applied. The comparative rankings in any particular table or all the rankings for an entire occupational group can, if need be, be subtracted from the cumulative tables here reproduced. Thus, for the reader interested only in the twentieth century, the order of finish (so to speak) in the Dictionary of American Biography, the comparative numbers in the table of Signers, in the delegates to the Constitutional Convention, in the table of American Physicians prior to 1900, etc., will have little interest; they can readily be calculated and then subtracted from the total first, second, third, fourth, fifth places, etc., here given. And the result will be a cumulative score card for leadership in the twentieth century. Vice versa, additional leadership tables (if they can be found) can be added to our deficient occupational categories and also to our cumulative totals. These additions or subtractions will necessarily alter the mathematical figures--but they will not, we believe, greatly alter the major balance and conclusions.

The same will prove true for our SUMMARY TABLE FOR THE GRADUATE AND PROFESSIONAL SCHOOLS (M-2), which documents the unquestionable preeminence of Harvard (84 first, second, or third places out of a possible 89). There can be, self-evidently, no arguing with such evidence. It can and indeed should be observed that Harvard's claims to leadership derive overwhelmingly from the drawing power of its Law School and (recently) its School of Business Administration, with some assistance also from its Graduate School and its Medical School. It can be regretted that university schools of divinity, of fine arts or music, of science or engineering, of agriculture or forestry, have registered so lightly in our tables. But that has been the fault not just of our selection of colleges; to a degree it has been also the consequence of a disproportion in American life. Just as our young women have sometimes seen no hope for fame but through Hollywood, so our young men, ambitious for power and public service, have felt

244

compelled to look to business or the law. And in the past century, the two schools at Harvard offered exceptional entrees or opportunities for preparation in those callings.

Whether the graduate and professional students from Columbia should rank second, ahead of their contemporaries from Yale, though mustering nine fewer leadership groups and manning these more often with nongraduates, may be debated, yet their achievement of a greater number of first and second places in my judgment qualifies them for the honor. The same consideration of outstanding excellence in a substantial group of listings has governed the ranking of Chicago ahead of Michigan, and Berkeley ahead of Princeton--though these and other ratings could be altered to accommodate a different emphasis on the professions or a different weighting of total mentions versus top performance.

What will, however, prove almost impossible to change-- and for cogent reasons--is the measure of relative contributions made by the graduate or professional school alumni of unversity 1 and (say) university 11, with Johns Hopkins alumni appearing 52 per cent as often as those from Harvard, but only 35 per cent as frequently in the top 10. Or again, one may note that the alumni of Columbia and Yale altogether figure 4 times as frequently in this professional register as those from Texas and Ohio State, but 23 times as often in the top 10.

The SUMMARY TABLE FOR THE UNIVERSITIES (M-3) attempts to rank our leading universities according to the frequencies and densities of their contributions of leaders (net totals, whether from college or professional schools or both) throughout the examined range of occupations and callings. And once again Harvard ranks a clear first, with Yale a strong second, and Columbia, Princeton, and Michigan next in order. Then come the alumni of Pennsylvania, Berkeley, and Chicago clustered together, with Cornell close behind, followed--at a somewhat greater remove--by Wisconsin in tenth place.

At that point appears a sharp break. And the second flight of university constituencies finds Johns Hopkins and M.I.T. in the lead, followed by Illinois, Stanford, Minnesota, and N.Y.U.

Still a third flight seems to be composed of Dartmouth, Virginia, Northwestern, and Williams: four excellent colleges with but limited university attachments or none at all. After which come Ohio State, Texas, and North Carolina--with one fifth as many contributing groups as Harvard or Yale but only one twentieth as many listings in the top ten.

M-2. SUMMARY TABLE FOR THE GRADUATE AND PROFESSIONAL SCHOOLS, 1865-1965

Ratings of alumni constituencies in 90 leadership listings (all periods and categories).

College or University	Number of Listings at Each Rank								
	1	2	3	4	5	6	7	8	9
HARVARD	57-TTTTT*	16-T	3-TT	1-T	1-T		T		
COLUMBIA	6-T	20-TT	13-TTTTT	8-TTTT	5	3	1-TTTTT	3	TT
YALE	1-TTT	6-TTTTT	16-TTTTT	9-TTTTT	6-TTT	9-T	TTT	2-TT	3-T
CHICAGO	4-TTT	4	9-T	6-TTTTT	6-TTT	5-T	3-T	1-T	4-T
MICHIGAN		3-TT	3-TTTT	8-TTTTT	8-T	7	6-TT	2-TT	1-TT
CALIFORNIA	7	8-TT	T	1-TTT	2-TT	TT	2-TTT	1-TTTT	4-TT
PRINCETON	T	TT	1-TT	7-TT	2-TT	6-TTT	5-TTTTT	2-TT	1-TT
PENNSYLVANIA	1-T	1	5-TTTTT	3-TTTT	1-T	2-TTT	1-TTTTT	2-TT	1-TT
WISCONSIN		T	6	3-TTT	4-TT	3-TT	2-T	4-TT	TT
CORNELL		1-T	T	1-TT	2-TT	3-T	2-TTTTT	3-TT	5-TTT
JOHNS HOPKINS	2	4	1-TT	2-TTT	3	1-TTT	2-TTT	1-TT	TT
M.I.T.	3	2-T	2-T	2-T	1-T	1	1	T	
MINNESOTA		2-T			T	T	T	2-TT	1-TTTT
STANFORD			T	1-T	2-T	1	1-TTT	TT	1-T
ILLINOIS	T			T		T	1-TTT	3-T	1-TT
N.Y.U.		T		TT	1-T	TT	1-T	T	1-TT
NORTHWESTERN		T	T	T		T	1	1-T	TT
TEXAS			T	T		T	1		T
OHIO STATE						T	T		

*The numeral indicates an undisputed rank, the "T" a tie at that rank. Thus 57-TTTTT means 57 undisputed first places and five ties for first.

10	11	12	13	14	15	16 or More	In Top 10	In Top 15	Total Mentions	Approx. Rank	
							89	89	89	1	HARVARD
						1	78	78	79	2	COLUMBIA
2	1	1-T	T		1	1	82	87	88	3	YALE
			T		1		58	60	60	4	CHICAGO
1	1-T	2-T	T	1-T		3	57	65	68	5	MICHIGAN
1	2-T	1-TTT		1		2	45	53	55	6	CALIFORNIA
3-TT	3-TT		TT	1	T	4	50	59	63	7	PRINCETON
1-T	2	3-TTT	1-TT	1-T	2-T	5	42	58	63	8	PENNSYLVANIA
4	1	2	T		TT		39	45	45	9T	WISCONSIN
4-T	4	T	5-T		1-T	1	39	52	53	9T	CORNELL
		4	T	1-T	TT	6	31	40	46	11	JOHNS HOPKINS
1	1-T	2-T	1-T	T	1	3	18	27	30	12T	M.I.T.
1-TT	1-TT	2-TTTTT	2-TT	3	1-TTT	5	18	40	45	12T	MINNESOTA
2-T	1	3	2-T	2	1	9	18	28	37	12T	STANFORD
2-T	5-T	3-T	1-TTT	T	T	4	17	33	37	12T	ILLINOIS
1-TT	1-TT		1		1-TT	7	16	23	30	16	N.Y.U.
	T	TTT	2-TT	2	1-T	8	9	20	28	17	NORTHWESTERN
1	1	T	TTT	T	T	8	6	12	21	18	TEXAS
	T	1	1-T	T	1-T	12	2	9	21	19	OHIO STATE

Ratings of alumni constituencies (net total of individuals attending one or more schools) in 111 leadership listings (all periods and categories).

College or University	Number of Listings at Each Rank								
	1	2	3	4	5	6	7	8	9
HARVARD	76-T*	19-T	4-T	4-T	2-T		1		
YALE	8	42-TTTTT	11-T	10-TTTT	4-TTTTT	8	1-T	2	2-T
COLUMBIA	5-T	9-TTT	19-TTTT	11-TTTTT	10-TTTT	7	4-TTTTT	6	1-T
PRINCETON	1	3-TT	17-TT	16-TTTTTT	8-TTT	5-TTTT	3-TTT	3-TT	2
MICHIGAN		1	4-T	12-T	13-TTTT	7-TTTT	6-TTTTT	2-TT	3-TTTT
PENNSYLVANIA	2	2-TT	4-T	3-TTT	3-TTT	1-TTT	2-TTTT	6-TT	5-TTT
CALIFORNIA	7	7-TT	4	3-TTTT	3	2-TTT	1-TTTTT	5-TT	4
CHICAGO	3-TT	3	11-T	5-T	7	5	3-TTT	3-T	4-TT
CORNELL		2-T	2-TT	3-TT	3-TTT	4-TT	7-TTTT	2-TTT	4-TTT
WISCONSIN			5	4-T	3-TTT	5-TTTT	3-TTT	8-TT	1-TT
JOHNS HOPKINS		5		2-T	1-T	4-TT	3-TT	2	TT
M.I.T.	5	1	3-T	1-TTT	3-TTT		3-TTT		
ILLINOIS		T		1	2	3-T	TT	3-TTT	2-TTTT
STANFORD				1-TT	2-TT	1-TT	1-TT	2-T	2
MINNESOTA		T		T	1		1-T	1-TT	3-T
N.Y.U.		1			TTT	1-T	2-T	TT	2-TTTTT
DARTMOUTH				T	2-TT	1	2-T	1-TT	TTT
VIRGINIA			TTT	1-T	TT	2-T		TT	
NORTHWESTERN				T	1			1	1-T
WILLIAMS					TT	1	1	TT	
OHIO STATE						T	1		
TEXAS		T			T		1	T	
NORTH CAROLINA					T	T	1		

*The numeral indicates an undisputed rank, the "T" a tie at that rank. Thus 76-T means 76 undisputed first places and one tie for first.

10	11	12	13	14	15	Over 15	In Top 10	In Top 15	Total Mentions	Approx. Rank	
							111	111	111	1	HARVARD
	2	1-T					106	110	110	2	YALE
T	TT	T				4	96	99	103	3	COLUMBIA
T	5-T	TT	T	1		2	81	91	93	4	PRINCETON
1-TTTT	3-T	3-T	T			3	74	83	86	5	MICHIGAN
4-TTTTT	2-TT	4-TT	1-T	1-T	3-T	4	58	76	80	6T	PENNSYLVANIA
2-TTT	2-T	1-TTTT	2-TT		1-T	1	57	71	72	6T	CALIFORNIA
2-T	1	TTTT	T	T	1	5	57	65	70	6T	CHICAGO
4-T	6	1-T	5-T	1		4	52	67	71	9	CORNELL
5-T	1-TT	2-T		TT	T	2	50	59	61	10	WISCONSIN
2-T		3-T	T	1-T	TT	7	28	37	44	11T	JOHNS HOPKINS
1	3-T	2-T	T	1	1	4	27	37	41	11T	M.I.T.
1-TT	4-TT	3-TT	2-TT	T	T	7	25	42	49	13	ILLINOIS
3-TTT	2	2-T	2	2	1	10	24	34	44	14	STANFORD
2-TTTT	TT	5-T	3-TTT	3-TT	3-TTT	7	18	43	50	15T	MINNESOTA
T	T	1-TT	2	T	1-T	14	19	28	42	15T	N.Y.U.
1-T	T	2		2-T		6	17	23	29	17	DARTMOUTH
1-TT		T		T	T	2	15	18	20	18	VIRGINIA
T	T		2-T	3-TT	1-TT	12	6	19	31	19	NORTHWESTERN
1-TT	1		T		1	7	9	12	19	20	WILLIAMS
2-T			1-T	T	1-T	18	5	10	28	21T	OHIO STATE
1-T	T	T	T	T		13	6	10	23	21T	TEXAS
1-T			1		T	14	5	7	21	23	NORTH CAROLINA

Reviewing these achievement records it becomes possible
to identify a leading five among the university constituencies,
then a second group of five, then at some remove in each case
a third group of six, a fourth group of four, and a final cluster of three. If we label these groups A, B, C, D, E, we can
say that on average performance these groups scored (in top
ten and in total appearances) as follows:

> A: 94 out of 101,
> B: 55 out of 71,
> C: 24 out of 45,
> D: 12 out of 25,
> E: 5 out of 24.

The observer may calculate his own group ratios and draw such
conclusions as seem warranted.

If we now compare our three Summary Tables, we find that
over the years and in all three tables the alumni of Michigan
have built up and maintained a more effective and successful
record of achievement than the alumni from any of the other
state universities. Among all constituencies, Michigan has
always ranked fifth: behind Harvard, Yale, Columbia, and
either Princeton or Chicago. By a smaller yet appreciable
cumulative margin, the men from Michigan have generally surpassed their rivals from Pennsylvania, Berkeley, and Chicago,
who in turn have produced more leaders than Cornell and Wisconsin. By their achievements these outstanding constituencies would seem to give us a top ten.

In this top ten may be identified five private or independent institutions (founded in 1636, 1701, 1746, 1754, and
1890), three public or state universities (founded in 1817,
1836, and 1868), and two of intermediate character (founded
in 1740 and 1865). Geographically, they are located: two in
New England, two in New York, one each in New Jersey and Pennsylvania, three in the Great Lakes region, and one on the
West Coast--a familiar if not universally popular distribution.

If the same analysis is extended to all 23 institutions
listed in our summary table for the universities, the results
will read: 12 private, 3 intermediate, and 8 public--with 6
of these institutions dating from colonial times, 8 from the
period 1783-1860, and 9 from 1860-1900, but not one founded
in the twentieth century. In turn the geographic distribution would show 5 from New England, 3 from New York, 3 from
the Middle Atlantic region, 7 from the Middle West, 2 from
the Far West, and 3 from the South.

Such a distribution perhaps suggests a much broader

balance of opportunity, particularly when the relative enrollments are taken into account. To illustrate: If we combine
the average registrations of full-time students for the decade
of the 1950's, the same 23 institutions would produce in rough
totals the following regional enrollments (by thousands): New
England 28, New York 41? (N.Y.U. estimated), Middle Atlantic
15, Middle West 124, Far West 25, and South 25.

By the same token, however, the chances for each individual student in the several regional groupings might be just
reversed--and for those in the Middle and Far West greatly
diminished. In attempting to estimate the comparative proba-
bilities we may recall Mr. Arthur E. Traxler's findings,
which showed that the different types of educational institutions seem to have diverged markedly in their ratios of productivity for Who's Who in America (see Table L-3). Thus 1
alumnus for every 25 (approximately) of the undergraduates at
H-Y-P in the years 1920-49 had achieved recognition in Who's
Who. This compared with 1 in 36 for Williams, 1 in 48 for
Dartmouth, 1 in 78 for Virginia, 1 in 82 for Michigan, 1 in
87 for North Carolina, 1 in 89 for Wisconsin, and 1 in 145 as
a median figure for the state universities as a group.

Pursuing this clue, if one could compare the totals of
production from our own cumulative accounting with the poten-
tials of the same institutions in terms of their student numbers, or better still in terms of the sizes of their respective alumni bodies, one might get some rather startling results. The achievements of the graduates of the universities
of Johns Hopkins, M.I.T., Stanford, Northwestern, and especially Dartmouth and Williams might seem far more considerable, the opportunities for individual students at certain of
the larger institutions proportionately diminished.

In an effort to test this possibility, yet hold the balance even, we have re-examined the total performance of certain of our colleges so as to give them credit for alumni who
in our original tables were counted in with the "also-rans"
(and therefore failed to achieve mention for the institution
among the listed leaders). This recounting shows that if we
take into account every appearance of an alumnus, in all our
usable statistical investigations for the colleges, Column 3,
Table M-4, the alumni of Williams would figure in 52 tables,
instead of the 19 "mentions" listed in our SUMMARY TABLE FOR
THE COLLEGES. And altogether 911 Williams men did appear in
the course of our investigations, as against a living college
alumni count for 1,930 of about 8,792: a hypothetical ratio
of 1 in 9.7. By the same somewhat arbitrary method of calculation, Dartmouth would rate 54 mentions and a total of 1,598
alumni "leaders" as against a total alumni constituency of

251

13,726: a ratio of 1 in 8.6. For Stanford the figures would
be 52 mentions and 1,155 "leaders" against a university alumni
count of 32,362, or 1 in 28; for Chicago, 54 mentions and
1,500 "leaders" against 22,407 alumni or 1 in 15; for M.I.T.,
44 mentions and 1,682 "leaders" against 18,920 alumni or 1 in
11.2; for Princeton, 72 mentions and 3,229 "leaders" out of
16,934 or 1 in 5.2; for Yale, 72 mentions and 5,298 "leaders"
out of 35,825 alumni, all told, or 1 in 6.8; and for Harvard,
73 mentions and 7,154 "leaders" out of 55,151 alumni or 1 in
7.7.

The foregoing ratios are deceptive in the last six cases
because the college leadership production is measured against
a total alumni constituency (graduate and professional alumni
included). If we now work out estimates for the living college alumni for 1929-30 for certain of the institutions above
named, we get the following leadership ratios: Stanford 1 in
22.7; M.I.T. 1 in 8.9; Princeton 1 in 4.6; Yale 1 in 4.6; and
Harvard 1 in 4.1.

Translating these ratios one may conclude that for every
100 chances the men of Harvard College have had, the undergraduates of Yale have had in the neighborhood of 89; the men
of Princeton, 89; of Dartmouth, 48; of Williams, 42; and the
men and women of Stanford, 18.

Still another and quite interesting method of comparison
is to notice the relative densities of contribution for the
leading seventeen colleges (Table M-4). If we omit for each
college those tables in which its contribution was either not
given or not known, we find that we can estimate the median
size of the alumni groups in our tables, using 74 tables for
Harvard, Yale, Princeton, and Columbia; 72 for Michigan; 71
for Pennsylvania and California; 68 for Chicago, Minnesota,
Illinois, and N.Y.U.; etc., etc. The median representation
then proves to be, for Harvard--17.50; for Yale--14.50; for
Princeton--8.25; for Columbia--5.50; for Michigan--3.93; and
the rest below. With a median figure of 3.00, the men of
Dartmouth did considerably better altogether than the graduates of a number of colleges which outranked them in total
formal appearances in our 85 tables. On the same basis,
Minnesota, N.Y.U., and Illinois would drop to the bottom of
the list, with Minnesota showing a median leadership delegation one tenth the size of Harvard, and Illinois one tenth
the size of Yale.

Such measurements can hardly be exact, given the unevenness and irregularity of our statistical samplings. Yet the
astonishing regularity and consistency of the returns should
warn us against too lightly discounting their import. And if

M-4. DENSITIES OF CONTRIBUTION, 17 COLLEGES

Tabulation of total numbers of alumni and their frequencies of distribution in 74-85 leadership tables.

| Colleges | Institutions- 85 Tables[a] | Individuals- 74 Tables[b] | Total Count of Alumni in 74 Tables | Number of Tables (out of 74)[c] Showing Alumni Represented at Indicated Levels of Concentration | | | | | | | | | | Median Size of Alumni Groups[d] |
				Not Given or Unknown	0	1 Rep.	2 Reps.	3 Reps.	4-9 Reps.	10-24 Reps.	25-49 Reps.	50-99 Reps.	100-up Reps.	
HARVARD	84	73	7,154	0	1	2	1	2	15	21	16	7	9	17.50
YALE	82	72	5,298	0	2	1	2	3	21	19	11	6	9	14.50
PRINCETON	70	72	3,229	0	2	6	7	3	26	13	9	2	6	8.25
COLUMBIA	71	66	2,181	0	8	9	6	6	19	17	4	2	3	5.50
MICHIGAN	62	65	2,526	2	7	8	10	8	24	5	4	3	3	3.93
PENNSYLVANIA	56	66	2,378	3	5	11	14	5	17	10	3	3	3	3.63
CALIFORNIA	48	56	2,046	3	15	8	8	6	18	9	2	2	3	3.25
CHICAGO	44	54	1,500	6	14	11	9	6	15	7	2	2	2	2.50
CORNELL	45	56	2,215	1	17	10	9	6	17	5	5	1	3	2.58
WISCONSIN	40	57	1,875	4	13	12	7	9	16	7	3	0	3	2.83
M.I.T.	30	44	1,682	4	26	5	13	2	7	9	4	1	3	1.81
DARTMOUTH	32	54	1,598	7	13	10	7	7	17	7	3	0	3	3.00
MINNESOTA	32	48	1,341	6	20	12	8	7	11	5	2	0	3	1.75
ILLINOIS	29	50	1,835	6	18	17	7	5	9	3	6	0	3	1.44
N.Y.U.	35	46	1,605	6	22	12	9	3	13	4	2	1	2	1.50
STANFORD	25	52	1,155	7	15	13	14	6	9	4	3	1	2	1.88
WILLIAMS	19	52	911	8	14	16	10	7	7	6	2	2	2	1.80

[a] Institutional rankings in 85 tables.

[b] Number of leadership groups in which alumni figured, out of 74 tables.

[c] Eleven of our tables have been omitted in this count: (a) the 4 Who's Who in America tables (L-2), plus the table showing increase in Who's Who, because these would produce a great duplication of names; (b) the 3 tables on Branches of the Federal Executive (B-5), because only per cent figures are given; (c) the parenthetical table on Great Educators before the Civil War (K-1); (d) the College Origins of the Younger American Scholar (K-17) and the Undergraduate Origins of Medical Students (D-8), because each of these represents, at most, a promise of performance rather than the achievement of leadership.

[d] Excluding tables in which the contribution of that constituency is unknown (Column 4).

we were to attempt a like comparison of _university_ performance for all those leaders who had studied at one level or another at each of our leading institutions, the disproportion in enrollments would certainly produce differences in ratios of achievement quite as marked.

All of which would seem to make plain the much higher opportunities for individual achievement at certain of our smaller private colleges and at certain of our independent universities, as compared with the massive state or city institutions. Aspiring freshmen and their parents, intending lawyers and men of affairs, Congressmen and foundation executives, presidents and directors of great industrial corporations, not least our public spirited citizens who are interested in the nourishment and preservation of excellence, may well take such disproportions into account.

From the point of view of society as a whole, of course, the gross totals of leadership production have been and will continue to be of the first significance. And these gross totals show, in scores of ways and repeatedly through the major professions and public occupations, the preponderance of contributions that have been made, and that continue to be made, by the colleges of Harvard, Yale, Princeton, and Columbia--by the graduate schools of Harvard, Columbia, Yale, and Chicago--and by the university constituencies of Harvard, Yale, Princeton, and Columbia, with Michigan following in all categories, at the head of a mixed company of public and private institutions: all dedicated to the service and the leadership of our democratic society.

CHAPTER N APPENDIX

HARVARD	1636 (1638)	U.S. NAVAL ACAD.	1845
		BELOIT	1846 (1847)
WILLIAM AND MARY	1693	GRINNELL	1847 (1848)
		C.C.N.Y.	1847 (1849)
YALE	1701 (1702)	IOWA	1847 (1855)
PENNSYLVANIA	1740 (1755)	NORTHWESTERN	1851 (1855)
PRINCETON	1746 (1747)	MINNESOTA	1851 (1869)
		ANTIOCH	1852 (1853)
COLUMBIA	1754	WASHINGTON (St. L.)	1853 (1854)
		M.I.T.	1860 (1865)
BROWN	1764 (1765)		
RUTGERS	1766 (1771)		
DARTMOUTH	1769 (1770)	WASHINGTON (Seattle)	1861
		VASSAR	1861 (1865)
		KANSAS	1864 (1866)
TRANSYLVANIA	1780 (1799)	SWARTHMORE	1864 (1869)
		OHIO STATE	1864 (1873)
UNION	1785 (1795)	LEHIGH	1865 (1866)
PITTSBURGH	1787	CORNELL	1865 (1868)
NORTH CAROLINA	1789 (1795)	PURDUE	1865 (1876)
GEORGETOWN	1789 (1812)	CARLETON	1866 (1870)
		WOOSTER	1866 (1870)
WILLIAMS	1793	ILLINOIS	1867 (1868)
HAMILTON	1793 (1812)	JOHNS HOPKINS	1867 (1876)
BOWDOIN	1794 (1802)	CALIFORNIA (Coll. of 1855-69)	1868
U.S. MILITARY ACAD.	1802	NEBRASKA	1869 (1871)
ANDOVER THEOL. SEM.	1807	SYRACUSE	1870 (1871)
MARYLAND	1807	WELLESLEY	1870 (1875)
MICHIGAN	1817 (1841)	SMITH	1871 (1875)
CINCINNATI	1819	VANDERBILT	1872 (1875)
VIRGINIA	1819 (1825)	RADCLIFFE	1879 (1882)
INDIANA	1820 (1824)	BRYN MAWR	1880 (1885)
ALABAMA	1820 (1831)		
		TEXAS	1881 (1883)
AMHERST	1821	STANFORD	1885 (1891)
GEORGE WASHINGTON	1821 (1822)	POMONA	1887 (1888)
TRINITY	1823 (1824)	BARNARD	1889
KENYON	1824	CATHOLIC U.	1889
WESTERN RESERVE	1826	CHICAGO	1890 (1892)
WESLEYAN	1831	CAL. TECH. (THROOP TO 1920)	1891 (1892)
N.Y.U.	1831 (1832)	RICE	1891 (1912)
OBERLIN	1833 (1834)		
HAVERFORD	1833 (1856)		
TULANE	1834 (1835)		
UNION THEOL. SEM.	1836	REED	1908 (1911)
EMORY	1836 (1837)		
MOUNT HOLYOKE	1836 (1837)	BENNINGTON	1925 (1932)
KNOX	1836 (1838)		
WISCONSIN	1836 (1849)	QUEEN'S (N.Y.C.)	1937
DEPAUW	1837 (1838)		
MISSOURI	1838 (1841)	BRANDEIS	1948
DUKE (TRINITY COLL. 1859-1924)	1839		

Note: The first date given is that in which the institution was established, chartered, or in some other official way given recognition. If
instruction at the college level was not achieved immediately, the year in
which it was begun is given in parentheses.

Average enrollments of full-time college students (so far as ascertainable) in representative colleges and universities through the first forty years of this century--together with percentage comparisons with the enrollment at Harvard.

College or University	Average Enrollments per Decade				Number of Students per Hundred at Harvard			
	1900-1909	1910-1919	1920-1929	1930-1939	1900-1909	1910-1919	1920-1929	1930-1939
BOWDOIN	281	375	516	600	11.4	15.4	16.1	16.6
CALIFORNIA (Berkeley)	2,587	4,420[a]	9,089[b]	10,034	104.9	182.0	283.7	277.8
CHICAGO	2,553	2,527	2,760	2,763	103.4	104.1	86.1	76.5
COLUMBIA	1,338	1,668[a]	3,051	3,350	54.2	68.7	95.2	92.7
CORNELL	2,571	3,969	4,742	5,113	104.2	163.5	148.0	141.6
DARTMOUTH	910	1,292[a]	2,058	2,354	36.9	53.2	64.3	65.2
HARVARD	2,468	2,428	3,204	3,612	100.0	100.0	100.0	100.0
ILLINOIS	2,182	3,694[a]	4,918	5,491	88.5	152.1	153.5	152.0
JOHNS HOPKINS	170	243[a]	685	793	6.9	10.0	21.4	22.0
MICHIGAN	2,441	3,925[a]	6,419	5,836	98.9	161.7	200.3	161.6
MINNESOTA	2,070	3,186[a]	5,342	6,321	83.9	131.2	166.7	175.0
M.I.T.	1,415	1,622[a]	2,693	2,493	57.3	66.8	84.0	69.0
PENNSYLVANIA	1,598	4,382[c]	5,501	5,033	64.7	180.5	171.7	139.3
PRINCETON	1,258	1,387	2,168	2,606	51.0	57.1	67.7	72.1
STANFORD	1,346	1,585[a]	3,001	3,116	54.5	65.3	93.7	86.3
TEXAS	897	1,727[a]	3,805	5,450	36.3	71.1	118.8	150.9
WILLIAMS	441	514[a]	718	797	17.8	21.2	22.4	22.1
WISCONSIN	2,622	3,862[a]	5,574	5,762	106.2	159.1	174.0	159.5
YALE	2,112	2.418	2,882	3,077	85.6	99.6	90.0	85.2

[a]Includes the years 1910-15, 1917, and 1919.   [b]1930-37 only.
[c]Includes the years 1910-13, 1915-18.

Sources: Annual Report of the Commissioner of Education, 1900-1915; Biennial Survey of Education, 1917-37, a publication of the Office of Education; Raymond Walters, "Statistics of Registration in American Universities and Colleges," published annually in School and Society since 1919; publications of the various institutions.

N-3. ESTIMATED UNIVERSITY ENROLLMENTS, 1900-1959

Average enrollments of full-time students (so far as ascertainable) in representative colleges and universities through the first sixty years of this century--together with percentage comparisons with the enrollment at Harvard.

College or University	Average Enrollments per Decade						Numbers of Students per Hundred at Harvard					
	1900-1909	1910-1919	1920-1929	1930-1939	1940-1949*	1950-1959	1900-1909	1910-1919	1920-1929	1930-1939	1940-1949*	1950-1959
BOWDOIN	374	421	505	598	897	799	7.9	8.4	6.8	7.0	8.5	7.6
BROWN	940	1,071	1,805	1,917	3,518	3,320	20.0	21.3	24.2	22.5	33.3	31.5
CALIFORNIA (Berkeley)	3,816	4,761	10,550	14,309	16,100[a]	17,505	81.1	94.6	141.4	167.9	152.5[a]	166.1
CAL. TECH.			536	771	1,204	1,111			7.2	9.0	11.4	10.5
CHICAGO	4,911	6,216[e]	5,327	5,857	6,275	5,559	104.3	123.5[e]	71.4	68.7	59.4	52.7
COLUMBIA	3,817	4,996	12,358	14,348	16,698	13,244	81.1	99.3	165.5	168.4	158.2	125.6
CORNELL	3,652	4,446	5,487	5,973	7,891	10,477	77.6	88.3	73.5	70.0	74.7	99.5
DARTMOUTH	994	1,332	2,121	2,418	2,648	2,930	21.1	26.5	28.4	28.4	25.1	27.8
HARVARD	4,708	5,033	7,461	8,521	10,558	10,541	100.0	100.0	100.0	100.0	100.0	100.0
ILLINOIS	3,782	5,507	10,568	12,001	19,827	21,449	80.3	109.4	141.6	140.8	187.8	203.5
JOHNS HOPKINS	713	1,232	1,397	1,765	2,118	2,324	15.1	24.5	18.7	20.7	20.1	22.0
M.I.T.	1,461	1,839	3,009	3,306	4,399	5,671	31.0	36.5	40.3	38.8	41.7	53.8
MICHIGAN	4,198	6,158	9,635	9,997	14,925	20,465	89.2	122.4	129.1	111.3	141.4	194.1
MINNESOTA	4,025	4,695	10,083	13,178	18,678	22,564	85.6	93.3	135.1	154.7	176.9	214.1
NORTH CAROLINA	721	966	2,247	2,942	5,535	6,622	15.3	19.2	30.1	34.5	52.4	62.8

PENNSYLVANIA	3,358	4,798	7,624	6,799	7,614	9,008	71.3	95.3	102.2	79.8	72.1	82.4
PRINCETON	1,357	1,456	2,357	2,636	3,172	3,403	28.8	28.9	31.6	30.9	30.0	32.3
REED		208	303	406	621	620		4.1	4.1	4.8	5.9	5.9
STANFORD	1,582	2,027	3,935	4,284	7,625[b]	7,190	33.6	40.3	52.7	50.3	72.2[b]	68.2
SWARTHMORE	278	465	545	629	903	898	5.9	9.2	7.3	7.4	8.6	8.5
TEXAS	1,526	2,573	5,020	7,407	13,695	14,782[c]	32.4	51.1	67.3	86.9	129.7	140.2[c]
U.S. MIL. ACAD.	496[d]	685	1,175	1,471	2,207	2,460	10.5[d]	13.6	15.7	17.3	20.9	23.3
WILLIAMS	469	491	738	803	989	1,060	10.0	9.8	9.9	9.5	9.4	10.1
WISCONSIN	3,426	4,876	8,189	9,414	15,396	15,346	72.8	96.9	109.8	110.5	145.8	145.6
YALE	3,198	2,994	5,024	5,632	7,349	7,589	67.9	59.5	67.3	66.1	69.6	72.0

*Omitting the years 1943, 1944, and 1945.

a Figures for 1940-42 and 1949.

b Figures for three postwar years only.

c Figures for 1950-55 only.

d Figures for 1905-09 only.

e Figures for 1910-16 and 1918--excluding unclassified and University College.

Sources: Annual Report of the Commissioner of Education, 1900-1915; Biennial Survey of Education, 1917-37, a publication of the Office of Education; Raymond Walters, "Statistics of Registration in American Universities and Colleges," published annually in School and Society since 1919.

N-4. TOTAL LIVING ALUMNI, 1900-1962

Estimates of living alumni for some representative colleges and universities through the first sixty-two years of this century--with estimates of comparative size expressed as percentages of the number of living Harvard alumni in 1909-12, 1929-31, and 1962.

College or University	Total Living Alumni								Comparative Size		
	1900	1909-1912	1919-1920	1929-1931	1939	1948-1950	1955	1962	1909-1912	1929-1931	1962
BOWDOIN	2,577[a]	2,847	2,887*	3,394*		6,397	7,454	8,604	8.8	6.2*	6.6
BROWN	4,800		5,600	9,000		11,874[b]		22,700		16.3	17.5
CALIFORNIA (Berkeley)		7,659[k]				100,000[b]		160,079[c]	23.8[k]		123.6[c]
CAL. TECH.	1,000*					5,578*		8,948*			6.9*
CHICAGO	1,050*	4,915[k]		22,407		60,000[b]		67,000*	15.3[k]	40.6	51.7*
COLUMBIA		17,832[k]		29,077		53,000[b]		93,997	55.4[k]	52.7	72.6
CORNELL	4,380[e]	16,500	30,000	45,000	59,591	71,689	91,493	105,000	51.3	81.3	81.1
DARTMOUTH		5,291	8,884	13,726	18,813	23,074	27,064	30,556	16.4	23.1	23.6
HARVARD		32,188	38,122	55,151	74,733[j]	93,330	109,945	129,500[m]	100.0	100.0	100.0
JOHNS HOPKINS		2,000[k]		11,592[f]				34,860[m]	6.2[k]	21.0[f]	26.9[m]
M.I.T.	2,050		18,920			39,126		51,445		34.3	39.7
MICHIGAN		20,205[k]				135,047		202,496[c]	62.8[k]		156.4[c]
MINNESOTA		7,183[k]					100,000	125,000	22.3[k]		96.5

260

N.Y.U.								164,398			126.9
NORTH CAROLINA	3,500		14,000			34,000		65,000		25.4	50.2
PENNSYLVANIA	15,000[k]		24,000[g]	48,350	57,260[d]	68,620	87,400	100,000	46.6[k]	87.7	77.2
PRINCETON	7,400[a]	9,432	13,247[g]	16,934	20,437		26,639	35,779	29.3	30.7	27.6
REED								8,636			6.7
STANFORD	2,800[k]			32,362				74,692	8.7[k]	58.7	57.7
SWARTHMORE	737		4,940				8,661	10,781		9.0	8.3
U.S. MILITARY ACAD.			5,645*		12,471*			17,384*		10.2*	13.4*
WILLIAMS	5,859		8,792					10,800		15.9	8.3
YALE	12,665[h]	22,829	28,165	35,825	46,330	54,843	65,627[i]	73,931	70.9	65.0	57.1

*Degree-holders only.

a 1902 b 1946 c 1963 d 1937 e 1898 f 1926 g 1924
h 1904 i 1956 j 1940 k estimate from Slosson m estimate

Sources: Alumni registers for H-Y-P, questionnaires and correspondence with registrars or alumni offices, and the estimates given in E. E. Slosson, Great American Universities, for 1909.

ABOUT THE AUTHOR

George W. Pierson is Larned Professor of History at Yale University and has been Director of Yale's Division of the Humanities since 1964. A Yale faculty member since 1926, he previously served as Chairman of the Department of History. Dr. Pierson has long been interested in the study of American educational history and in the development of American civilization. His courses on the foreign relations of American civilization stemmed from an early interest in the experiences of Alexis de Tocqueville and Gustave de Beaumont, which led him to publish Tocqueville and Beaumont in America.

Mr. Pierson's other books include Tocqueville in America, Yale College: An Educational History, 1871-1921, and Yale: The University College, 1921-1937. He contributed to The Modern University (edited by Margaret Clapp) and has published articles in Yale Review, American Historical Review, New England Quarterly, and American Quarterly, among others.

Mr. Pierson received his Ph.D. degree from Yale University.